CONTEMPORARY AFRICAN LITERATURE AND THE POLITICS OF GENDER

The influence of colonialism and race on the development of African literature has been the subject of a number of studies but the effect of patriarchy and gender, and indeed the contributions of African women, have up until now been largely ignored by critics. *Contemporary African Literature and the Politics of Gender* is the first extensive account of African literature from a feminist perspective.

In this radical and exciting work Florence Stratton outlines the features of an emerging female tradition in African fiction and dedicates a chapter each to the works of four women writers: Grace Ogot, Flora Nwapa, Buchi Emecheta and Mariama Bâ. In addition she provides challenging new readings of canonical male authors such as Chinua Achebe, Ngũgĩ wa Thiong'o and Wole Soyinka. *Contemporary African Literature and the Politics of Gender* thus provides the first truly comprehensive definition of the current literary tradition in Africa.

Florence Stratton received a Ph.D. in African Literature from the School of Oriental and African Studies in London. She taught literature at Njala University College in Sierra Leone for nineteen years and is currently at the Catholic Worker in New York.

CONTEMPORARY AFRICAN LITERATURE AND THE POLITICS OF GENDER

Florence Stratton

London and New York

First published 1994
by Routledge
11 New Fetter Lane, London EC4P 4EE

Simultaneously published in the USA and Canada
by Routledge
29 West 35th Street, New York, NY 10001

Typeset in Bembo by ROM-Data Corporation Ltd., Falmouth,
Cornwall
Printed and bound in Great Britain by Clays Ltd, St. Ives plc
Printed on acid-free paper

British Library Cataloguing in Publication Data
A catalogue record for this book is available from the British Library

Library of Congress Cataloging in Publication Data
Stratton, Florence.   Contemporary African Literature and the Politics of
Gender / Florence Stratton.
     p.   cm.
  Includes bibliographical references and index.
  1. African literature (English)—Women authors—History and criticism.
  2. African literature (French)—Women authors—History and criticism.
  3. Feminism and literature—Africa—History—20th century. 4. Women and
literature—Africa—History—20th century. 5. Sex role in literature.   I.   Title.
PR9340.5.S77   1994
   809'.8896'082—dc20   93-11947

ISBN 0-415-09770-3 (hbk) ISBN 0-415-09771-1 (pbk)

PERMISSIONS

Acknowledgement is made for permission to reprint, in slightly different form,
' "Periodic embodiments": a ubiquitous trope in African men's writing', by Florence
Stratton, *Research in African Literatures*, 1990, 21.1; and to reprint portions of 'The
shallow grave: archetypes of female experience in African fiction', by Florence Stratton,
Research in African Literatures, 1988, 19.2, by permission of Indiana University Press.
   Acknowledgement is made for permission to quote from the following:
Christopher Okigbo, *Labyrinths*, London, Heinemann, 1971. By permission of
Heinemann Publishers (Oxford) Ltd. Léopold Sédar Senghor, *Léopold Sédar
Senghor: Prose and Poetry*, trans. and ed. John Reed and Clive Wake, Oxford
University Press, 1965. By permission of Oxford University Press.
   I regret that I have been unable to trace the copyright holder of Okot p'Bitek, *Song
of Lawino*, Nairobi, East African Publishing House, 1966; and of Ousmane Sembène,
Tribal Scars and Other Stories, trans. Len Ortzen, London, Heinemann, 1974.

CONTENTS

ACKNOWLEDGEMENTS

This book grew out of the years I spent teaching literature at Njala University College in Sierra Leone. While it takes as its subject the development of contemporary African literature in relation to its social context, it is marked by the impact that living in the Njala community had on my own personal and intellectual development. I am particularly indebted to the members of the Department of Language Education at Njala for introducing me to African literature, getting me involved in the debates in the field, and inspiring me to take on this project. To Amy Davies, Jamie Dennis, Max Gorvie, Siaka Kroma, Morie Manyeh, Francis Ngaboh-Smart, Joe Pemagbi, Julius Spencer, thanks also for providing the very best of company.

I am also intellectually indebted to Fredric Jameson for his *The Political Unconscious: Narrative as a Socially Symbolic Act* and to Abdul R. JanMohamed for his *Manichean Aesthetics: The Politics of Literature in Colonial Africa*. These works provided the theoretical framework for my study. *Manichean Aesthetics* has been largely ignored by students of African literature. The reason for this is difficult to discern, for JanMohamed engages complex theoretical issues in lucid terms. And while I am critical of him for ignoring gender as a social and analytic category, my own analysis is meant not to refute but to complement his in defining the characteristics of contemporary African literature.

For her advice and support throughout my research, I am very grateful to Liz Gunner. Her suggestions were indispensable and her enthusiasm and friendship made working with her a pleasure.

The encouragement of Lyn Innes, Bernth Lindfors, Len Moody, Rowland Smith, and Richard Taylor aided me in significant ways. I also want to thank the Social Sciences and Humanities Research Council of Canada, the London House Association of Canada, and the Committee of Vice-Chancellors and Principals of the Universities of the United

Kingdom. They made my research possible by providing financial assistance. I would also like to thank friends at William Goodenough and London House in London and Maryhouse in New York for allowing me to share in the life of their communities while working on this project.

For assistance of various kinds, I am grateful to Tamara Aboagye-Kwarteng, Amy Z. Davies, Belinda Hale, Helen Hawley, Katy McCrone, Tim O'Shaughnessy, Joan Sandomirsky, Alison Sutherland, and Kassie Temple. But most of all, I thank them for their friendship.

In this same connection, I want to thank Mo Agrawal, Michael Allie, Padma Anagol, Joseph Biancalana, Helen Burrows, Grant Curtis, Peter Dane, Mary Donaghy, Ambrose Ganda, Anil Jagtiani, Moma Lati, Jean and Roger Mitchell, Gretchen Mosher, Agnes Roberts, Ruth and Sam Robinson, Clarissa Stephen, Tunde and Willie Taylor, Maria and Joe Tucker, Peter Wilkinson, and Susanne Wise.

I would also like to thank Suraya, Fred, Mayah, and Krishna Stratton who, in various ways, also helped to make this book possible. To my mother, Kathleen Stratton, I owe an enormous debt of gratitude.

INTRODUCTION
Exclusionary practices

This book is about the place of African women writers in African literature. Its primary aim is to provide a more comprehensive definition of the contemporary African literary tradition than is available in current criticism, a definition that includes, rather than excludes, women's writing.

In characterizing African literature, critics have ignored gender as a social and analytic category. Such characterizations operate to exclude women's literary expression as part of African literature. Hence what they define is the male literary tradition. When African literary discourse is considered from the perspective of gender, it becomes evident that dialogic interaction between men's and women's writing is one of the defining features of the contemporary African literary tradition. Such a redefinition has important implications for both critical and pedagogical practices. What it indicates is that neither men's nor women's writing can be fully appreciated in isolation from the other.

This study also has two secondary aims: to supplement current definitions of the male literary tradition and to define the features of the emerging female tradition in African fiction. I will begin, however, by examining some of the ways in which women writers have been written out of the African literary tradition.

African women writers and their works have been rendered invisible in literary criticism. General surveys have neglected them as have more theoretical works such as Abdul R. JanMohamed's *Manichean Aesthetics*. The first book-length treatment of African fiction, Eustace Palmer's *An Introduction to the African Novel*, refers only once to a woman writer – a reference to Flora Nwapa that labels her 'an inferior novelist' (61). Women authors are also notably absent from Palmer's *The Growth of the African Novel*, as they are from other standard surveys such as David Cook's *African Literature: A Critical View* and Gerald Moore's *Twelve African Writers*. In his introduction,

Moore goes so far as to plead with critics 'to step beyond what have already become the "safe" writers' and then expresses regret that space does not permit him to include in his own study 'such new writers' as Nuruddin Farah, Ebrahim Hussein, Kole Omotoso, and Femi Osofisan (8). In light of this list of men writers, it is worth noting that by the late 1970s there were several women writers who could no longer be described as 'new' – writers such as Bessie Head and Flora Nwapa, each of whom had three novels and a collection of short stories to her credit. But Moore shows not the slightest compunction about excluding them from his study.

Similarly, the African authors JanMohamed treats are all men: Chinua Achebe, Ngũgĩ wa Thiong'o, and Alex La Guma. So too are the writers Ngũgĩ refers to in 'Writing against neo-colonialism', an essay in which he outlines the development of African literature since the Second World War. This same practice is evident among critics who theorize 'third-world' or 'post-colonial' literatures, although they do refer to African men authors. Thus Fredric Jameson, in elaborating his 'theory of the cognitive aesthetics of third-world literature' ('Third-world literature' 88), cites only men writers (two of whom are African). In *The Empire Writes Back*, Bill Ashcroft, Gareth Griffiths, and Helen Tiffin do at least make passing reference to two women writers – Jean Rhys and Doris Lessing – and they also discuss in some detail one novel by the New Zealand writer, Janet Frame. But this is in the course of an extended treatment of a large number of men (including African men) writers.

African women writers have fared no better in critical journals. To take just one example, *African Literature Today* did not publish a full-length article on a woman writer until its seventh volume (1975). It published its second in its eighth volume (1976) and did not include another until its twelfth volume (1982). Recently, the trend has been toward 'special issues' – issues devoted mainly to women writers, like the fifteenth volume of *African Literature Today*: *Women in African Literature Today* (1987). Considering the content of succeeding volumes, such issues are open to the charge of tokenism. For the established pattern of issues, which, although they are not labelled 'special', are devoted exclusively to men writers, tends to reassert itself, as is the case with the sixteenth (1989) and seventeenth (1991) volumes of *African Literature Today*. Special issues also raise the question of ghettoization, as Ama Ata Aidoo indicates when she asks: 'why a special issue on the work of women writers especially as these supposed special issues never come out at all, or once in a half decade?' (162). This same kind of question can be raised in relation to the two book-length studies of women writers which have been published – Lloyd W. Brown's insightful *Women Writers in Black Africa* and Oladele Taiwo's trite and ill-informed

Female Novelists of Modern Africa:[1] Why are the titles of these books marked for feminine gender? Or conversely: Why is Gerald Moore's book not entitled 'Twelve African men writers'?

Palmer justifies his selection of texts for inclusion in *An Introduction to the African Novel* by claiming that he has 'concentrated . . . on the dozen or so novels which seem to be of some importance, and which are gradually finding their way into school and university syllabuses' (xv). But texts become important and find their way into syllabuses – are, in short, admitted to the literary canon – when they are written about. This is the point Bernth Lindfors emphasizes in presenting the results of one of the tests he has devised for measuring the literary stature of Anglophone African writers:

> The unexamined literary career is not worth much in a noisy marketplace of ideas. To be famous, to be reputable, to be deemed worthy of serious and sustained consideration, an author needs as much criticism as possible, year after year after year. Only those who pass this test of time – the test of persistent published interest in their art – will stand a chance of earning literary immortality.
>
> ('Famous authors' 143)

Considering their invisibility in the dominant critical tradition, it is not surprising that women writers have not gained admission to the literary canon. Lindfors analyses two types of data in order to establish a writer's canonical status: the frequency with which, between 1936 and 1986, an author was discussed by literary critics ('Famous authors' reputation test'); and the frequency with which in 1986 an author was included in the literature syllabuses of Anglophone African universities ('Teaching of African literatures'). The result in each case is an all-male canon. Achebe, Ngũgĩ, and Soyinka (not necessarily in that order) are the three top-ranking authors, while the next seven positions on the combined-ranking scale are occupied by Ayi Kwei Armah, John Pepper Clark, Okot p'Bitek, Christopher Okigbo, Peter Abrahams, Alex La Guma, and Dennis Brutus. Ranking fifteenth and eighteenth respectively, Aidoo and Head are the only women who come close to acquiring canonical status ('Teaching' 54). Thus Soyinka is speaking from a privileged position – from within as well as on behalf of the dominant literary tradition – when he complains in a paper he presented at the 1986 Stockholm African Writers' Conference that African literature has been subjected to too much criticism:

The amount of criticism of African literature, which is now probably

3

about a thousand fold of the actual [literary] material being put out,
really constitutes a barrier, not only to the literature itself, but in fact
to the very personalities of the producers of literature.

('Ethics' 26)

Speaking at the same conference, but from quite a different position – from
the margins of the canon and on behalf of women writers – Ama Ata Aidoo,
by contrast, is bitter about the literary establishment's neglect of women
writers. Making a plea not for less but for more criticism, she claims that
what most distinguishes African women from African men writers is the
vast difference in the amount of critical attention paid to them:

> [I]t is especially pathetic to keep on writing without having any
> consistent, active, critical intelligence that is interested in you as an
> artist. . . . Therefore, it is precisely from this point that African writing
> women's reality begins to differ somewhat from that of the male
> African writer. Once we have faced the basic fact of the oppression
> and marginality that is almost endemic in the lives of . . . Africans,
> we also begin to admit that at least, some people are interested in the
> male African writer. These include African, non-African, male and
> female literary critics, different categories of publishers, editors,
> anthologists, translators, librarians, sundry academic analysts, and all
> other zealous collectors of treasures! ('To be' 158)

Lindfors clearly subscribes to the conventional formalist view of the
canon as the corpus of texts that defines excellence – classic texts
produced by great writers. Thus, for example, he labels authors who score
badly on his tests as 'second-rate talents' ('Famous authors'' 133). Recently critics concerned with marginalized literatures have challenged
this view and insisted that literary canons, rather than reflecting objective
judgements of literary merit, are artificial constructs that are imposed by
an elite and that operate to reproduce and reinforce existing power
relations. What these critics argue is that biases are embedded in the
prevailing critical paradigms and that these work to marginalize or
discredit certain perspectives. As Arnold Krupat puts it in his discussion
of Native American literature: 'there are unmistakable connections between critical paradigms and canon formation' (91).[2] What I hope to
show in the pages that follow is that sexism has operated as a bias of
exclusion in African literary criticism.

As Biodun Jeyifo indicates, New Critical formalism has been the
reigning point of view in African literary studies since the 1960s, its
proponents, who include both western critics like Lindfors and Cook, and

African ones like Eustace Palmer, Eldred Jones, and Daniel Izevbaye, advocating 'an "objective" literary scholarship based on truly "aesthetic", formal criteria of evaluation' (43). The main charge that has been levelled against this mode of criticism from within African literary studies is that of Eurocentrism, the most influential formulation of this accusation being that of Chinweizu, Onwuchekwa Jemie, and Ihechukwu Madubuike who argue that the universal values New Criticism purports to embody are, in fact, 'provincial, time-and-place bound *European preferences*' (4); and that to judge African literature by these criteria is therefore to define it 'as an appendage of European literature' (10). Ashcroft and his colleagues make a similar point. New Criticism's false claim to objectivity, they state, facilitated the 'assimilation of post-colonial writers into a "metropolitan" tradition' which retarded the development of indigenous theories, as works were not considered 'within an appropriate cultural context' (160–1).

In its claims to objectivity and universality, New Criticism has also been challenged by western feminists. Rejecting 'universal' values as masking male preferences, they have confronted New Criticism with its andro- or phallocentrism. This same male bias is apparent in New Criticism's reading of African literature. Most evidently, the texts it privileges – the titles that make up the all-male canon – encode a reactionary gender ideology. Revealing this hidden ideology – making explicit the gender codes of canonical texts – is the main undertaking of my first two chapters. What can be noted here is that it is not only New Criticism that fails to mention this reactionary ideology. Other modes also suppress it which suggests that there is a coincidence between this ideology and that of a variety of non-feminist critical positions.

New Criticism's method of evaluating texts is also revealing. As Chinweizu and his colleagues indicate, it betrays its Eurocentrism by only endorsing texts which conform to western standards. But there is also a tendency within the New Critical paradigm to assess works written by women differently from those written by men. For whereas the general practice has been to compare the latter to canonical (usually male-authored) European texts, the former have tended to be compared to valorized male-authored African ones. In the second case, that comparison, in my reading, is always derogatory. This is not surprising given the fact that women's texts are being assessed on the basis of standards established first by western and then by African men writers, and it illustrates the extent to which African women writers have been alienated from the African literary tradition. New Criticism's exclusionary methods will be considered in more detail in later chapters where, as part of a discussion of women writers' critical reception, a number of reviews written in the New Critical mode will be examined. As we shall see, works by women writers have been trivialized, distorted, and maligned as a result of their non-conformity to standards that are both Euro- and androcentric.

Lindfors considers the African literary canon to be 'still in a state of creative gestation' with only Achebe, Ngũgĩ, and Soyinka being quite secure in their standing ('Teaching' 55). If the tradition of New Criticism can be seen to have led to the exclusion of women writers from the canon, as Lindfors's data (which are current to 1986) represent it, what is the likelihood of their gaining admission as the canon changes?

It is evident that New Criticism is finally giving way to other paradigms and it is to a consideration of some of those that are gaining currency that I will turn in addressing this question. These include a number of models which are subsumable under the rubric of historicist or cultural criticism – JanMohamed's, Ngũgĩ's, Jameson's, and that of Ashcroft and his colleagues, all of which theorize African/'post-colonial'/'third-world' literature as having been shaped by a particular set of socio-political conditions. As we have already seen, these critics do not treat any African women writers in their discussions. The question is, then, do their models preclude such a treatment? Do they manifest an underlying bias of exclusion?

Like New Criticism, this historicist criticism represents itself as universal, although only in terms of gender. Thus the critics use generic terms such as 'the African writer' and '"post-colonial"/"third-world" writing'. Thus, too, none of these critics treats gender as a socio-political category. Ashcroft and Jameson's sole category of analysis is coloniality, while Ngũgĩ privileges class and JanMohamed race. Moreover, the only socio-political conditions they consider in relation to the literary structures produced by African/'post-colonial'/'third-world' writers are the conditions of colonialism or neo-colonialism, and these they represent as being universal as to gender. Thus JanMohamed, drawing on Fanon's insight into the structure of colonial society, posits 'a manichean allegory of white and black, good and evil, salvation and damnation, civilization and savagery, superiority and inferiority, intelligence and emotion, self and other, subject and object' (4) as the source of 'such a powerful socio-political-ideological force field that neither colonial nor African literature is able to escape or transcend it':

> [Writers] may decry or simply depict its existence and effects, they may try to subvert it or overcome its consequences, or they may valorize it; but regardless of the overt thematic content of their writing, they cannot ignore it. (277)

In criticizing JanMohamed for ignoring gender, Susan Z. Andrade observes that while his 'allegorical model is useful in deciphering race

6

relations', it 'seems capable of addressing only one category of analysis at a time, which requires that marginalized categories be assimilated into, rather than accommodated by, the model, which remains fixed' (93). It is, however, perhaps more a failure to insert other categories that is the problem. The model the authors of *The Empire Writes Back* elaborate – a model based on the spatial metaphor of centre and margin or periphery – suffers from the same kind of limitation.[3]

As a result of the assimilation of gender into other categories, the African/'post-colonial' subject (including the writing subject) is constructed as male in these models. For, as feminist scholars in various fields have argued, colonialism is not neutral as to gender. Rather it is a patriarchal order, sexist as well as racist in its ideology and practices. What these studies indicate is that women's position relative to men deteriorated under colonialism. They also show that, while pre-colonial women had more freedom than their colonized descendants, male domination was nonetheless an integral part of the societies they lived in.[4] Under colonialism, then, African women were subject to interlocking forms of oppression: to the racism of colonialism and to indigenous and foreign structures of male domination.

JanMohamed's use of the 'generic' pronoun is telling. For it is precisely this difference between men's and women's experience of colonialism that his characterization of the dilemma created for Africans by colonialism suppresses:

> [Colonialism] puts the native in a double bind: if he chooses conservatively and remains loyal to his indigenous culture, then he opts to stay in a calcified society whose developmental momentum has been checked by colonization. If, however, the colonized person chooses assimilation, then he is trapped in a form of historical catalepsy because colonial education severs him from his own past and replaces it with the study of the colonizer's past. (5)

But records show that the second option – assimilation through education – was relatively inaccessible to the gendered 'native'. For example, the figures Ifi Amadiume quotes in her discussion of male bias in colonial education show that the ratio of boys to girls in school in the Eastern Province of Nigeria in 1906 was more than 5:1 and in the Central Province more than 20:1. Amadiume also notes that the *Annual Colonial Report* of 1911 records 'a figure of 1,160 boys to 20 girls in 29 schools' (*Male Daughters* 134–5). On the same subject, Carole Boyce Davies observes how colonial policies in combination with indigenous attitudes operated to deny girls access to education:

7

The selection of males for formal education was fostered by the colonial institutions which made specific choices in educating male and female. Then too, the sex role distinctions common to many African societies supported the notion that western education was a barrier to a woman's role as wife and mother and an impediment to her success in these traditional modes of acquiring status. With few exceptions, girls were kept away from formal and especially higher education. The colonial administrations were therefore willing accomplices because they imported a view of the world in which women were of secondary importance.

('Feminist consciousness' 2)

Furthermore, Amadiume has shown how the transportation of 'Victorian ideology . . . into Igboland by the British missionaries and educationalists' undermined women's traditional autonomy. 'It was', she says, 'from their ideologies that the expression "a woman's place is in the home" was derived', a 'slogan [that] has ever since been a popular topic for school debates in Nigeria' (*Male Daughters* 136).

The 'double-bind', then – an aspect of colonial experience which, in JanMohamed's view, must be taken into account for 'the development of the African novel' to be 'adequately appreciated' (5) – is essentially a male bind, as colonialism created quite a different set of problems for women. Moreover, the conclusion Christine Obbo reaches in her study of East African women's attempts to adapt to the radical social changes inaugurated by colonialism indicates that one of the ways in which men have resolved their own dilemma is by developing a theory of separate historical roles for men and women – a theory which serves to justify and reproduce the structures of male domination which continue to deny girls and women equal access to education and other resources:[5]

[I]t seems that women's own attempts to cope with the new situations they find themselves in are regarded as a 'problem' by men, and a betrayal of traditions which are often confused with women's roles. Women must act as mediators between the past and the present, while men see themselves as mediators between the present and the future. (143)

As we shall see, this same resolution to the double bind of calcification or catalepsy is enacted by men writers in their texts: the identification of women with 'petrified' cultural traditions and the allocation to male characters or narrators of the role of regaining control over the historical development of their societies.

The authors of *The Empire Writes Back* are more blatant than JanMohamed in their designation of the 'post-colonial' subject and writer as male – a designation which exposes their inclusion, by name at least, of three women writers as a token gesture. As they see it, '[women] share with colonized races and peoples an intimate experience of the politics of oppression and repression, and like them they have been forced to articulate their experiences in the language of their oppressors' (174–5). This same logic requires that feminism be designated a western phenomenon. Hence, in their view, there is a '[striking] parallel between the situation of post-colonial writing and that of feminist writing' in that each engages from a marginalized position with a dominant culture – western imperial culture in the case of 'post-colonial' writing and patriarchal culture in the case of feminism (7). In a separate article in which he homologizes further between feminist and 'post-colonial' writing, Ashcroft expresses the hope that 'a genuine post-colonial feminism' will emerge 'through the gaps and absences of [his] paper' ('Intersecting marginalities' 33). One has already emerged through the lacunae in Ashcroft's thinking in the form of the writing of any number of 'post-colonial' feminists, that of Doris Lessing, for example, a writer whom Ashcroft and his colleagues do refer to (in passing) in *The Empire Writes Back*, or of Margaret Atwood or Flora Nwapa.

In his 'Writing against neo-colonialism', Ngũgĩ claims in a note that '[t]he terms "he" and "his"', which he uses throughout the essay to refer to 'the writer', 'are not meant to denote the "maleness" of a person' (103). But this is precisely what they do, Ngũgĩ's conscious refusal to generalize gender reference being symptomatic of an a priori resistance to recognizing women as writers or as equal subjects. Ngũgĩ delineates 'three ages' in the development of African literature since the Second World War: 'the age of the anti-colonial struggle; the age of independence; and the age of neo-colonialism' (92). The writing of 'the first age', the 1950s, he says, was self-assured and optimistic as 'the writer and his work were part of the African revolution' (94), while that of the 1960s 'was characterized by a sense of despair' as the writer responded to 'the moral decay of the new states' (97–8). The 1970s, on the other hand, 'the third age', saw the writer 'coming face to face with neo-colonialism. . . . Further he was beginning to take sides with the people in the class struggle in Africa' (100). This periodization of contemporary African literature is based on men's writing; and it operates to exclude women's literary expression as part of African literature. For, as a result of their placement in the social order, women writers have been engaged in a sexual, as well as a class/race struggle from the beginning. Hence works like Nwapa's *Efuru* (1966) and Emecheta's *The Joys of Motherhood* (1979) do not fit Ngũgĩ's 'three ages' theory. At the same time, Ngũgĩ's account of the development of African literature suppresses the ongoing history of women's writing.

At least when it is applied to African literature, Jameson's characterization of 'third-world' literature can also be seen to work to exclude women's literary expression. 'All third-world texts', Jameson declares, 'are necessarily . . . allegorical'. Unlike 'first- and second-world' texts, 'they are to be read as . . . *national allegories*' so that '*the story of the private individual destiny is always an allegory of the embattled situation of the public third-world culture and society*' ('Third-world literature' 69). Jameson prefaces this statement with a description of 'third-world' socio-political conditions. 'Third-world' states, he says, are defined by 'the experience of colonialism and imperialism' (67). It is this which distinguishes them from 'first-and second-world' states and which, it would seem, is also responsible for their nationalism, nationalism having long since been abandoned in 'first- and second-world' nations. As Aijaz Ahmad points out, Jameson's theory 'rests . . . upon a suppression of the multiplicity of significant difference among and within both the advanced capitalist countries and the imperialised formations' (3). In my reading of African literature, one of the differences that has been suppressed is gender difference. For while 'national allegory' is a frequent (but not exclusive) form of narrativity in contemporary African literature, this is only the case in literature written by men. This difference in representational strategy is, I would suggest, the result of two interrelated factors. First, as sociologists like Helen Ware, Eleanor R. Fapohunda, Kamene Okonjo, and Ifi Amadiume indicate, women in many African states are marginal to national politics and, more generally, to the public life of their nations.[6] Hence, as writers, women would be less concerned than men, at least for some of whom nationalism did become an urgent ideological preoccupation, with representing 'the embattled situation of public . . . culture' than with portraying the anti-national experience of their gender. Second, this difference can be seen as resulting from an antagonistic response on the part of women writers to the 'national allegories' produced by some of their male counterparts – allegories which, as I will indicate in my second chapter, encode gender definitions which operate to justify and maintain the status quo of women's exclusion from public life.[7]

According to JanMohamed, a dialogue on race with colonial discourse constitutes 'a fundamental component of contemporary African literature' (279). Ashcroft and his colleagues' characterization of 'post-colonial' writing is quite similar. '[T]he process of literary decolonization', they write, 'has involved a radical dismantling of the European codes and a post-colonial subversion and appropriation of the dominant European discourses. . . . These subversive manoeuvres . . . are the characteristic features of the post-colonial text' (195–6). Again, if African literature is representative, then what both JanMohamed and the authors of *The Empire Writes Back* provide is a (partial) definition of African men's writing. For while African women writers' texts do establish a dialogic relation – or, in Ashcroft's terms, engage in subversive manoeuvres – with western texts, the interaction is as much concerned with gender as it is with race or coloniality. Furthermore, the primary engagement of these texts is with the African male literary tradition, as women writers have responded to the reactionary gender ideology embedded there.

JanMohamed's and Ashcroft's models even fail to characterize men's writing adequately. For they obscure intra-regional or intra-national exchanges between African/'post-colonial' men writers, exchanges on issues which may be rooted in the experience of colonialism but which have acquired regional or national importance. In other words, they mask the intertextuality produced by African/'post-colonial' men writers' engagement with *each other's texts*. In the case of African literature, the debate among authors over the language of its expression is obscured – a debate which has engaged Ngũgĩ as the main proponent of the exclusive use of African languages for African literary expression, and other writers, such as Achebe, who argue that European languages can be made to carry the weight of African experience.[8] So too are the exchanges between authors such as Ngũgĩ, as well as critics, who take up a Marxist position in their writing and those such as Soyinka and Achebe who oppose Marxism.[9] More crucially, they also obscure the influence of the literary dialogue initiated by women writers on men's writing.

Finally, we might note that these models operate on the assumption (and give the impression) that African and other 'post-colonial' literatures lack an internal dynamic, that they are unable to generate their own experience. But as Achebe reminds us, 'every literature must seek the things that belong unto its peace, it must, in other words, speak of a particular place, evolve out of the necessities of its history, past and current, and the aspirations and destiny of its people' (*Morning* 7). African literature does, as Chinweizu puts it, present 'a community discussing its experiences with itself' (4). And while, as Ashcroft and his colleagues claim, 'the process of literary decolonization' can be seen to have 'involved a radical dismantling of the European codes', it has also involved the establishment of internal dialogues, dialogues which, *because they are internal*, can be seen to mark the progress that has been made toward decolonization. The literary dialogue between men and women is particularly significant in this regard in that it is occasioning major changes in the orientation of the African literature – a turning away from a concern with the issue of race to a concern with the

11

issue of gender, as well as a turning away from an interrogation of European texts to an interrogation of or interaction with other African texts. As the initiators of this dialogue, women writers have earned a place in African literary history, one which has been denied them because gender has been ignored as a factor in the development of African literature.

Feminist criticism has also recently gained currency in African literary studies, so much so that it can be credited with placing Emecheta and Head among the writers who, in Lindfors's terms, have since 1981 'displayed the greatest upward mobility' ('Famous authors'' 142). While this criticism can be seen to be improving African women writers' status in relation to the canon, it has generally not tried to situate them within the African literary tradition. One of its concerns has rather been with their placement in a wider female aesthetic. Such is the case with Chikwenye Okonjo Ogunyemi's 'Womanism: the dynamics of the contemporary Black female novel in English' which posits a 'black womanist aesthetic' encompassing African and African American women's literature (64), and with my own 'The shallow grave' which suggests the possibility of there being 'a female literary tradition that transcends all cultural boundaries' (144). Susheila Nasta's critical anthology, *Motherlands*, has a similar perspective in its desire 'to compare and contrast women's writing in English from Africa, the Caribbean and South Asia' (xix). Such cross-cultural readings are usually quite valid. But it is evident to me now that African women's writing cannot be thoroughly appreciated unless it is juxtaposed to African men's literature. The converse is also the case: African men's writing cannot be fully appreciated in isolation from African women's literature. For each provides a primary context for the development of the other. Furthermore, by removing works from the cultural context in which they were produced, such criticism retards the development of theories of African literature.

More crucially, the prevailing trend in feminist criticism has been for African women's texts to be assimilated into a white feminist problematic. This is a practice which Gayatri Chakravorty Spivak describes in a warning she issues to 'first-world' feminists as 'fall[ing] back on a colonialist theory of most efficient information retrieval' (*In Other Worlds* 179). It is also one which privileges the concerns and modalities of western feminism, as well as the African texts that conform to those modalities, and which implicitly if not explicitly presents feminism as a western phenomenon. As has been shown by feminist scholars from a variety of disciplines who, like Spivak, identify with a different constituency of women, white western feminist research is generally marked by Eurocentrism.[10] It may, like the historicist criticism we have been examining, represent itself as universal, in this case in terms of race, but in so doing it overlooks its own cultural and historical specificity, including, as Andrade reminds us, its 'inscription within a European system of thought which is saturated by imperialism' (92).

Well aware of the Eurocentrism/racism of mainstream western feminism, African writers like Flora Nwapa and Buchi Emecheta have rejected the feminist label or insisted on qualifying it.[11] Making a similar move, Filomena Chioma Steady formulates a specifically African feminism. Rather than being a western import, Steady argues, feminism is a strategy that African women have developed and consistently adopted for their survival in the face of race, class, and sex oppression:

> True feminism is an abnegation of male protection and a determination to be resourceful and self-reliant. The majority of the black women in Africa and in the diaspora have developed these characteristics, though not always by choice. (35)

Therefore, Steady asserts, the claim can be made that 'the black woman is . . . the original feminist' (36). Ifi Amadiume reaches the same kind of conclusion in her analysis of Igbo society. Whereas 'militant feminism' is 'a comparatively new phenomenon in the Western world', she writes, it has been 'a constant reality for women in traditional Igbo societies' (*Male Daughters* 10). The question of the racial politics of feminist literary criticism will be taken up again in later chapters where I will examine in some detail several critical essays in which a western feminist perspective has been adopted in the treatment of African women writers.

The main undertaking of the chapters that follow, however, is to write African women writers back into the African literary tradition. As we shall see, the inclusion of this writing alters conventional views of the tradition. On the related issue of the canon, my concern will be less with the incorporation of works by women into the established canon than with canon reconstruction through alternative modes of reading. As will be evident, in relating to the male literary tradition, women writers themselves provide alternative readings of canonical authors.

Like JanMohamed's, my study derives from Fredric Jameson's work on 'narrative as a socially symbolic act' and is in accordance with Jameson's view that all literature is informed by 'the political unconscious' and that the primary function of literary analysis is 'the unmasking of cultural artifacts as socially symbolic acts' (*Political Unconscious* 20). In Jameson's Marxian analysis, the political unconscious is constituted by the individual subject's placement in the class hierarchy, while in JanMohamed's it is the subject's racial designation that is the determining factor. For, he says, 'in the colonial situation the function of class is replaced by race' (7). As I have tried to indicate, because JanMohamed ignores gender, his characterization of contemporary African literature encompasses only men's literature. In my analysis of socio–literary relations, two facets of subject constitution will be considered: determination by the social category of race and determination by gender. The focus will, however, be on the latter, as my intention is to complement, as well as to revise, analyses like JanMohamed's. What needs to be emphasized, however, is the heterogeneous character of subject constitution.

The first, or political, horizon of interpretation in Jameson's scheme is constituted by the historical context of the text. Within this horizon, the text is construed as 'the rewriting or restructuration of a prior historical or ideological *subtext*' (81). This transformation of the subtext comprises the 'symbolic act' of the text. For Jameson, then, literary texts are both aesthetic and ideological discourses: 'the aesthetic act is itself ideological, and the production of aesthetic or narrative form is to be seen as an ideological act in its own right, with the function of inventing imaginary or formal "solutions" to unresolvable social contradictions' (79).

Manichean Aesthetics in part fills the critical gap JanMohamed makes reference to at the beginning of his study: namely the gap created by the practice of studying colonial and African literatures 'in a socio–political vacuum', by the 'refusal . . . of literary critics to come to terms with the colonial situation' (1). Of the remaining gaps,[12] the most gaping, it seems to me, is the one created by the failure of critics of African literature to come to terms with the patriarchal situation in both its indigenous and colonial or foreign dimensions. Within the political mode of interpretation, then, my primary concern is with the nature of the influence of patriarchal social structures, both indigenous and imported, on the literary structures of fiction produced by contemporary African writers, men as well as women. I will, however, also consider the influence of the racial dimension of colonial structure on African women's writing.

While all contemporary societies can be classified as patriarchal, in that each operates a social system characterized by male dominance, they are differently patriarchal, for each constructs gender differently. There is also evidence to indicate that some societies are more flexible than others in their construction of gender. This is what Amadiume and others have argued was the case in a number of African societies until the beginning of this century when, under colonialism, rigid European gender definitions were imposed, which altered male–female power relations to the detriment of women. While some specific variations will become evident in the chapters that follow, I will begin, as JanMohamed does in his treatment of colonialism, with a description of the generic patriarchal situation in contemporary Africa, relying in this undertaking on Omolara Ogundipe-

Leslie's analysis of the condition of women in Africa in her essay 'African women, culture and another development'.

'African women', she says, 'are weighed down by superstructural forms deriving from the pre-colonial past' when 'gender hierarchy or male supremacy . . . was known or taken for granted' (133). These 'traditional ideologies of patriarchy or male domination' were themselves 'negatively encouraged' under colonialism as 'nineteenth century European ideas of patriarchy' were imposed on African societies. The introduction of Islam also disrupted traditional societies, 'creating new oppressed and subjugated stati and roles for women'. Thus African women are also 'weighed down' by the 'male-dominated structures' and 'the hardened attitudes of male superiority' introduced through foreign incursions (130–1). On the cultural outcome of the changes that have occurred in political structures, Ogundipe-Leslie makes the following observations:

> Women are 'naturally' excluded from public affairs; they are viewed as unable to hold positions of responsibility, rule men or even be visible when serious matters of state and society are being discussed. Women are viewed to need tutelage before they can be politically active; politics is considered the absolute realm of men; women are not considered fit for political positions in modern African nation-states, though their enthusiasm and campaign work are exploited by their various political parties. (130)

As we shall see, the experience of marginality is reflected in the thematic preoccupations of African women's literature, while men's literature tends to be full of ideological valorizations of the status quo of male domination.

As we have already seen, JanMohamed, following Fanon, characterizes colonial society as a manichean structure organized according to a racial allegory – an allegory of white and black, good and evil, superiority and inferiority. But there is evidence to suggest that a sexual allegory – an allegory of male and female, good and evil, superiority and inferiority, subject and object, self and other – also organizes the structure of African colonial, as well as 'post-colonial' societies. This is the substance of Ogundipe-Leslie's observation that '[t]he ideology that men are naturally superior to women *in essence* and in all areas, affects the modern day organization of societal structures' in Africa (133).

The operation of this binary code is, perhaps, nowhere so clearly evident than in the ordinances enacted in various parts of Africa during the colonial period to keep single women out of urban areas. Thus Patricia Ruddy reports that under the Southern Rhodesian Natives Registration Act of 1936 'a pass system for women was instituted to, as the Conference of Native

Commissioners stated, "put a check on the influx [to urban centres] of young women who evade parental control and enter all too easily into an immoral life"' (4). From this perspective, then, 'an immoral life' is a wholly female affair. And while women are viewed as being easily corrupted by the city, no contradiction is perceived in men being moral and being in the city. Similarly, Kenneth Little indicates that a chiefs' conference in Sierra Leone in the early 1940s resolved that 'women strangers in a town should be "signed for" by their landlords' with whom they were then required to stay 'until collected by the husband or his representative' (16–17). And Christine Obbo reports that in Kampala during the 1950s

> there were laws requiring the repatriation of all single women found 'loitering' in town. All single female migrants were branded as 'prostitutes' or 'loose' women who were intent on satisfying the sexual needs of the male migrants and consuming some of their money, but who were not destined for marriage. (26–7)

As Ruddy observes, the efforts to keep women in the rural areas served 'a number of both colonial and male African interests':

> On the colonial side, keeping women – and thus African family life – situated firmly in the villages prevented the full proletarianization of African men labouring in the towns; senior men in the villages shared this interest, for with women/wives tied to the rural areas the junior men who had migrated to the towns would continue to make remittances. . . . Male migrants themselves had an interest in leaving their wives and families in the villages, for in this way they could both earn urban wages and retain their foothold in the rural economy. (3)

Such ordinances, then – ordinances made in the name of female 'morality' – contributed to the process of women's economic marginalization by relegating them to the rural economy, which in practice often meant subsistence farming.

Ruddy also writes of the mass arrests of 'unaccompanied women' in the cities of a number of 'post-colonial' African nations – Gabon, Zimbabwe, Mozambique, Zambia – and of their transportation to rural areas in order to demonstrate the wide currency of the notion that 'control of female "immorality" may be achieved through repatriation to the villages' (2). Writing in a similar vein, Amadiume tells of a northern Nigerian state 'which outlawed rented accommodation for single women, considering them all to be prostitutes against whom punitive action should be taken' (*Male Daughters* 199). And Carolyne Dennis tells of how, in its 'War Against

Indiscipline', the Nigerian Federal Military Government in 1984–5 'singled out as being the cause of "indiscipline"' three categories of women: 'petty traders, single women, and working women with children' – categories which 'would appear between them to encompass most Nigerian women' (19).

Thus the patriarchal situation, as these types of incidents delineate it, puts the African woman in a particular kind of double bind. For if, in order to improve her economic status, she chooses to migrate to the city or seek employment, she is labelled a 'prostitute' or singled out as the cause of national 'indiscipline'. If, on the other hand, she elects to stay in the village or be a housewife, she is economically marginalized. The patriarchal situation also creates difficulties for men – reconciling the fact of women's participation in the liberation struggle with that of their exclusion from national politics, and of accommodating the notions of freedom and equality upheld by the liberation movements with the actual subjugation of women in 'post-colonial' nations. Men writers, as we shall see, have found several ways of 'resolving' their dilemmas – the identifi- cation of women with 'tradition', for instance, or the idealization of conventional female roles. And while men writers tend to valorize the sexual allegory by, for example, invoking what Ruddy refers to as 'the theme of redemption through repatriation [to the village]' (7), women writers attempt to subvert it.

The second or social horizon of interpretation in Jameson's model is constituted by the discoursal context of the text as viewed from the perspective of class. Here the text is 'refocused as a *parole* or individual utterance, of that vaster system, or *langue*, of class discourse' and hence is seen 'as a symbolic move in an essentially polemic and strategic ideological confrontation between the classes' (85). Jameson's analysis of the structure of class discourse, which following Mikhail Bakhtin he characterizes as 'dialogical' (84), provides the basis for my study of intertextual relations. However, as JanMohamed does with the allegorical model he derives from Fanon, so Jameson inserts only one category into his Saussurean model. Hence, it cannot account for Bakhtinean polyphony, for a text's or a literature's participation in more than one dialogical system. Nor can it account for the shifts in allegiances and changes in status that occur when texts or literatures are transferred from one system to another, or for the dialogic relation between texts of the same status.

Although my primary concern is with the dialogical system constituted by gender discourse, other dialogical systems are invoked in intertextual readings of men's and women's narratives. What I most hope my analysis within this mode of interpretation makes evident is that the dynamics of none of these or of other related systems, including the system constituted by race discourse that JanMohamed considers, can be adequately understood if the systems are examined in isolation from one another.

On the basis of his analysis of class discourse, Jameson characterizes 'the normal form of the dialogical' as 'essentially an antagonistic one' (84), thus deviating from Bakhtin's view of the dialogical as taking several forms: agreement or affirmation, as well as antagonism or negation, and relativization or ambivalence (*Problems* 125–6, 183–99). As I hope to show, the relationship between African literary texts of the same status is often one of affirmation. In her examination of the intertextual relation between Nwapa's *Efuru* and Emecheta's *The Joys of Motherhood*, Andrade provides one example (although I shall query her reading of *Efuru* in a later chapter). What Andrade concludes is that 'the relation of the second text to the first is not a violent rewriting. Rather, their intertextual relation is one that ultimately emphasizes the affinities that marginalized women writing in a shared tradition must acknowledge' (105).

Following Jameson, JanMohamed characterizes the relationship between colonial and African (male) literature as an antagonistic one (13). But even here there are instances of intertextual ambivalence or affirmation. Such instances become evident when the patriarchal dimension of colonial structure is taken into consideration, as they occur when the sexist aspects or formulations of colonial racism are adopted with little or no revision by African men writers. Kathleen McLuskie and Lyn Innes provide an example of this type of dialogical interaction in their discussion of the context in which African women began to write. 'The coloniser's mythologising of Africa as the Other, as Female', they state, 'was all too often transformed into recognizably related forms by African male writers in the name of nationalism' (4). This essentially nonparodic reiteration in African men's writing of the conventional colonial trope of Africa as Female can best be understood as an expression or function of that writing's change in status from a nonhegemonic literature in its relation to colonial discourse to a hegemonic literature in its relation to women's writing.[13] Other such instances of intertexual affirmation will become evident in the chapters that follow. As we shall also see, combatants on both sides in the sexual struggle which is taking place within African literature and which has influenced its development have made efforts to diminish the level of antagonism in the dialogue.

This book is divided into three sections. The first, 'Aspects of the Male Literary Tradition', seeks to elicit the gender definitions embedded in the literary, as well as in the critical texts of the contemporary African male literary tradition. In Chapter 1, I consider the most canonical of African texts, Chinua Achebe's *Things Fall Apart*, first as it has been acclaimed by the critical establishment and then as its sexual codes are revealed in a feminist reading. In Chapter 2, I consider the status of the Mother Africa trope – 'the mythologising', in McLuskie and Innes's terms, 'of Africa as . . . Female' – as a convention within the African male literary tradition, first tracing the trope's history from the time of its occurrence in the poetry of the Negritude movement through the revisions it undergoes in later texts, and then investigating the sexual politics of the convention.

The second section, 'Room for Women', focuses on the attempts of four women writers – Grace Ogot, Flora Nwapa, Buchi Emecheta, and Mariama Bâ – to dismantle the gender codes inscribed in the male tradition. However, intertextual relations between African women's texts and colonial literature are also considered, as are intertextual relations within African women's literature and trends in the criticism of that literature.

In the third section, 'Men Write Back', I examaine two fairly recently published novels by men writers: Ngũgĩ's *Devil on the Cross* and Achebe's *Anthills of the Savannah*. These works mark a new moment in African literary history: men writers' engagement in the dialogue on gender women writers have initiated.

Finally, a brief word on my choice of authors. In geographical terms, the selection is somewhat comprehensive in that the writers come from two different regions – East and West Africa – and from a number of different countries. Those whom I treat in some detail include: Ngũgĩ wa Thiong'o and Grace Ogot from Kenya; Nuruddin Farah from Somalia; Okot p'Bitek from Uganda; Chinua Achebe, Cyprian Ekwensi, Buchi Emecheta, Flora Nwapa, and Wole Soyinka from Nigeria; Ayi Kwei Armah from Ghana; Camara Laye from Guinea; Mongo Beti from Cameroun; and Léopold Senghor, Ousmane Sembène, and Mariama Bâ from Senegal. This geographical spread also encompasses several different forms of western colonial imperialism: Italian, British, and French in the case of Somalia; and either British or French in the case of the other countries. I have not included any works from southern Africa, as it seems to me that, because of the racial politics of the area, its literature would, for the meantime, benefit from separate treatment. The men writers I have chosen are mainly canonical authors, while the women writers are well-established (though unrecognized) authors. The ratio of men to women writers is nearly 3:1, a reflection of the facts of publishing on the continent. I have, however, allocated more chapters (and more pages) to women writers, an 'act' undertaken to promote their proper placement within the African literary tradition.

Part I

ASPECTS OF THE MALE LITERARY TRADITION

1

HOW COULD THINGS FALL APART FOR WHOM THEY WERE NOT TOGETHER?

Chinua Achebe's first novel, *Things Fall Apart* (1958), is the most important work by an African author. 'Over five million copies' of the book have been sold and it has been translated into thirty languages.[1] Its influence on the development of the contemporary African literary and critical tradition has been substantial. In the view of H. L. B. Moody, Elizabeth Gunner, and Edward Finnegan, it can be taken 'to mark the beginning of modern African literature' (vii), while for C. L. Innes, its author 'may be deemed the "father of the African novel in English"' (19).

As numerous critics have noted, *Things Fall Apart* provided a model for succeeding writers to follow. Thus David Cook states that it 'has become an early landmark . . . because it is a worthy archetype' (65). And while Kofi Awoonor writes of how Achebe's 'style and thematic preoccupations . . . inspired a whole new school of writers who may be referred to as the "clash of cultures" novelists' (279–80), C. L. Innes and Bernth Lindfors speak of the 'School of Achebe' (6). Similarly, Lewis Nkosi states that in his reconstruction of the past – his establishment of 'history as the "hero" of the African novel' – Achebe 'blazed a trail large enough to be followed by other writers' (33); and that in his innovative handling of language, he '[set] an example which has influenced many younger writers' (53). *Things Fall Apart* also provided a model for critics. In the words of Gerald Moore:

> [Its] appearance . . . in 1958 won for its author a position of eminence in African literature which for a long time led to his being elevated above his fellows, in his own and the succeeding generation. The book was quickly recognized as a classic and tended to be used as a yardstick with which to measure the many Anglophone novels, Nigerian and other, that followed it.
>
> (*Twelve African Writers* 123)

Things Fall Apart, then, has been a very influential novel, founding a new era in African literature, providing a pattern for countless other novels, and serving as an arbiter of critical standards.

Achebe's own later comments on colonial fiction and on the role of the African writer suggest that he was himself aware when he was writing that he was creating a new literature. While studying at Ibadan, he says, 'I read some appalling novels about Africa . . . and decided that the story we had to tell could not be told for us by anyone else no matter how gifted or well-intentioned' (*Morning* 70). One of those novels was Joyce Cary's *Mister Johnson* and another, Conrad's *Heart of Darkness*, works which he has accused of racism in various speeches and essays. Achebe is especially emphatic in his condemnation of *Heart of Darkness*:

> Conrad was a bloody racist. That this simple truth is glossed over in criticism of his work is due to the fact that white racism against Africa is such a normal way of thinking that its manifestations go completely undetected. Students of *Heart of Darkness* will often tell you that Conrad is concerned not so much with Africa as with the deterioration of one European mind caused by solitude and sickness. . . .
>
> Which is partly the point: Africa as setting and backdrop which eliminates the African as human factor. Africa as a metaphysical battlefield devoid of all recognizable humanity, into which the wandering European enters at his peril. Of course, there is a preposterous and perverse kind of arrogance in thus reducing Africa to the role of props for the breakup of one petty European mind. But that is not even the point. The real question is the dehumanization of Africa and Africans which this age-long attitude has fostered and continues to foster in the world. And the question is whether a novel which celebrates this dehumanization, which depersonalizes a portion of the human race, can be called a great work of art. My answer is: No, it cannot.
>
> ('Image of Africa' 788)[2]

More recently, Achebe has recounted how reading Cary, Conrad, and other colonial writers, including Rider Haggard, made him realize 'that stories are not innocent; that they can be used to put you in the wrong crowd, in the party of the man who has come to dispossess you' ('African literature' 7).

In the face of colonial derogation, the prime duty of the African writer in the first few years after independence was, according to Achebe, to restore dignity to the past, to show

that African people did not hear of culture for the first time from

Europeans; that their societies were not mindless but frequently had a philosophy of great depth and value and beauty, that they had poetry and above all, they had dignity. It is this dignity that many African people all but lost during the colonial period and it is this that they must now regain. The worst thing that can happen to any people is the loss of their dignity and self-respect. The writer's duty is to help them regain it by showing them in human terms what happened to them, what they lost. There is a saying in Ibo that a man who can't tell where the rain began to beat him cannot know where he dried his body. The writer can tell the people where the rain began to beat them.

('Role of the writer' 8)

I have quoted Achebe extensively on the issue of the racial politics of literary texts because his comments provide a context for my discussion of the sexual politics of Achebe's own most celebrated text. In *Things Fall Apart*, the Carys and Conrads of colonial Africa are represented by the District Commissioner whose own version of the story of imperial conquest is to be told in a book entitled '*The Pacification of the Primitive Tribes of the Lower Niger*' (187), a book in which Africans are to be represented as primitive savages, and the destruction of a sophisticated culture rendered as 'pacification'. Achebe subverts and dismantles the racial codes of this paradigmatic colonial text by contextualizing it in an alternative discourse – one which seeks to restore 'dignity and self-respect' to 'African people'. For Achebe's own version of the story – *Things Fall Apart* – tells of the tragic consequences of imperialism, of the destruction of a culture which manifested 'great depth and value and beauty'. The question is, however: Does Achebe attempt to restore 'dignity and self-respect' to African women? Does he tell his female readers 'where the rain began to beat them'?

Part I of *Things Fall Apart* is primarily concerned with the restoration of humanity to African society through the recreation of pre-colonial social, political, and religious institutions. We might therefore begin our analysis by examining the first scene in the novel that focuses on the women of Umuofia. The young Okonkwo, having inherited nothing from his father – 'neither . . . a barn nor a title, nor even a young wife' (17) – has come to borrow seed yams from his clansman, Nwakibie. Before they settle down to business, the palm-wine Okonkwo has brought is shared among the men present. Nwakibie calls in his wives:

Anasi was a middle-aged woman, tall and strongly built. There was authority in her bearing and she looked every inch the ruler of the womenfolk in a large and prosperous family. She wore the anklet of her husband's titles, which the first wife alone could wear.

24

She walked up to her husband and accepted the horn from him.
She then went down on one knee, drank a little and handed back
the horn. She rose, called him by his name and went back to her hut.
The other wives drank in the same way, in their proper order, and
went away. (18–19)

Eustace Palmer chooses this excerpt as one of the passages he particularly
admires, stating that from it 'the reader gains a sense of an alien, but
nevertheless strong, self-assured, and civilized society' (*Introduction* 51). But
where in this passage is the gendered African reader to locate herself? For
while she will immediately recognize the strength and self-assurance of the
male culture of Umuofia, she will have no such experience of its female
culture. Might she not wonder if the abject servitude of women is the
hallmark of a 'civilized society'?

In its representation of male–female power relations, this passage is
emblematic. For with the notable exception of Chielo, the powerful
priestess of Agbala, Achebe's women are, indeed, 'down on one knee', if not
both, before their menfolk and they are regularly making an exit, no doubt
'in their proper order', from all the spaces in which power, economic or
otherwise, is exercised.

The status of women in Umuofia is very low: 'He had a large barn full
of yams and he had three wives' (6). They are mere objects circulated among
their menfolk, willed, for example, by a father to a son as part of an estate,
or traded for a bag full of cowries. The only escape, it would seem, from
this demeaning classification is for a woman to outlive the men who could
own her. This might explain the position of *widow* Chielo.

Women are also systematically excluded from the political, the economic, the judicial, and even the discoursal life of the community. This is
indicated not only through the composition of the governing council of
elders, the *ndichie*, or the membership of the powerful *egwugwu* cult, which
is, in both cases, all male. For a repetition of the meaning underlying the
closing sentence of the passage Palmer admires so much – 'The other
wives . . . went away' – provides the novel with a kind of semantic refrain.
For example, when a townswoman is killed by a neighbouring clan, the
town-crier disturbs the slumbering people of Umuofia: 'And this was the
message. Every man of Umuofia was asked to gather at the market-place
tomorrow morning' (9). Or the people gather to witness the court
proceedings in a marital dispute: 'It was clear from the way the crowd stood
or sat that the ceremony was for men. There were many women, but they
looked on from the fringe like outsiders' (79). Or, the women repair the
exterior of the *egwugwu* house: 'These women never saw the inside of the

hut. No woman ever did. . . . No woman ever asked questions about the most powerful and the most secret cult in the clan' (80). As another passage which reiterates the refrain indicates, women are even excluded from their own betrothal ceremonies:

Akueke [entered] carrying a wooden dish with three kola nuts and alligator pepper. She gave the dish to her father's eldest brother and then shook hands, very shyly, with her suitor and his relatives. . . .
    When she had shaken hands, or rather held out her hand to be shaken, she returned to her mother's hut to help with the cooking. (64–5)

And sadly, but almost predictably, the one ceremony which is designated 'a woman's ceremony' (100) excludes women from all but the cooking:

Then the bride, her mother and half a dozen other women and girls emerged from the inner compound, and went round the circle [of men] shaking hands with all. The bride's mother led the way, followed by the bride and the other women. . . .
    When the women retired, Obierika presented kola nuts to his in-laws. (106)

While women are excluded from the male domain of community power, men are permitted to intrude into the domestic domain. Moreover, if Okonkwo is representative, the intrusion is often violent. Thus, when his third wife fails to produce her afternoon meal at the prescribed time, Okonkwo goes to her hut, then interrogates his other wives, and eventually beats the delinquent spouse. The prohibition on women from so much as approaching the male arena is, on the other hand, so absolute that even speech is forbidden them. This is the case not only when, as with the *egwugwu*, a secret male ritual is involved, but also when the concern is domestic. Thus in response to her query on how long she is, as she has been ordered, to look after Ikemefuna, Okonkwo's first wife is informed: 'Do what you are told, woman. . . . When did you become one of the *ndichie* of Umuofia?' (11).

We might pause for a moment in our analysis to consider, along with Ifi Amadiume, the authenticity of Achebe's representation of male–female power relations in pre-colonial Igbo society, not so much with a view to questioning the mimetic adequacy of the novel but in order to examine the relationship between the novel and the patriarchal situation which provided an important component of its generative ambience. 'The famous Igbo novelist, Chinua Achebe . . . a product of Western education, is no less guilty of the masculinization of the water goddess, whom he describes in his novel *Things Fall Apart*, as "god of water"', than are male historians and anthropologists (121). So writes Amadiume in *Male Daughters, Female Husbands*, her revisionist study of gender relations in Igbo society. In his most recent novel, *Anthills of the Savannah* (1987), Achebe himself acknowledges that he was in error in assigning masculine gender to the deity. For he devotes a chapter to the water *goddess* Idemili. He also implies through his characterization of the novel's heroine, Beatrice Okoh, herself an unwitting avatar of Idemili, that his ascriptive failure can be attributed to his western education:

> Beatrice . . . did not know [the] traditions and legends of her people because they played but little part in her upbringing. She was born . . . into a world apart; was baptized and sent to schools which made much about the English and the Jews and the Hindu and practically everybody else but hardly put in a word for her forebears and the divinities with whom they had evolved. (105)

The son of Christian converts, of a father who was a catechist for the Church Missionary Society, Achebe was himself 'born . . . into a world apart', and he attended church schools from an early age.[3]

At the same time, it should be noted that *Things Fall Apart* was written and published in the years immediately preceding Nigerian independence in 1960, a transitional period when political power was being transferred from the colonial masters to a Nigerian male elite. *Things Fall Apart* legitimizes this process whereby women were excluded from post-colonial politics and public affairs through its representation of pre-colonial Igbo society as governed entirely by men.

In Amadiume's analysis, Idemili was 'the central religious deity' (27) of the Igbo living in the Nnobi area of Eastern Nigeria where both she and Achebe were born. Associated with female industriousness, assertiveness, and prosperity, as well as other qualities, Idemili embodied the matriarchal principle, a principle which, in its ideological opposition to the patriarchal principle embodied in 'the cult of ancestral spirits' (53) (Achebe's *egwugwu*), ensured that Igbo gender construction was flexible. Furthermore, the qualities associated with Idemili ensured that women were not marginalized either politically or economically. Hence the 'male daughters' and 'female husbands' of Amadiume's title – women who, through inheritance or self-generated wealth, acquired the status and power of men. There was also a title reserved for women, the *Ekwe* title, which was associated with Idemili and which prosperous women could take, after which they 'would wear a string anklet . . . like all titled men' (43) and become members of the Women's Council. This Council, Amadiume writes, 'appears to have been answerable to no one', not even to '*ozo* titled men' (Achebe's elders or *ndichie*), its special strength residing in its authority to order mass strikes by all women (67).

The central divinity in Achebe's Umuofia is also a female deity, the Earth Goddess, Ani. The values Ani embodies, however, do not serve women's interests. Okonkwo commits a number of crimes against Ani for which he is punished: beating his youngest wife during the Week of Peace; participating in the killing of Ikemefuna, the boy who calls him father; and accidentally shooting another teenaged boy. But Ani does not even protect women from male brutality. For Okonkwo's first crime is not the beating of his wife, wife-battering being sanctioned by the goddess, but the perpetration of an act of violence during the Week of Peace.

Reading *Things Fall Apart* from the vantage of *Male Daughters, Female Husbands* uncovers silences in Achebe's narrative. Achebe himself generally avoids questioning the hierarchical nature of gender relations in Umuofia society, an indication of his attitude toward the status quo of male domination. Problems do, however, arise on at least two occasions, but in each case the narrative backs away from the issue. One concerns the story of Ndulue, whose wife dies immediately after she learns of his death. 'It was always said that Ndulue and Ozoemena had one mind', Okonkwo's friend Obierika recalls. 'I remember when I was a young boy there was a song about them. He could not do anything without telling her' (62). Okonkwo is incredulous when he learns that Ndulue had also been a renowned warrior. While the novel does take up as one of its primary concerns the issue of the over-valuation in Umuofia of masculine qualities to the exclusion of feminine ones, it retreats from a consideration of the issue of the imbalance of power in gender relations which the story of Ndulue and Ozoemena also raises.[4]

Another occasion concerns the efforts of Okonkwo's uncle, Uchendu, to reconcile his nephew to the punishment he has received as a result of his accidental shooting of a young man: exile in his 'motherland'. 'We all know that a man is the head of the family and his wives do his bidding', Uchendu says to Okonkwo. 'A child belongs to its father and his family and not to its mother and her family. A man belongs to his fatherland and not to his motherland. And yet we say Nneka — "Mother is Supreme". Why is that?' Uchendu answers his own question by explaining that a mother's supremacy resides in her role as protector. Just as a child 'seeks sympathy in its mother's hut', so a man 'finds refuge in his motherland' (121–2). As Lloyd Brown states, Achebe offers in this passage 'an important distinction between . . . a mythic concept of supreme motherhood and the limited status of the woman who is required to do her husband's bidding in her day-to-day life' (8–9). However, Achebe is not critical of this contradiction. For although the narrative momentarily focuses on the discrepancy between woman in myth and woman in reality, it eschews treatment of the issue as it relates to gender inequality.

As if to reflect their social insignificance, women are marginalized in the text. Achebe does not even bother to name Okonkwo's wives until the narrative is well under way. At the end of Chapter One they are merely numbers, representing an apparently minor part of Okonkwo's achievement:

> Okonkwo was clearly cut out for great things. He was still young but he had won fame as the greatest wrestler in the nine villages. He was a wealthy farmer and had two barns full of yams, and had just married his third wife. To crown it all he had taken two titles and had shown incredible prowess in two inter-tribal wars. (7)

It is not until Chapter Four that it is revealed that Okonkwo's first wife is called 'Nwoye's mother' and his third 'Ojiugo'. His second wife is not named Ekwefi until after she has, in anonymity, first been beaten and then narrowly escaped being murdered by Okonkwo.

Innes states that 'Achebe's characters', in contrast to Joyce Cary's portrayal of Africans, 'are complex individuals, types rather than archetypes, the resolution of whose conflicts is central to the plot' (22). But this assertion is valid only with regard to Achebe's male characters. For while a fair number of the male cast – Okonkwo, Unoka, Nwoye, Ikemefuna, Obierika, Uchendu – are complex personalities, of the female characters, all but Ekwefi, her daughter Ezinma, and Chielo, the priestess of Agbala, remain shadowy figures. Furthermore, the portrayals of Ekwefi and Ezinma collapse into stereotypes, while Chielo is a feminine archetype.

The primary function of Ekwefi and Ezinma is to reveal Okonkwo's well-hidden capacity for tender feelings and hence to ensure that, despite his violent temperament, he retains the sympathy of readers. This leads to a tension in their characterization between masculine assertiveness and feminine passivity and dependence, a tension which is ultimately resolved in favour of the feminine stereotype. Ekwefi and Ezinma gain Okonkwo's affectionate interest in the first instance because they exhibit characteristics which are atypical of their gender as Okonkwo conventionally defines it. Thus, whereas, in Okonkwo's view, his son Nwoye is 'degenerate and effeminate' (140), Ezinma 'has the right spirit' (60): 'He never stopped regretting that Ezinma was a girl' (156). Okonkwo attempts to make both children conform to conventional definitions of their respective genders, encouraging Nwoye, for example, to listen to 'masculine stories of violence and bloodshed' (48) and ordering Ezinma to 'Sit like a woman!' (40). But he succeeds only with Ezinma. For in contrast to Nwoye who ultimately rebels against his father's strict model of masculinity, she submits to his definition of her gender, taking on the role of the tractable, serviceable, selfless daughter. Thus, for example, she agrees to reject all suitors until the family returns from exile to Umuofia when it will give a much needed boost to her father's prestige to have a marriageable daughter in his house.

Similarly, Ekwefi, who runs away from her first husband so that she can live with Okonkwo, is passive in her response to the beatings she receives from him and even to his attempted murder of her. She is, it would seem, content with her condition as a battered wife.

As the Priestess of the Oracle, Agbala, Chielo is the one woman in Umuofia who has power. Speaking of 'the Chielo–Ezinma episode' – the episode in which Okonkwo follows his wife and daughter when the latter is taken by Chielo on a late-night journey to the Oracle's shrine – Carole Boyce Davies observes that it 'is one of those situations over which Okonkwo has no control. . . . His machete, the symbol of male aggression, is of no use at all in this context' ('Motherhood' 247).

Innes pays scant attention to this episode and JanMohamed glosses over it all together. This is possibly partly because both critics read *Things Fall Apart* dialogically solely through Cary's novels. However, as I hope to show, for this episode to be fully appreciated, the novel must be examined in juxtaposition to other colonial fiction, in particular to Rider Haggard's novels. What such a reading indicates is that Chielo is a latter-day descendant, following Conrad's 'savage and superb' African woman in *Heart of Darkness* (101), of the female figure in Haggard's *She*.

Chielo, the Priestess, is a femme fatale, sharing with Ayesha of *She* many of the features of this feminine archetype as Sandra M. Gilbert and Susan Gubar outline them in their discussion of Haggard's novels (3–41). Like Ayesha, the Priestess of Agbala is 'She-who-must-be-obeyed'. 'Beware', she screams at Okonkwo when he pleads with her not to carry Ezinma off. 'Beware of exchanging words with Agbala. Does a man speak when a god speaks?' (91). Like Ayesha, too, the Priestess makes demands that are cruel and irrational: that a sickly child be taken away from its parents and on a long journey in the middle of the night. It is also Agbala who orders the execution of Ikemefuna. In addition, the Priestess speaks an enigmatic language through the command of which she manifests her power and mystery, and she dwells in a cave, as does Ayesha. Furthermore, as Haggard does in both *King Solomon's Mines* and *She*, Achebe feminizes and eroticizes the landscape 'She' inhabits. Thus Agbala's 'house' is 'in the hills and the caves' (92); and while the way to the shrine is through 'a circular ring [of hills] with a break at one point' (97), the way into the shrine is through a small 'round hole at the side of a hill' (15). The Priestess 'crawl[s] out of the shrine on her belly like a snake' (101). Confronted with this phallic woman, Okonkwo is, of course, as Davies has indicated, rendered impotent, deprived of *his* powers, as are Haggard's male protagonists in similar encounters.

What we have here, then, is an instance of intertextual affirmation. How does this representation of female power function in its new context – in an African, as opposed to a colonial, text? The first thing we might note is that there is no contradiction between Achebe's feminization of the landscape and his professed desire to help 'African people' regain 'their dignity and self-respect', even though, in so sexualizing the terrain, Achebe has taken over what David Bunn refers to as 'one of the most recurrent enabling metaphors of colonialism' (11). For the landscape that is feminized is very localized, the territory marked as 'alien' being confined to that in the immediate environs of the Oracle's shrine, the Priestess's seat of power. Further, Achebe counters the conventional colonial practice of feminizing Africa and Africans with a representation in which African society is masculinized.

The characterization of Chielo, however, seems to be based on contradictory impulses: on the one hand to show that African cultures have 'great depth and value and beauty', and on the other to demonstrate that women are incapable of exercising power responsibly. For what Achebe implies through the portrayal of Chielo is that women in positions of power are despotic and destructive because they are irrational. By contrast, men in positions of power are shown to be reasonable, impartial, and constructive, as in the court scene in which the *egwugwu*, 'the fathers of the clan' (82), settle disputes. Again, it should be noted that *Things Fall Apart* was written during the transitional years between colonial rule and independence following which women were to be given equal franchise with men. The Chielo–Ezinma episode can in this light be seen as an expression of Achebe's fear of female power. Achebe's success in anathematizing female power is suggested by Palmer who describes the scene as 'blood-chilling' (*Growth* 74).

At the very end of the scene, Achebe symbolically restores Okonkwo's virility by having Ekwefi recall her first meeting with him after she has run away from her first husband: 'He just carried her into his bed and in the darkness began to feel around her waist for the loose end of her cloth' (99). Shortly after, Achebe drives Chielo out of his novel. And while, in comparison with Haggard's 'willed destruction of Ayesha by a phallic pillar of fire' (Gilbert and Gubar 46), Achebe's treatment of the Priestess looks quite innocuous, Chielo's absence from the second half of the novel plays, as we shall see, a key role in the novel's performance of its function of legitimating male domination.

Underlying the portrayals of Ezinma, Ekwefi, and Chielo is one of the manichean allegories that defines Achebe's society – the sexual allegory of male and female, good and evil, superiority and inferiority, rationality and irrationality, activity and passivity. The frequent association of women with children in the narrative is another manifestation of the allegory. Thus we are told that Okonkwo's 'wives and young children were not as strong [as he was], and so they suffered' from the work regimen he imposed (13). We also learn that '[t]he women and children . . . took to their heels [when the *egwugwu* appeared]. It was instinctive. A woman fled as soon as an *egwugwu* came in sight' (80–1).

Commendation of Achebe for the impartiality with which he recreates Igbo society is a critical commonplace. In the words of JanMohamed, Achebe reproduces 'a version of Igbo society in an objective rather than an idealist or subjective manner' (161).[5] This claim loses a certain amount of credibility, however, when the treatment of female characters in the narrative is considered. As I have already indicated, a subjective bias is evident in the portrayal of women. Furthermore, the narrator does not always maintain an objective stance on the issue of gender relations, but instead aligns himself with the sexist views of the male characters. Thus according to the narrator, when Ojiugo does not return from her friend's house in time to serve Okonkwo his afternoon meal, Okonkwo is 'provoked to *justifiable* anger' (26, emphasis added). In beating Ojiugo, Okonkwo breaks the sacred peace of Ani, but the beating itself is implicitly sanctioned by the narrator. By contrast, the narrator is quite scrupulous about distancing himself from the views of Okonkwo on other matters. For example, after noting that Nwoye has a tendency toward laziness, he adds: 'At any rate, that was how it looked to his father' (13). While this distancing manoeuvre creates space in the narrative for the telling of Nwoye's side of the story, the coincidence between the narrator's and male characters' attitudes toward women leaves no room for Ojiugo to express her viewpoint. And while space is provided for the viewpoint of a sensitive boy on what it is like to live under Okonkwo's harsh authority, no such provision is made for Okonkwo's wives and daughters. This limits the reader's sympathy for and interest in the female characters.

Innes argues that 'authorial consciousness' is to be distinguished from 'narrative voice', that while the former corresponds to 'the questioning and alienated vision of Nwoye', the latter 'represents a collective voice' and articulates 'the values and assumptions of [the] community' (32, 35). Palmer, on the other hand, evidently considers author and narrator to be similarly positioned in the novel. For he, too, exonerates Okonkwo from blame when he beats Ojiugo: 'On this occasion he has a plausible excuse [for the sacrilege he commits], the girl being clearly in the wrong' (*Introduction* 55). The question of the relationship between author and narrator is, however, relatively unimportant for my analysis. What is significant is that nothing in the novel constitutes a serious challenge to the view of either the narrator or the male characters on women. This view therefore becomes invested with authority.

Achebe does not, however, idealize Igbo society, but as we shall see, his criticism does not encompass the condition of women in Umuofia. As the novel progresses the emphasis shifts from a concern with recreating pre-colonial Igbo society to the question of the reason for its rapid capitulation to the invading colonial forces. Achebe presents the collapse as being due not solely or even primarily to British military superiority, but also to an internal disorder. There is general critical agreement on the nature of that disorder: the clan's failure to maintain a balance between masculine and feminine values.[6] This imbalance accounts for the social sanctioning of such cruel practices as the killing of war hostages like Ikemefuna and the sacrifice of twins.

There is also substantial critical agreement on Okonkwo's function in the novel as the embodiment of Umuofia's values.[7] But his character is defined not so much by 'the subject–object dialectic' as that dialectic is constituted by the colonial situation, which is what JanMohamed claims (273). Rather it is the relation between Self and Other in a patriarchal situation that defines Okonkwo's character. Okonkwo provides a classic example of male psychology in a patriarchal society, from the perspective of which women are inferior because of their otherness. Insisting on sexual otherness, Okonkwo projects on to women those qualities he most despises in himself. Thus, when a man who has taken no title contradicts him in a meeting, Okonkwo 'call[s] him a woman' (24). Thus, too, when thinking of Nwoye, Okonkwo wonders how he, who at Nwoye's age 'had already become famous throughout Umuofia for his wrestling and his fearlessness', could 'have begotten a woman for a son' (140). And when Okonkwo concludes that his anguish over his involvement in the killing of Ikemefuna is a sign of weakness, he curses himself with the very worst words of abuse he can think of:

'When did you become a shivering old women', Okonkwo asked himself, 'you, who are known in all the nine villages for your valour in war? How can a man who has killed five men in battle fall to pieces because he has added a boy to their number? Okonkwo, you have become a woman indeed'. (59)

The primary motive of Okonkwo's existence is to avoid being thought effeminate like his father who was called *agbala*, a word which Okonkwo is mortified to learn not only means 'a man who had taken no title', but is also 'another name for a woman' (13). It is this fear – a fear of femininity – that impels Okonkwo to participate in the killing of Ikemefuna, the act which inaugurates his own decline.

Okonkwo is not unique in defining himself in opposition to women, even though he is sometimes extreme in his reactions because of the peculiarities of his upbringing. That he is simply conforming to a cultural norm is emphasized by the double-meaning of the word '*agbala*'. It is in order to prove to themselves that they are strong and not weak like a woman that the men of Umuofia callously and routinely commit acts of brutality. These are the 'things' which, when the white man 'put[s] a knife' on them, cause Umuofia to fall apart (160).

The imbalance in Umuofia society, then, does not pertain to the power imbalance between men and women but is located within the male personality. Bu-Buakei Jabbi refers to it as a 'manliness complex' (135). But the nature of the disorder is more adequately conveyed by Juli Loesch's terms 'penisolence' and 'testeria', for these account both for the acts of destructive aggression committed by the men of Umuofia and for their repression of tender or sympathetic feelings.[8] It is for this suppressed element in the male personality that the feminine stands in the novel, for male thoughts and feelings that have no expression in the culture: Obierika's silent musings on cultural injustices; Nwoye's unspoken outrage at the killing of Ikemefuna and the sacrifice of twins; and Okonkwo's inner torment over his part in the slaying of the boy who called him father. Indeed, the feminine is, in the words of the text, the 'silent and dusty chords in the heart of an Igbo *man*' (133, emphasis added).

But this male heart is not moved by the oppression of women, by their degradation in their definition as chattel, or by their marginalization in society. Nor is Achebe's. For although he avoids idealization by including in the novel an implicit criticism of certain aspects of life in Umuofia, that criticism, which is in part expressed through the reflections of male characters such as Nwoye and Obierika, does not cover the condition of women in Umuofia. Moreover, not only does the male inner voice fail to question the harsh injustice done to women, the female inner voice is utterly mute. The defection from the community of some of its members performs the same critical function as the reflections of the male characters. But while some of Achebe's female characters convert to Christianity, they do so not because they resent their oppression *as women* in Umuofia society but because they are the mothers of twins or members of the *osu* caste.

The women of Umuofia, then, are content with their lot. In their silence they assent to their status as the property of a man and to their reduction to a level lower than a barn full of yams in their role as signifiers of their husbands' wealth. So, too, does Achebe. For although he exposes, through the defection of *osu*, the injustice of Umuofia's social class system, he remains silent (mute like his women) on its gender hierarchy. And while critics continue to eulogize Achebe for the balance he has achieved in his portrayal of Umuofia's strengths and weaknesses, they have generally avoided pointing to the subjugation of women as one of those weaknesses or to the novel's failure to make the same point. This critical silence on the work's sexism can be attributed to the same cause as that to which Achebe assigns responsibility for the silence on Conrad's racism: sexism 'is such a normal way of thinking that its manifestations go completely undetected'.

Moreover, just as Achebe's women are silent in the face of their oppression under Igbo patriarchy, so, too, they express no opposition to the imposition of a regime which will add racial to further sexual oppression. This is true of Ezinma who, according to her father, 'has the right spirit', and even of Chielo who, as the Priestess of Agbala, stands to lose her considerable prestige and power to the priests of the Christian religion who, in affirmation of the manichean allegory of race, see 'things in black and white. And black [is] evil' (166).

Abena P. A. Busia has shown that what she calls 'the voicelessness of the black woman' is a recurring trope in colonial fiction (90). She sees *The Tempest* as providing the model for a number of later figures, including Kurtz's African woman in *Heart of Darkness*, in its portrayal of Caliban's mother, the silent, absent Sycorax. But such figures are not confined to colonial discourse, for in their 'inactive silence' the female characters in *Things Fall Apart* also conform to the model as Busia defines it (86).

Of course, women all over Africa did, in fact, participate in the struggle against colonialism, sometimes as leaders. In Nigeria there were mass protests by Igbo women against the British and their agents which began in 1925 and culminated in the Women's War of 1929–30.[9] The question of the authenticity of Achebe's representation can, however, be most dramatically focused by comparing Amadiume's account of an incident which took place in Nnobi 'towards the middle of this century' to Achebe's version of the same or a similar incident: the killing by a Christian zealot of the sacred python, which is, in his story, 'the emanation of the god of water', and in hers, 'a totemic symbol of those who worship the goddess Idemili'. This is the 'people's' response in his story: 'the [male] rulers and elders of Mbanta assembled to decide on their action', their decision being 'to ostracize the Christians' (144–5); while in hers: the women of Nnobi 'demonstrated their anger by . . . marching half naked to the provincial headquarters, Onitsha, to beseige the resident's office' and then 'returned to Nnobi, went straight to the [home of the man who killed the python] and razed it to the ground'. This was, Amadiume adds, 'the indigenous Igbo female custom of dealing with offending men' (*Male Daughters* 121–2).

By failing to imagine either a sister for Okonkwo, a female nationalist hero, or a female counterpart for Nwoye, a woman in revolt against Umuofia's definition of her gender, Achebe alienates Igbo women from history. Thus, if 'history' is 'the "hero" of [this] African novel', if, in other words, the novel features, as Nkosi claims, 'history as a collective working out of a people's destiny' (31), then that hero and those people are male. Alienated from history, women are relegated to 'tradition', their inferiority naturalized by the ahistorical identity Achebe has constructed for their gender: woman as a passive object, acted upon, never acting in her own right.

As Achebe says, 'stories are not innocent'. '[T]hey can be used to put you in the wrong crowd.' For where in this story is the African woman reader to locate herself? If, as the novel leads her to do, she identifies with the hero, Okonkwo, she identifies against herself, with a hero for whom woman is the Other. Even Nwoye who cherishes feminine values does not provide the woman reader with a self-affirming image, for like other Umuofia males he is not critical of the gender hierarchy. Is she, then, Ezinma who remains passively at home, as indifferent to the newly imposed colonial restrictions as she has always been to those of Igbo patriarchy, while her brother goes off to the school that has been set up 'to teach young Christians to read and write' (139)?

JanMohamed argues that Cary's fiction can best be understood in terms of racial romance, using 'romance' as Northrop Frye defines it in *Anatomy of Criticism*.[10] He also claims that '[t]he major function of [Achebe's] novels as symbolic *acts* is the refutation of Cary's romances through his own realism' (273) and that '[h]is realism . . . makes Achebe the best contemporary African writer' (179). It could be argued, however, that *Things Fall Apart* is also a version of romance, the gender romance, for it, too, conforms to some of the criteria of the genre as Frye outlines them. Briefly, like Cary's African characters, Achebe's female ones are not realistically portrayed. For, as we have seen, they do not change in response to their specific social or historical situations, but instead remain true to conventional gender characteristics. Further, Chielo, who, arguably, is the central female character in the novel, is a stylized figure, a psychological archetype; she is also a shadow, a demonic parody of powerful men, despotic and destructive. Finally, the subjective bias of romance is evident in the coincidence of the narrator's and male characters' attitude toward women, but most especially in the absence of anything in the novel to undercut Okonkwo's stereotypical view of women.

Quite clearly, then, *Things Fall Apart* has another function in addition to that of refuting Cary's romances, one which I will try to highlight once again by considering Achebe's masculinization of Igbo society from two different perspectives. When *Things Fall Apart* is read dialogically through Haggard's and Conrad's novels, the characterization of Umuofia as an aggressively masculine society appears as Achebe's response to colonial writers who, in their feminization of Africa and Africans, contributed to the justification of the colonial presence in Africa. But when the novel is read with a view to examining its relation to patriarchal ideology, the portrayal appears as a means of legitimizing male domination. For, despite his critical stance, Achebe does not relate the brutality of masculinity to the excess of power a patriarchal society makes available to men. Hence, what he advocates is not a dismantling of the structures of male domination but the incorporation into the male personality of qualities conventionally associated with the feminine.

What we have, then, is a story whose concern is wholly for men and their dilemmas, one in which what happens to women is of no consequence. Even the folktale which Ekwefi is assigned the role of telling to Ezinma – the story of the visit paid to the sky by the birds and the crafty tortoise – relates only to male behaviour. A cautionary tale which tells of the consequences of over-weening pride, of challenging one's *chi* in the idiom of the larger narrative, it serves to foreshadow the decline of Okonkwo's fortunes.[11]

As we have seen, in Achebe's view, a novel which valorizes racist ideology cannot be 'called a great work of art'. As we have also seen Achebe attempts to undermine the authority of such canonical western texts as *Heart of Darkness* by giving an account of his own experience of reading them and by providing alternative readings – ones which identify the race bias not only in colonial fiction but also in western criticism. As JanMohamed has shown, *Things Fall Apart* is also a conscious attempt on Achebe's part to refute colonial authors like Joyce Cary. However, while seeking to subvert the manichean allegory of race, Achebe valorizes a version of the sexual allegory. This, then, has been my project in this chapter: to challenge the authority of Achebe's most canonical novel by offering an alternative reading of it, one which reveals its male bias as well as that of Achebe criticism.

Achebe does not tell African women 'where the rain began to beat them'. Nor does he attempt to restore 'dignity and self-respect' to African women. However, although women have been explicitly excluded from Achebe's constituency of readers, they have, in contrast to his female characters, refused to remain silent. As writers they have undertaken the task of refuting Achebe, of presenting an alternative view of colonization and of African society, one which challenges Achebe's underlying assumption that things could not fall apart for African women because they never had been and never would be together.

2
THE MOTHER AFRICA
TROPE

Léopold Sédar Senghor is probably Francophone Africa's most famous writer. A poet and a politician, he was a founding member of the Negritude movement and the president of Senegal for the first twenty years after independence. The publication of his first volume of poetry in 1945 can be said to mark the beginning of the modern period in African literature. In presenting Negritude in his poetry, Senghor frequently employs a trope which also occurs, though sometimes in a different guise, in contemporary male-authored writing: the embodiment of Africa in the figure of a woman. The first stanza of his much-quoted poem 'Femme noire' provides a prototypical example:

Naked woman, black woman
Clothed with your colour which is life, with your form which is
    beauty!
In your shadow I have grown up; the gentleness of your hands was
    laid over my eyes.
And now, high up on the sun-baked pass, at the heart of summer,
    at the heart of noon, I come upon you, my Promised Land.
And your beauty strikes me to the heart like the flash of an eagle.
    (105)

The trope is deeply entrenched in the male literary tradition, the sexual imperatives it encodes shaping the writing of such diverse authors as Senghor, Soyinka, and Ngũgĩ.

My aim in this chapter is partly identification: to demonstrate the frequency of the trope's occurrence in the African male literary tradition. I also hope to show how the trope functions within several different dialogical systems. It is to this trope that McLuskie and Innes refer when they speak of African men writers' transformation of the 'coloniser's mythologising of Africa as the Other, as Female, as treacherous and seductive . . . into recognizably related forms' (4). Part of my project, then, will be to consider the function of some of these 'related forms' relative to colonial writing. But the trope also has a history *within* African literature. For one thing, as I have already noted, there are indications that it is indigenous to African artistic expression, occurring in the orature and plastic arts of at least some cultures. This being the case, then the trope's function in relation to African oral cultures also needs to be considered. Furthermore, the trope has acquired an identity and history *specific* to the African male literary tradition, as men writers have revised and reiterated each other's versions of it. It is on this level that I focus in the discussion that follows where, in an attempt to convey something of the dynamics of the intertextual process, I present a chronological record of some of the high points in the trope's history from the time of its occurrence in Senghor's poetry. I conclude the chapter with a discussion of the implications of the trope for female creativity – for the creation by women of literary texts and of national visions. What I hope to show is that the trope operates against the interests of women, excluding them, implicitly if not explicitly, from authorship and citizenship.

As Senghor defines it, '*negritude is the sum total of the values of the civilization of the African world. . . . [I]t is culture*' (99). Countering the myth of the inherent inferiority of the black race – a myth which provided the ideological rationale for European imperialism, Senghorian Negritude celebrates African culture, defining it as the heritage of African values, a pre-colonial African essence as yet uncontaminated by western culture. 'The chief celebrant' of this heritage or essence is, as Kofi Awoonor puts it, 'the Black Woman, the Earth Mother, the anthropomorphic symbol of primal sensuality' (155). For 'the Black Woman' as 'symbol', as embodying figure, serves as a generic marker in Negritude poetry, featuring in many of the poems of the period, including, as we have seen, Senghor's 'Femme noire', as well as his 'Nuit de Sine', 'I will pronounce your name', and 'Spring song' and David Diop's 'To my mother' and 'To a black dancer'. In this poetry, the trope functions both formally and thematically to valorize African culture. It also operates to refute colonial representations of Africa. For even though a conventional colonial mode of representation is replicated, a negative image of Africa as savage and treacherous is replaced by a positive one: an image of Africa as warm and sensuous, fruitful and nurturing.

The Senghorian vision has, however, been bitterly contested, one of the most serious objections arising from its engagement of western categories of thought. For in asserting the distinctive characteristics of African culture, Senghorian Negritude resorts to the binary logic of the western philosophical tradition, opposing feeling or emotion, which it equates with African civilization, to reason, which it identifies with western culture. Hence it reproduces and reinforces the racist stereotypes of western discourse. It is on these grounds that Soyinka charges Negritude with manicheism:

> In attempting to refute the evaluation to which black reality had been subjected, Negritude adopted the Manichean tradition of European thought and inflicted it on a culture which is most radically anti-Manichean. It not only accepted the dialectical structure of European ideological confrontations but borrowed from the very components of its racist syllogism.

> (*Myth, Literature and the African World* 127)

Lurking within Negritude, however, is another manichean allegory, one which also underlies Soyinka's writing: the allegory of male and female, domination and subordination, mind and body, subject and object, self and other. For the trope defines a situation that is conventionally patriarchal. The speaker is invariably male, a western-educated intellectual. The addressee is always a woman. She is pure physicality, always beautiful and often naked. He is constituted as a writing subject, a producer of art and of socio-political visions; her status is that of an aesthetic/sexual object. She takes the form either of a young girl, nubile and erotic, or of a fecund nurturing mother. The poetry celebrates his intellect at the same time as it pays tribute to her body which is frequently associated with the African landscape that is his to explore and discover. As embodying mother she gives the trope a name: the Mother Africa trope.

In the contemporary period, the trope is ubiquitous, to be found in the works of most major men writers, where, as I hope to show, it follows two lines of development. One, following the model provided by Senghor, analogizes woman to the heritage of African values, an unchanging African essence. This line, which I call 'the pot of culture' strand,[1] is illustrated with reference to Okot p'Bitek's *Song of Lawino* and Ayi Kwei Armah's 'An African fable'. The other, which I call 'the sweep of history' strand, revises the Senghorian analogy, for woman now serves as an index of the state of the nation. This is exemplified in Ousmane Sembène's 'La noire de. . .', Nuruddin Farah's *From a Crooked Rib*, and Mongo Beti's *Perpetua and the Habit of Unhappiness*. Soyinka's *Season of Anomy* and Ngũgĩ's *Petals of Blood* are also examined as instances of texts which incorporate both forms of the trope. In Jameson's terms, all of these works are 'national allegories'. What distinguishes them as a special class within African literature is that in each case it is 'the private individual destiny' of a female figure that serves as 'an allegory of the embattled situation of the public . . . culture and society'.

Sembène's short story, 'La noire de . . .' (1962),[2] provides one of the most striking examples of intertextual revision in response to changing historical conditions and conflicting ideologies. For the black woman of Sembène's title is Senghor's 'femme noire' transported to France at the time of the transition in Senegal from French colonial rule to what is, as Sembène perceived it, neo-colonialism under the leadership of the nation's first president, Léopold Senghor. The story is set in the months preceding the 1958 Referendum in which the French colonial territories voted on whether to maintain formal ties with France within the framework of a French community dominated by France, an alternative for which Senghor successfully campaigned, or to sever them completely in favour of immediate independence, the option supported by Sembène. Sembène alludes to the Referendum in the opening sentence of his story and he concludes it with a poem written in the Negritude tradition and addressed to his 'femme noire', Diouana, who has committed suicide while working in France as the servant of a French family. The final stanza of the poem reads as follows:

> Diouana,
> Our sister,
> Light of the days to come,
> One day soon
> We shall say,
> These forests,
> These fields,
> These rivers,
> This land,
> Our flesh,
> Our bones
> Are ours alone.
> Image of our Mother Africa,
> We lament over your sold body,
> You are our
> Mother,
> Diouana. (101)

Taken together, the story and poem subvert the Senghorian Negritude ideology of cultural assertion, exposing what, for Sembène, are its inadequacies in the face of neo-colonialism. In the process Senghor's version of the Mother Africa trope undergoes a revision, being transformed into a sweep of history.

Diouana leaves for France grateful to her employers for their kindness in giving her an opportunity to make her fortune, only to discover that they have been motivated entirely by self-interest. They exploit her economically, making her do 'the work of six people', 'all for a pittance'. They also exploit her culturally, appropriating for themselves her Negritudeness as they parade her from villa to villa as if she were 'some trophy'. She soon loses her personal identity, for she is not referred to by her name but as 'their black servant' (97), and she begins to withdraw into herself, viewing 'her skin', 'her blackness' with 'terror' (95). Her eventual suicide thus represents what for Sembène are the dire consequences for Senegal of Senghor's policy, pursued even after independence, of cultural and economic 'co-operation' with France. A celebration of black culture sidesteps the issue of the cultural and economic exploitation of Africa. Thus Diouana, in her apotheosis in the poem as 'Mother Africa', represents not a precolonial African essence but rather a post-neo-colonial Africa free of foreign domination – 'Light of the days to come', the promised land of the future.

In Okot p'Bitek's *Song of Lawino* (1966), the trope reverts to Senghorian type. Like Sembène, Okot was writing in response to 'post-colonial' conditions, in this case, those of Uganda, but like Senghor he saw as his task the revaluation of African culture. This is the basis for his argument in *Africa's Cultural Revolution* that, if the goals of African nationalism are to be achieved after political independence, Africa 'must discover her true self, and rid herself of all "apemanship". For only then can she begin to develop a culture of her own' (vii).

The target of attack in the poem is the 'apemanship' of Ocol, a representative of Africa's educated elite which assumed power at independence. Okot gives dramatic expression to this class's rejection and suppression of Africa's cultural traditions through Ocol's repudiation of his first wife, Lawino, whom he abandons in favour of Clementine. A woman of 'the old homestead' (30), Lawino is Africa's 'true self'. She is identified with the fertile African earth: her body is 'The rich red soil' that periodically 'Swells with a new life' (99); she is 'the mother of many' (94). Clementine, on the other hand, is 'a modern girl' (21). Her 'breasts are completely shrivelled up' (25), she has no children, and she lives in the city. Ocol has been emasculated by his 'marriage' to Clementine, his 'testicles . . . smashed', his 'manhood . . . finished' (208). In order to regain his virility, to acquire 'A new spear with a sharp and hard point' (213), he 'must remove the road block / From [Lawino's] path' (215) and reimmerse himself in 'The rich red soil' of Mother Africa. Thus will a cultural revolution be inaugurated.

If, in Sembène's story, Mother Africa, so revered by the Negritude poets, is in servitude, and if she is abused and abandoned in Okot's poem, her fate in succeeding works is often even more degrading. Such is the case in Armah's paradigmatic tale of post-independence disillusionment, 'An African fable' (1968). Published two years after *Song of Lawino*, this little-known work is also the quintessential tale of 'apemanship'. For in the form of a historical allegory it tells of the new ruling elite's imitation of their colonial predecessors in defiling Africa's cultural heritage. The story is of a young African warrior's quest for what Armah was several years later, in *Two Thousand Seasons*, to call 'the way': authentic African socio-political systems based on the principles of reciprocity and the inter-connectedness of all things in a cycle of regeneration. These are, as in *Song of Lawino*, embodied in the figure of a woman.

Wandering south through desert, savannah, and forest, the Warrior traverses the landscape of Africa in his search, finally arriving at the sea which proves to be his destination. For on the shore he finds a woman, beautiful but grieving, who has 'about her . . . the stamp of the permanence of things that move in cycles, beginning and ending, springing and dying and then springing' (192). While the woman is pleased to see the Warrior, she is also wary, for she has 'welcomed many like him before' and 'watched the promise always fade into the ashen blandness of disillusionment' (193). On his part, the Warrior is frustrated by his 'impotence' to comprehend or alter the woman's being. '[H]is powers of penetration' incapacitated, he wanders off, and, then moved by an overwhelming compulsion, returns, this time to find the woman being raped by an older warrior, a stranger to him. His strength renewed by this sight, he slays the other warrior. But now, flushed with a sense of his own power and still frustrated by his inability 'to pierce' the woman's 'night-like beauty', he is 'filled with a feeling' of both 'love and desire' and 'contempt and repulsion' for her. The Warrior rapes the woman. The woman, so the story ends, gazes during this act of violation past the Warrior's head at the sea thinking, 'there was no separation between now and then, nothing at all between the present and the depths of ages that should long have been forgotten' (194–6).

The degradation continues in Nuruddin Farah's *From a Crooked Rib* (1970). In this case, Mother Africa ends up as a whore. Farah has been quite explicit about the literary value with which he invests his female figures, having stated in an interview that '[l]ike all good Somali poets I used women as a symbol for Somalia' (Kitchener 61). In *From a Crooked Rib* the 'sweep of history' form of the trope is played out in the plot. On one level, it tells the story of Ebla, a young woman who abandons her nomadic roots in the Ogaden for life in the city; on another, it presents the history of Somalia from the colonial period to the time of independence. As is made evident by the introduction of references to history at each turn of the plot, Ebla's misadventures as she seeks to escape from her oppression represent the fate of Somalia as it was partitioned and swapped by the Italians, British, French, Egyptians, and Ethiopians under colonialism, whereas her strategy of resistance reflects the politics of independence. In her varying conditions, Ebla serves as an index of the state of the nation from the time of colonialism until independence.

Against the background of the story of the defeat of the British forces under Corfield by the Somali hero Sayyed Mohamed Abdulle Hassan, Ebla flees from her grandfather who has offered her in marriage to an old man in exchange for some camels. Having taken refuge with a male cousin in a nearby town, she discovers, at the same time as she learns that Somalia is now under Italian jurisdiction, that he intends to settle his debts by marrying her to a broker who has tuberculosis. Still determined to control her own fate, she elopes with Awill, an educated young man who carries her off to Mogadishu and then departs for Italy to prepare for independence. Then, when Ebla finds out that Awill is having an affair with an Italian woman, she takes a second husband. Immediately after this episode she learns that her home in the Ogaden is now part of Ethiopia. At this point she wonders when her own 'kind of going from one hand to another would come to an end' (128). What she eventually concludes is that the best she can do is to develop a strategy that will at least serve her own interests too: 'With her hand, she felt down her body, naked under the sheet; she scratched her sex, then chuckled. "This is my treasure, my only treasure, my bank, my money, my existence"' (160). As prostitute, Ebla represents Somalia at the time of independence, her nominal autonomy and actual dependence depicting the nature of nationhood in the 'post-colonial' era. The novel then ends on a note of uncertainty with Ebla's discovery that she is bearing a child whose father she cannot identify.

Wole Soyinka has also been explicit in an extra-literary context about the function of his female figures. They serve, he says, primarily as 'symbol and essence' (Bryan 119). Through Ofeyi, the hero of *Season of Anomy* (1973), Soyinka also articulates a theory of the relationship between male creativity and woman's body, one which encompasses the trope's operation in all of the works examined in this chapter. Ofeyi is watching his partner of the night, Iriyise, as she performs 'her rites of transformation' from night-time lover to vestal of the morning:

> Conjurer, incantatory words floated through Ofeyi's lips. . . . And why not, thought Ofeyi? Vision is eternally of man's own creating. The woman's acceptance, her collaboration in man's vision of life

results time and time again in just such periodic embodiments of earth and ideal. (82)

As in so much of the literature of the period, literature that has been shaped by history, by colonialism and the making of new nations, '[m]an's vision' in this text is of national re-vision. Specifically it is of the redemption of the nation from the prevailing 'season of anomy' by a transformation in the construction of nationhood from an ideology predicated on tyranny and exploitation to one engendering freedom. Woman's role is the conventional collaborative one: to embody that vision. As one of 'such periodic embodiments', Iriyise is 'earth and ideal', prostitute and virgin, 'Madammadonna', as Zaccheus, Ofeyi's friend and fellow-gazer, names her (83). She is thus an embodiment of the nation both as it has been degraded, tainted, corrupted – prostituted – down through the ages, and as it is re-envisioned by man (Soyinka–Ofeyi) – a kind of virgin land.

In performing this role, Iriyise not only serves as an index of the state of the nation – its actual and its potential or envisioned condition; she is also identified with the heritage of African values. Her major and original metamorphosis, a transformation which is echoed in the scene of her dressing, occurs when she leaves the capital city Ilosa, the power-base of the corrupt and tyrannical military-industrial cartel which rules the nation, and arrives in the agrarian setting of Aiyéró where traditional communalistic values have been maintained. Her contact with Africa's regenerative soil, with which she now, in the Negritude tradition, becomes closely associated, transforms her from a city prostitute, symbol of the nation in its present debased state, to a Mother Earth/Africa figure, symbol of the nation restored:

> Iriyise abandoned the circuit of Ilosa's lights, the earth of Aiyéró held her deeper than any bed of eiderdown.
> In wrapper and sash with the other women of Aiyéró, her bared limbs and shoulders among young shoots, Iriyise weaving fronds for the protection of the young nursery. . . . Her fingers spliced wounded saplings with the ease of a natural healer. Her presence, the women boasted, inspired the rains. (20)

However, shortly after her transformation, Iriyise is abducted by the forces of the cartel, and from this point on the plot structure of the novel is, like that of Armah's fable, shaped by the male quest story. As most commentators have indicated, Ofeyi's quest for Iriyise is modelled on the Hellenic myth of Orpheus's epic quest for Eurydice. However, like Armah's Warrior, the aim of Ofeyi's quest is to redeem the values of African civilization as these have been preserved in Aiyéró and are now embodied by Iriyise. In contrast to both Orpheus and the Warrior, Ofeyi succeeds in his mission. For after a nightmare journey through the depraved under-world of military-capitalist tyranny, he rescues the now comatose Iriyise and carries her back to Aiyéró.

The conversion of the Mother Africa trope into a prostitute metaphor is itself a recurring feature of the contemporary tradition in men's fiction. We have already seen it in Farah's *From a Crooked Rib* and Soyinka's *Season of Anomy*. It is found again in the Cameroun writer Mongo Beti's *Perpetua and the Habit of Unhappiness* (1974) where once more it expresses the degradation of Africa. In this text also, as in Armah's and Soyinka's, the trope is linked with the male quest motif, but in this case it is the 'sweep of history' form of the trope that is played out in the quest plot. On the literal level, this story tells of the protagonist Essola's inquest into the death of his beloved younger sister, Perpetua. This death occurred while Essola was in prison for his support of Rubenist resistance to the regime of Baba Tura who collaborated with France in a typical neo-colonialist relationship. The real object of Essola's quest, however, is to discover what has happened to his nation during the first decade after independence. And Perpetua's story, which he reconstructs, is an allegory of that history.

In her optimism and enthusiasm as a school girl and in her ambition to train as a medical doctor so that she can replace the expatriates she believes will soon be leaving, Perpetua embodies the national mood and the nationalist goals of the Rubenists at the time of independence. As Essola is to discover, however, there are even more expatriates '[i]n the army, in the hospitals, in the schools, on the railway, in the shops, in the port, every-where . . . .. almost ten years after Independence' (216). Perpetua is with-drawn from school by her mother, Maria, a peasant woman who is herself a degraded form of the formerly idealized African mother – a mother who favours profligate sons who will, she believes, further her own selfish interests. In order to raise the money so that Perpetua's other brother, the besotted Martin, can marry, Maria sells Perpetua in marriage. Perpetua's husband, Edward, is a dim-witted petty official in the police department. He initially uses his wife as a servant, then attempts to starve her into submission, and finally prostitutes her to a high-ranking civil servant in order to gain a promotion. In the eyes of the ruling party stalwarts, Edward is a 'man with an astonishing genius for peacemaking, so malleable in the hands of his masters, so uncompromising to those he dealt with – a model of Baba Tura himself, who sold out his birthright and the dignity of the nation' (192).

Perpetua does eventually revolt against her oppression by taking a lover, the footballer Zeyang, a Rubenist supporter. Yet her rebellion is short-lived. For when Edward discovers her treachery, he subjects her to daily beatings and imprisons her in his house where she dies heavily pregnant with a child fathered by Zeyang. Although Essola murders Martin and thus avenges the death of Perpetua and of the assassinated founder of the Rubenist movement, the novel, unlike *Season of Anomy*, ends pessimistically. Not only is Perpetua, the embodiment of nationalist aspirations, dead, but Zeyang has been executed and Essola himself has compromised with Baba Tura's regime. The struggle for nationhood, for freedom from neo-colonial exploitation, comes to an end in Beti's bitter novel of 'post-colonial' disillusionment.

The manipulation of the trope by Ngũgĩ in *Petals of Blood* (1977) marks another high point in its history. It is the last to be discussed here and it is a fitting text with which to conclude this overview. For not only does Ngũgĩ incorporate both forms of the trope into his text, but in so doing he reiterates and revises earlier treatments producing a manifest intertextuality. In this way the history of the trope is inscribed in the text.

Like Perpetua, Ngũgĩ's Wanja enacts through her story the 'post-colonial' history of the nation, in this case Kenya, her condition, like Perpetua's serving as an index of the state of the nation. As we shall see, the pattern of her life coincides at many points with that of Perpetua, although Ngũgĩ's novel allows for a transformation and transcendence of this pattern in its optimistic ending. As an aspiring school girl at the time of the Mau Mau War for national liberation, Wanja is seduced by one of her father's friends, an entrepreneur and a supporter of the British side in the struggle. Pregnant, she drops out of school and leaves home, and when she gives birth, she disposes of the baby in a latrine. This act marks the end of a period of national optimism, the abandonment of a hope that the new nation would be founded on socialist principles of distributive justice.

In the years following independence, the pattern of Wanja's life repeatedly shifts between two alternative modes. Sometimes she lives in Kenya's cities where, as a barmaid–cum–prostitute, she continues to be abused and exploited by the men of the new ruling class. Eventually she acquiesces in her complete degradation by adopting the '[e]at or you are eaten' (293) ideology of her oppressors: she becomes a whorehouse madam. Through Karega, another of Wanja's early lovers, Ngũgĩ makes explicit the analogy between prostitution and national degradation:

> [I]n a world of grab and take, in a world built on a structure of
> inequality and injustice, in a world where some can eat while others
> can only toil, some can send their children to schools and others

cannot . . . in a world where a man who has never set foot on this land can sit in a New York or London office and determine what I shall eat, read, think, do, only because he sits on a heap of billions taken from the world's poor, in such a world, we are all prostituted. (240)

At other times, Wanja inhabits the rural countryside, represented in the novel by Ilmorog prior to its 'development' and by Wanja's 'old hut' which she returns to in the end after the mansion she has built on the proceeds from prostitution burns down (337). Near the beginning of the novel, Wanja, having spent years in the city, goes to Ilmorog to visit her grandmother, Nyakinua. Longing now to become pregnant, but seemingly barren, she is in search of a new beginning. In this setting she undergoes a transformation which is reminiscent of Iriyise's when she arrives in Aiyéró. In both cases, the catalyst is 'contact with the soil':

[H]er eyes had become less exaggeratedly bright, more subdued, with a different kind of softness, no longer caressing people in the first hour of contact. She had become a less fully fleshed beauty, more of an angular beauty of a peasant women. (243)

As she works in the fields with Nyakinyua, Wanja is, like Iriyise, closely associated with the earth and its fecundity. And in her relationship with Nyakinyua, that indomitable old woman whom the community hails as the 'mother of men' (123), she becomes an embodiment of the nation's African heritage, an emblem not only of communalism but also of active resistance to exploitation and oppression.

Like Soyinka and others before him, then, in his recreation of history in fiction, in his creation of his 'vision', Ngũgĩ conflates in one body the figures of Africa as mother and whore. And just as Ofeyi approves of the oxymoronic designation 'Madammadonna' for Iriyise, so in *Petals of Blood*, the Mau Mau hero and Wanja's final lover, Abdulla, marvels at the paradox of the 'barmaid-farmer' (61).

Wanja's union at the end of the novel with Abdulla, which, not incidentally, takes place in her 'old hut', is reminiscent of Perpetua's relationship with Zeyang. Both men are revolutionary heroes and, like Perpetua, Wanja becomes pregnant. But unlike Beti, Ngũgĩ is not cynical as there is no doubt about Wanja's survival. Furthermore, through his union with Wanja, Abdulla regains his manhood, for he had been a man 'without one limb' (338), one who has been 'unmanned' by history – twice dispossessed of his national heritage, first by the British and then by the nation's new ruling elite after independence. The relationship between him and Wanja signifies the regeneration of potency in the struggle for freedom from oppression and exploitation in present-day Kenya. Abdulla's reflections recall Ofeyi's thoughts as he watches Iriyise dressing. They also reproduce the association of landscape and woman's body as in Negritude poetry. In essence, Wanja is his promised land:

> [F]or him now, a woman was truly the other world: with its own contours, valleys, rivers, streams, hills, ridges, mountains, sharp turns, steep and slow climbs and descents, and above all, movement of secret springs of life. Which explorer, despite the boasts of men, could claim to have touched every corner of that world and drunk of every stream in her? Let others stay with their own worlds: flat, grey, without contours, unexpected turns, or surprises – so predictable. A woman was a world, the world. (315)

Her pregnancy – preceded by an act of infanticide on the eve of independence and followed by years of barrenness – is the promise of the rebirth of the nation.

The same trope occurs in works by other writers like Camara Laye, Cyprian Ekwensi, and Meja Mwangi. The trope is, moreover, not just a periodic feature of the male literary tradition, it is one of its *defining* features. For it does not occur in works by African women writers. Why would women writers repudiate a convention so entrenched in the literary tradition they have inherited and one which, furthermore, from a (masculinist) formalist critical perspective is usually seen as making a work richer, more integrated, more complex, more intriguing? Does the trope serve the interests of men? Is it detrimental to the interests of women?

Feminist criticism has thus far failed to cope with the trope. Relying on the methodology of 'images of women' criticism, feminist critics have, in their treatment of the texts or authors I have discussed in this chapter, denounced Senghor and Okot for their reductive, stereotypical images of women, lauded Sembène, Farah, Beti, and Ngũgĩ for their portrayal of complex, realistic, or politically committed women, and given Soyinka mixed reviews.[3] There is a correlation here, on the one hand, between images that are condemned in the criticism as sexist and what I have called 'the pot of culture' form of the trope and, on the other, between images that are commended as liberating and the 'sweep of history' form of the trope. This correlation may be related to the fact that the 'pot of culture' form of the trope analogizes woman to a bygone culture which is usually conceptualized as immutable, rendering the female figure static, conservative, and ahistorical, whereas the 'sweep of history' form allows for change. More evidently, the socio-political ideologies of the favoured authors are of the type usually considered progressive or radical. They thus seem amenable to the feminist agenda. Furthermore, their texts, unlike those by Senghor, Okot, and others, treat such issues as the economic exploitation and sexploitation of women. Both Farah and Ngũgĩ have, in fact, made non-literary declarations in favour of the emancipation of women. In a continuation of his statement quoted earlier, Farah claims that the reason he 'used women as a symbol of Somalia' is '[b]ecause when the women are free, then and only then can we talk about a free Somalia' (Kitchener 61); and Ngũgĩ has written in condemnation of 'the double oppression of women' (*Barrel* 41). What I hope to show, however, is that the distinction feminist critics have made among texts and authors is a false one.

What emerges from a survey of the trope's operation across texts is an intertext that dominates the texts, a mastertext that neutralizes the differences in their ideological projects. For underlying the trope that is embedded in all of the texts is that same old manichean allegory of gender we uncovered in Negritude poetry. In other words, the ideological function of each text is identical. For each reproduces in symbolic form the gender relations of patriarchal societies. The trope elaborates a gendered theory of nationhood and of writing, one that excludes women from the creative production of the national polity or identity and of literary texts. Instead, woman herself is produced or constructed by the male writer as an embodiment of his literary/political vision. As Soyinka so neatly puts it: 'Vision is eternally of man's own creation'; woman's function is one of 'collaboration in man's vision'. So constructed, woman is defined as her body, as her sexuality: she is an ideal virgin-mother figure and/or a prostitute, 'Madammadonna', 'a barmaid farmer'.

The feminization of Africa by Senghor and his literary successors serves the same function as Achebe's masculinization of Igbo culture: while poems of the Negritude period like 'Femme noire' prepared the way for post-independence male governance, the 'post-colonial' writing I have examined justifies the perpetuation of male domination. In all of the works, the national subject is designated as male. A feminized Africa thus becomes the object of the male gaze, just as Iriyise is the object of that gaze in *Season of Anomy*. The relationship is one of possession. He is the active subject-citizen. She is the passive object-nation. She symbolizes his honour and glory or his degradation as a citizen. Sometimes he is a questing hero, Africa a woman in distress. To ensure that there is no mistake about the source of his power, he links male sexual potency with male political potency. This correspondence, always implicit, becomes quite explicit in 'An African fable', *Song of Lawino*, and *Petals of Blood*. Also in *Petals of Blood* and in Negritude poetry, he draws verbal maps of Africa on woman's naked body.

Thus he stakes out his territory. So he claims mastery. Africa is his to rule in perpetuity.

The trope also legitimates the critical practice of excluding women from the creation of culture, of writing them out of the literary tradition. For the author, too, is identified as male. He is the subject-artist, she is the aesthetic object, the repository of his meaning. Whether it is Senghor's Negritude or Ngũgĩ's socialism, her function is to embody his vision. And whether she is canonized as a mother or stigmatized as a prostitute, the designation is degrading, for he does the naming and her experience as a woman is trivialized and distorted. Metaphorically she is of the highest importance, practically she is nothing. She has no autonomy, no status as a character, for her person and her story are shaped to meet the requirements of his vision. One of these requirements is that she provide attractive packaging. She is thus constructed as beauty, eroticism, fecundity, the qualities the male Self values most in the female Other. She is the emblem of male desire. Wanja's claim in *Petals of Blood* that '[i]f you have a cunt . . . instead of it being a source of pride, you are doomed to either marrying someone or else being a whore' (293) would seem to be valid. This is, in fact, one of the points at which Ngũgĩ's text begins to fray at the edges. For although this identification of woman with her body is condemned as a product of capitalism, the rhetoric of Ngũgĩ's socialist text identifies woman in precisely this way. In other words, Wanja is her sexuality: she is virgin, whore, or mother. This sexualized representation raises the question of the writer's projected constituency, for it would seem that it would be a male readership that would find a vision thus packaged seductive.

Another requirement is that the woman bear the writer's interpretation of history, just as she might bear his baby. Now she is an emblem of male potency or power and a sexual/political allegory is produced in which her story is transformed into his story. The analogy becomes explicit in the (authorial) impregnation of Ebla, Perpetua, and Wanja near the end of Farah's, Beti's, and Ngũgĩ's novels. In each case, she is pregnant with his meaning. In particular, her pregnancy signifies the possibility of new life for his nation – the birth of a new Somalia, Cameroun, or Kenya that he will have fathered by the potency of his vision. But because Farah is uncertain about the future, he leaves Ebla in a quandary, unable to resolve the question of paternity. Beti's cynicism, on the other hand, dictates that Perpetua must die before delivery, while Ngũgĩ's Marxist certainty allows Wanja to live to give birth to the baby.

Men writers also use the trope to resolve the cultural calcification/historical catalepsy dilemma colonialism imposes on them. This resolution is in part achieved by the identification of women with tradition. As Senghor does with his *femme noire*, so Okot associates Lawino, Soyinka Iriyise, and Ngũgĩ Wanja with the heritage of African values – values that are timeless, impervious to history. These same authors then allocate the task of mending the breach in the historical continuum to their male narrators and/or characters. This is, for example, the role of Ofeyi in *Season of Anomy* and of Karega in *Petals of Blood*.

As it operates intertextually, the main function of the prostitute metaphor, the flip side of the Mother Africa trope, is to reproduce the attitudes and beliefs necessary for preserving the otherness of women and hence to perpetuate their marginalization in society. Not only Soyinka, Farah, Beti, and Ngũgĩ, but also Cyprian Ekwensi in *Jagua Nana*, Thomas Akare in *The Slums*, Sembène in *God's Bits of Wood*, Meja Mwangi in *Going Down River Road*, and many other male writers people (or woman) their texts with prostitutes. In these texts, prostitution is not related to the female social condition in patriarchal societies. Rather it is a metaphor for men's degradation under some non-preferred socio-political system – a metaphor which encodes women as agents of moral corruption, as sources of moral contamination in society. As I have already suggested in the Introduction, this perception of women plays a part in Nigeria's 'War Against Indiscipline' and the 'clean-up' campaigns of various African governments. Patriarchal ideology and practice are further reinforced in Ekwensi's, Soyinka's, and Ngũgĩ's novels by the invocation of the theme of redemption through repatriation to the village as a means of resolving the good women (virgin–wife–mother)/whore dichotomy that is at the heart of each text's sexual/political allegory. Thus Jagua, Iriyise, and Wanja are transported by their authors from the city to the village. Wanja's final move is from the mansion she has built to the 'old hut' which belonged to her grandmother. Redeemed at last, she is rewarded with motherhood by Ngũgĩ who suppresses the question of how she is going to support herself and the baby.

The trope also exploits the male–female power relations of domination and subordination. For women's oppression in texts like Farah's, Beti's, and Ngũgĩ's is used as a paradigm for the fate of Africa since the time of colonialism. This fact raises the question of whether the interest of these writers really lies in exposing the injustices done to women, for they seem to have been attracted primarily by the metaphorical potential of the situation of women.

More insidious, perhaps, is the trope's exploitation of female sexuality, which, in its replication of men's exploitation of women's bodies in patriarchal societies, reinforces and justifies that exploitation. *Petals of Blood* provides a striking example. For Wanja is made to bed down with nearly every man in the text so that her author can compare the potency of his own ideology with that of his competitors: with Kimeria, Mzigo, and Chui's capitalism, with Munira's early liberalism and his later Christian fundamentalism, and with Karega's youthful nationalism. Abdulla's African socialism apparently wins the competition, although once again the text begins to unravel. For the mature Karega, now a socialist of Marxist persuasion, spurns Wanja. Is this Ngũgĩ's way of indicting orthodox Marxism for its rigidity? Or is Wanja too tainted to embody his vision? The latter would seem to be the case, as Karega is supplied with a brand new woman: a 'girl' who looks 'shy' (343), a virgin. In either case, Wanja is most obliging, submitting without complaint to this textual sexploitation. If I have singled out Ngũgĩ for criticism, it is because he is the male writer who has been most lionized by feminist critics. But his text, too, is subsumed by the mastertext.

As has already been suggested, across texts, the prostitute metaphor is particularly illuminating. For rather than being related to women's social condition, prostitution is equated to men's degradation. And certainly the male literary tradition from Senghor to Ngũgĩ has exploited the metaphorical potential of woman's reproductive capacity. These texts are written on woman's body.

But contrary to what Soyinka imagines, her collaboration in this inscription has not been voluntary. On the contrary, she has been conscripted. For as a writer, she has repudiated the trope. This is a subversive act, a declaration of citizenship and of authorship, of her status as the subject of literary texts and of national visions. It is an attempt to undermine the manichean allegory of gender. It is also a refusal to collaborate with men in the exploitation of her sex. Moreover, by repudiating the trope, women writers reject the national vision the trope engenders, for such a vision implicitly gives men licence to exploit, rape, oppress, and dominate nations. This has been the nightmare of African history since at least the time of European imperialism when Africa, 'dark' and 'mysterious' like a woman, was 'penetrated' by European men.

In 1959, one year before Senegal's independence, Senghor made the following claim: that '[c]ontrary to what is often thought to-day, the African woman does not need to be liberated. She has been free for many thousands of years' (45). It is to claims such as this that Mariama Bâ was responding when she spoke in an interview about the role of the African woman writer:

> The woman writer in Africa has a special task. She has to present the position of women in Africa in all its aspects. There is still so much injustice. . . . In the family, in the institutions, in society, in the street, in political organizations, discrimination reigns supreme. . . . As women, we must work for our own future, we must overthrow the

status quo which harms us and we must no longer submit to it. Like men, we must use literature as a non-violent but effective weapon. *We no longer accept the nostalgic praise to the African Mother who, in his anxiety, man confuses with Mother Africa.* Within African literature, room must be made for women . . ., room we will fight for with all our might.

(cited in Schipper 46–7, emphasis added)

What Bâ is saying is that in their idealization and romanticization of African womanhood, Senghor and other men writers belie the actual 'position of women in Africa', that through the Mother Africa trope, they mask the subordination of women in the patriarchal socio-political systems of African states from which they do, indeed, need to be liberated. As I have tried to show, the trope, in its various forms and guises, also justifies and therefore serves to perpetuate the status quo of male domination. But ubiquitous as woman is as embodying figure, she continues to have difficulty gaining access to men's texts as a dominant, autonomous character. Moreover, as a writer, she has had difficulty gaining recognition from the male dominated critical establishment. As Bâ says: 'Within African literature, room must be made for women'.

Part II

ROOM FOR WOMEN

3

MEN FALL APART
Grace Ogot's novels and short stories

Like 1945 and 1958, 1966 is a significant date in African literary history. For in that year Grace Ogot's *The Promised Land*, the first novel by a woman to be published by the East African Publishing House, and Flora Nwapa's *Efuru*, the first work by a woman in the Heinemann African Writers Series, both appeared. The year 1966 can thus be said to mark the advent of a contemporary female tradition in fiction. This event has not been written into the literary records, as critics have tended to treat the publication of the two novels as a non-event. Recently, however, several feminist critics, with no reference to Ogot's *The Promised Land*, have assigned paradigmatic status to Nwapa's text. Thus according to Susan Andrade: '*Efuru* [is] the first published novel by an African woman and the text that inaugurates an African women's literary history' (97). It is 'the "mother" text of (anglophone) African women's literature' (100).[1] In ordering my chapters, I have given priority to Ogot, partly because she has a legitimate claim to it in that she became a published author before Nwapa, with several of her short stories appearing in journals in the early 1960s.[2] I also hope to show that, in terms of the strategies of resistance it inscribes, *The Promised Land*, too, can be deemed a '"mother text"'.

Ogot is the most forgotten of the women writers I examine. She also provides a particularly striking example of the invisibility of African women writers. Bernth Lindfors describes her as 'Kenya's best-known female writer' ('Interview' 57). But as his own data on the canonical status of African authors shows, the title 'best-known female writer' is an empty epithet. For Ogot's ranking on the first of Lindfors's two tests is only twenty-ninth – whereas that of Kenya's 'best-known' male writer, Ngũgĩ, is third ('Famous Authors'' 141–2); and she scores so poorly on his other test – where Ngũgĩ moves into second place – that her name doesn't appear at all ('Teaching' 54–5).

Ogot has had a fairly productive career as a writer. She has to her credit two novels – *The Promised Land* and *The Graduate* (1980) – as well as three volumes of short stories – *Land Without Thunder* (1968), *The Other Woman* (1976), and *The Island of Tears* (1980) – in English. But the critical establishment as well as feminist critics have tended to ignore these works. Ogot has also produced a number of works in Dholuo. Of these, Oladele Taiwo states:

> The writings in Luo – *Ber Wat, Miaha, Aloo Kod Apul Apul, Simbi Nyaima* – may be new to many outside Kenya, but they have proved extremely popular at home. For example, a recent dramatisation of *Miaha* in Luo-speaking areas of Kenya excited the people and showed to what extent drama could be used as a medium of transmitting indigenous culture. (128)

Miaha has recently been translated into English under the title *The Strange Bride* (1989).

Ogot's stance on the language issue is not essentially different from Ngũgĩ's. As early as 1968 she stressed the need for African writers from 'an urban environment' to attempt to bridge the 'great cultural gulf' which separates them from 'the overwhelming majority of the population who live in the villages' ('African writer' 37). And in 1983, she stated that she was prompted to start writing in her first language by her mother's remark on the publication of *The Graduate* that 'If only you could write in Luo you would serve your people well'. She also indicates that she has remained committed to writing in Dholuo so that her work can 'be read by all my people' and her language preserved and not 'swallowed up by English and Kiswahili' (Burness 60). Ogot's decision has not, however, generated any of the interest or debate Ngũgĩ's resolve did a few years earlier to begin writing in Gĩkũyũ. The debate has, in fact, been characterized as a wholly male affair, and Ogot's act has been negated by the absence of critical commentary on it.

Speaking to Lindfors about how she and Ngũgĩ came to write their first novels, Ogot suggests that a kind of regional nationalism inspired them both when they were made aware at the 1962 Makerere conference on African literature of the relative 'literary barrenness' of East Africa ('Interview' 58). Ngũgĩ's *Weep Not, Child* (1964) was much more widely reviewed than Ogot's *The Promised Land*, possibly partly because it was the first novel by an East African to be published. It was also much more favourably received than *The Promised Land*, which was condemned by the critics. Charles R. Larson reviewed both books. *Weep Not, Child* he praises highly, referring to it as one of those 'remarkable first novels' ('Things' 64). Of *The Promised Land* he says, after having criticized Ogot for her handling of theme, plot, mood, dialogue, and character, that it is 'one of the most disappointing African novels in a long time' (Review 44). As is so often the case with mainstream criticism, the condemned text is one which attempts to subvert the manichean allegory of gender, while the one which is commended valorizes it. *Weep Not, Child* is a conventional male narrative – as Taban lo Liyong inadvertently reveals in his review when he contrasts the role of the male characters, the fathers and sons of the story, with that of 'the mothers'. While the former engage in historical struggles, the latter, he observes, 'are symbolic of "mother earth": they give and preserve life and are wise' (43). Or as Elleke Boehmer says of Ngũgĩ's characterization of women in his first two novels: 'We see here Ngũgĩ upholding the patriarchal order by establishing archetypal roles and patterns of relationships that will continue, albeit in transmuted form, into the later novels' ('Master's dance' 12–13).

The reviews of *The Promised Land* and the commentaries on it in overviews of East African literature display many of the trends that are evident in the criticism of African women's writing. The supercilious tone Gerald Moore adopts in his review is typical of male critics' attitude toward women writers. 'Grace Ogot', he opines, 'would be advised to return to [the short story] form, which she has handled with some skill, and to abjure all attempts to give the visions of her essentially fantastic imagination a realistic dress' (Review 95). Moore's review also shows evidence of a careless reading, but Douglas Killam who, in his analysis, confuses, in name at least, the main male character of Ogot's novel with its female protagonist, highlights the insensibility with which some (male) critics read women's novels (126).

From the convention they adopt in naming Ogot, it is evident that Moore and Killam, as well as Larson, were actively aware of gender when they were reading her novel. For Ogot is always either 'Grace Ogot' or 'Miss/Mrs Ogot' (there is critical dissention over her marital status), whereas Ngũgĩ, whom Killam also mentions, is never 'Mr Ngugi', only occasionally 'James Ngugi', and almost always 'Ngugi'. Such namings may look inno- cent, devoid of significance, but they, too, uphold the patriarchal order. The semantic rule underlying the convention is what Dale Spender refers to in her analysis of sexist bias in the English language system as the rule of 'the male-as-norm' (3). Masculinity is the unmarked form, the assumption being that writing is a male activity. Hence, while on first mention or for emphasis it might be 'James Ngugi', it is almost always simply 'Ngugi'. Femininity is the marked form. In other words, the naming is gendered – 'Grace/Miss/Mrs Ogot' – to show a deviation from the norm. The convention therefore not only marks the woman writer for her gender; it also rebukes her for transgressing the norm by daring to take up the pen.

Even more insidiously, it names her not a writer but a woman, the implicit message encoded in the naming being that it is marriage/motherhood that is her true vocation and not writing.

The rule of 'the male-as-norm' would also seem to underlie the critics' readings of *The Promised Land*. All three critics complain of inconsistencies and improbabilities in the plot. 'But, worse than that', according to Moore, the story lacks 'force and point' as the male protagonist, Ochola, rather than being 'a tragic figure' is 'merely a misguided one' (Review 94); while for Larson the story's 'end destroys the mood of what could have been an idyllic memoir of African agrarian life' (Review 44). But it is precisely such male literary representations as Moore and Larson evidently have in mind – Moore of the Okonkwo-type tragic hero and Larson of idealized, Mother-Africa-type evocations of the past such as Camara Laye's *The African Child* – that *The Promised Land* (the title is ironic) challenges. The problem would seem to be, then, not that Ogot's plot is improbable or pointless but that her narrative does not conform to the characteristics of the conventional male narrative.

It is, however, Maryse Conde, one of the few feminist critics to treat Ogot, who offers the most perverse reading of her writing. Conde, too, complains that Ogot's stories lack credibility:

> Grace Ogot lacks neither style nor imagination. But her talents are totally wasted. She is so blinded by her respect for the European codes of behaviour, so confused as to the place of her traditional beliefs, that her female characters possess neither coherence nor credibility. . . . She may believe that she is an emancipated woman 'who reads books' but what she offers her fellow-countrywomen is a dangerous picture of alienation and enslavement. One feels tempted to advise her to join some Women's Lib. Movement to see how European females question the code of values and behaviour imposed upon them, and to replace her Bible by Germaine Greer's book. (142)

In the advice she offers Ogot, Conde overlooks the cultural and historical specificity of western feminism which she represents as universal. Indeed, it would seem to be Conde herself who is 'blinded by her respect for European codes of behaviour'. For at the same time as she condemns Ogot for adhering to western values (of which, in fact, as we shall see, Ogot is highly critical), she urges her to take western feminists as her model.

As Lloyd Brown observes, Conde's reading of Ogot is also skewed by the prescriptive demands of the mode of feminist analysis she employs, the images mode, which requires that writers provide a positive role model for women:

The critic's ideal of social equality or female independence ought not to distort or obscure the degree to which a writer, any writer, succeeds in depicting the less than ideal lives of women. . . . Conde seems to assume that an uncompromising realism is incompatible with a thorough-going commitment to the ideal of women's equality. (11)

As this excerpt suggests, Brown's own criticism is grounded in what Rita Felski calls 'a reflectionist model' (26), a mode of criticism which subscribes to the notion of representation as unmediated, and which measures a work by its ability to reproduce female experience realistically. As Felski observes, such a model is unable to account for the relation between literature, ideology, and the social domain or for the shaping influence of aesthetic structures (8–9, 28). Brown also glosses over some of the subtleties of Ogot's texts, but his analysis is, on the whole, perceptive, and I draw on it in the discussion of Ogot's short stories and novels that follows.

The main ideological function of Ogot's fiction is to undermine patriarchal ideology by means of a reversal of the initial terms of the sexual allegory. Such an inversion – female and male, good and evil, subject and object – does not resolve the problems of gender, but it is, nonetheless, a subversive manoeuvre. For it exposes the sexist bias of the male literary tradition and creates space for the female subject. As we shall see, inversion is a strategy that other women writers have also employed in their attempt to combat patriarchal manicheism.

In Ogot's writing, inversion is effected in part by the designation of the national subject as explicitly female. Thus Ogot counters both colonial and African male representations of women as passive and ahistorical, as well as providing a critique of colonialism and indigenous patriarchy. I will briefly consider how this and Ogot's other major strategy, the discrediting of the male subject, operate in a number of her short stories, as well as in *The Strange Bride*, before treating *The Promised Land* and *The Graduate* in some detail.

'The old white witch'[3] is set during colonial times at a mission hospital where male and female nurses are being trained under the supervision of Matron Jack, the 'old white witch' of the story's title. Much to the Matron's consternation, she finds that her female charges do not conform to the colonial definition of African womanhood:

She wished the African women folk were as obedient as their men. She had been told again and again that African men were little Caesars who treated their women like slaves. But why was it that she found the men co-operative and obedient? It was these headstrong females whom she found impossible to work with. (17)

As Nwapa also does in *Efuru*, in this story Ogot casts men in the role of colonial collaborators and portrays women as being foremost in offering resistance to colonial domination. But she is, in this respect, even more confrontational than Nwapa. For having designated women as subjects of African nationalism, she foregrounds their defiant action in her narrative.

The conflict centres on the Matron's requirement that the female nurses conform to English hospital practice and administer bedpans, a ruling which the nurses resist as it contradicts the social conventions of their own cultural heritage which exempt women from what is quite literally the shit-work of their communities and would result, if adhered to, in their social ostracism. The Matron, however, who, in her validation of the racial allegory, epitomizes colonial society, insists that administering bedpans is the nurses' Christian duty. 'Having accepted Christ', she says, 'you must face the challenge and lead your people who are still walking in darkness and are governed by taboos and superstitions' (10).

Although the male nurses and other African male members of the hospital staff are privately incensed with the Matron for 'treating them like little children' (20) and excluding them from administrative participation, they remain silent about their grievances and identify with the hospital authorities in the dispute. Echoing the sentiments of Matron Jack, their spokesman, the Reverend Odhuno, admonishes the nurses when they threaten to take strike action to 'return to your rooms, change into your uniforms and continue to work in the Lord's Vineyard' (11). As he puts it to the other men: 'We should give our missionaries support' (16). By contrast, the female nurses under Monica's leadership act to liberate themselves from 'the iron rule' of Matron Jack (18). Branding the men 'traitors' (9), they call a strike and decide to leave the hospital and return to their homes for its duration. For, Monica reasons: 'Is it not true that [the Europeans] give orders while we work? Then let them carry urine and faeces – they will not do it for a week. When they are desperate . . . they will call us back, on our terms' (13).

However, as is the case with Okonkwo, history is on the side of Monica's adversaries, which makes a tragic ending to her story also inevitable. For colonial power relations do not permit the emergence of African national subjects of either gender. Monica falls ill while she is at home and her people take her to the hospital 'against her wish' (25). Having lost consciousness, the once 'headstrong' Monica is as 'co-operative and obedient' as her male colleagues have always been in the face of colonial authority. '[Y]ou can keep your Christianity', she had once told Matron Jack (10), but the last sacrament, 'the best parting gift that a dying Christian can receive', is administered to her while she lies helpless, the object of the Matron's ministrations. Regaining consciousness just before her death and recognizing that she has been defeated, she tells her mother to return home, for 'I am staying with the Old White Witch' (25).

In 'Elizabeth' it is post-independence patriarchal relations which reduce the story's eponymous heroine to object status. Like several of the male-authored texts discussed in the previous chapter, 'Elizabeth' is a story of 'post-colonial' disillusionment. But Ogot counters the conventional male account of post-independence experience which, as we have seen, takes the primacy of the male subject for granted, with an account of women's anti-national experience.

Because of sexual harassment, Elizabeth leaves her job first with an American and then with a European employer. Assured by the Labour Officer 'that working for a fellow African with the country's progress at heart would be different' (199), she accepts the job she has been offered in Mr Jimbo's office, hoping that she will now be able to contribute to national development. At first Jimbo seems like 'an angel' (196), a man who respects her for her abilities. But her claim to national subject-hood is soon thrust aside and she finds herself once again fixed in the male gaze. She is 'loveable', 'beautiful', 'feminine', Jimbo tells her (195–6). Then he rapes her.

Elizabeth's final employer is Mother Hellena, a nun who runs an orphanage, the only kind of employer, Ogot bitterly implies, under whom a woman can work and maintain her integrity. But the damage has been done and Elizabeth hangs herself when she discovers she is pregnant. She is not, however, portrayed as a passive victim of male oppression. Her suicide is less an act of despair than one of defiance and vengeance, a means of reasserting her status as a subject. For Elizabeth is not voiceless and she insists on telling her story. She attaches a note to the door of Jimbo's house stating, 'I have come to stay', and then hangs herself in his laundry room where his wife and children will see her. She also leaves her personal journal telling of her 'life in the city' with Mother Hellena who hands it over to the police (203). Thus she asserts her superiority over the Jimbos of Kenya and exposes their hypocrisy.

Ogot is quite emphatic about the unexceptional nature of Elizabeth's experience. '[M]y heart is full to the brim', the Labour Officer tells Elizabeth, 'with story after story of you women who have suffered shame and cruelty in this city' (199). It is also not very different from the experience of Ngũgĩ's Wanja. But in contrast to the latter, Elizabeth is the subject of her author's story. She is portrayed to represent herself and to define the experience of women under patriarchy.

In *The Strange Bride*, Ogot combats one of the major orthodoxies of male literature: the representation of women as outside history. The story is set '[i]n the distant ancestral days, [when] our god, Were Nyakalaga, lived on the earth with his own people' (1), and it tells of the introduction of change into a society which had been bound by the same laws from time immemorial. Inverting conventional role assignments, Ogot identifies men with tradition and casts a woman, Nyawir, the 'strange bride' of the story's title, in the role of change agent.

Nyawir's husband, Owiny, the man who will succeed the present ruler of Got Owaga, articulates the viewpoint of the conservative majority:

[A]s the roots are the strength of a fig tree, giving it life and energy, so our forefathers are the strength of our nation, because Were Nyakalaga put all the commandments which govern our nation in their hands. That is why when we try to alter our customs, we are breaking the commandments of Were Nyakalaga; and we are destroying the earth. (122)

Nyawir, on the other hand, is an advocate of change. 'Generations succeed one another', she tells Owiny, which implies that 'what an elder did when he was a child, his own child will one day try to do better and in an easier way'. 'That . . . is what development involves', she says, and it is 'the increase in knowledge which builds a nation' (123).

By wilfully breaking one of Were Nyakalaga's commandments, Nyawir forces the people of Got Owaga to enter into history. And while her act does have one negative effect in that the growing of crops now requires human labour, the majority of the changes which occur – cattle are introduced as is tobacco, and fishing becomes an additional form of gainful employment – are beneficial. Thus Ogot attempts to counter the male myth of the 'traditional woman'. She identifies her female protagonist with change and development and grants her historical agency.

Discrediting the male subject is Ogot's other major strategy in her assault on the sexual allegory, a strategy that complements the tactic of privileging the female subject. In 'The green leaves', for example, the greed for wealth of an already prosperous man undermines his clan's defence against colonial domination by generating mistrust among clan members. In accordance with the laws of their society, Nyagar and other men of the clan bring a cattle thief to justice by beating him, or so they think, to death. Later, Nyagar sneaks back to the spot with the intention of robbing the thief and hence of making himself richer than his companions. But the thief turns out to be very much alive and he kills Nyagar whose corpse the people find in the morning.

Nyagar's death sows seeds of discord among the members of the once united clan despite the clan leader's plea that it should not be allowed to 'break up our society' (98). For it makes all clan members, in each other's eyes and also in those of outsiders, murder suspects, and Nyagar's wife, who is convinced that her husband was killed by his clansmen, intimates as much to the colonial police. In the words of the clan leader: 'The white man's tricks work only among a divided people' (95–6).

It is, however, the eponymous Tekayo who is Ogot's archetype of masculine egocentrism, avidity, and rapacity. Tekayo develops a 'savage appetite' for human liver after he has quite accidentally had a taste of it (56). He becomes so obsessed that he neglects his cattle, loses his sexual desire, and finally begins to slaughter his own grandchildren so that he can eat their liver. A patriarch of the clan, he is a father who quite literally consumes his own children.

Several of Ogot's other male characters are patterned on this same model, including Jimbo whom Elizabeth initially regards as 'the fatherly boss' (193) and who, just before he rapes Elizabeth, tells her, 'I like you like my own child' (195). The philandering Mica of 'The wayward father'[4] and the lecherous Jerry of 'The other woman'[5] also conform to the model. Mica, for example, impregnates a girl young enough to be his daughter and causes such distress to his own children that the younger ones begin to fall behind in school and the eldest daughter threatens suicide. 'Woe unto defenceless children of the world', is the heartfelt cry of Anastasia, his wife (18).

As she does in 'Elizabeth', Ogot privileges the female voice in these stories and gives it moral authority. At the same time she indicates how this voice has been suppressed by the patriarchal conventions governing relations between men and women. Thus Anastasia turns over in her mind the code of conduct which regulates her behaviour as a wife:

> [S]he knew fully well that she should never argue, that she ought not to question the husband about where he had been, even when he turned in well after midnight. She knew that she was supposed to wake up humbly, with a smile, and ask him if he had eaten where he had been, and if he had not, to quickly warm his food and serve him. This was the ideal Luo woman, treasured and respected by all men, whose praises were echoed wherever men gathered. (9)

But both she and Jerry's wife, Jedidah, refuse to be passive and subservient. They speak their anger and eventually they succeed in imposing their will on their errant and destructive husbands.[6]

In two of her stories Ogot celebrates male heroes – in 'Island of tears', the Luo nationalist Tom Mboya, and in 'The hero', the first African medical consultant in Uganda. What is especially notable is that these stories commemorate the untimely *deaths* of these heroes, Mboya's at the hands of assassins and the doctor's from polio. It is also the case that the positively portrayed, pivotal male figures in 'Allan Mjomba' and 'Love immortalized' have both died long before the stories open. Is it, then, only dead men who, in Ogot's view, are worthy of celebration?

In *The Promised Land* and *The Graduate*, Ogot employs the same kind of strategies we have seen in the short stories, privileging the female voice and discrediting the male subject. The structure of these works is the key to their understanding. For in each case the normative male subject is displaced and replaced by a female subject. There is, however, an increase in female subjectivity from the earlier to the later novel, as women are granted more agency.

Like Achebe's and Ngũgĩ's first novels, *The Promised Land* is set in the colonial period. And like her male predecessors, Ogot seeks to undermine colonial manicheism. Thus, for example, when Ochola contracts a strange disease, western remedies prove to be entirely inefficacious and it is what the English doctor who is treating him brands ' "heathen" practices' and ' "superstitious" ideas' (179) that ultimately effect a cure. Ogot's primary concern, however, is with combating sexual stereotyping and with promoting the acknowledgment of gender as a social and literary issue.

The novel opens on a scene which not only privileges the female voice but also involves contestation at the thematic level. For by questioning the existing basis of male–female relations, it treats a subject that has been suppressed in the dominant (male) tradition. It is a 'bitterly cold' night and Nyapol, a new bride, is alone for the first time in her marital home, a hut in her husband Ochola's village. Feeling 'frightened and lonely', she wonders how she will be able to 'exist in this isolated village' (7–8). For Nyapol, marriage produces the conditions of exile. Transported from her home village where she lived in a female-centred community, to an alien environment where she must learn to live within male-defined parameters, she experiences feelings of alienation, dislocation, and displacement. Becoming aware that her situation is not unique, she attempts to find comfort in the thought that 'there were hundreds of wives whose husbands were away earning money in the town, while they were left to fend for themselves in lonely isolated villages' (12).

Migration is the dominant motif in the novel. For the main plot deals with Ochola's decision to leave his village and settle in Tanganyika, a decision which places him in circumstances that are analogous to those marriage imposes on Nyapol. The cross-gender comparisons – comparisons which are to the detriment of the male subject – are a structural component of the novel and they valorize the emergence of the female subject.

In the scenes that follow, Nyapol continues to reflect on marriage. For a woman, she comes to recognize, it means permanent displacement. She does ask Ochola 'to let me go free so that I may return to my people' when he is so preoccupied with his plans to emigrate that he ignores her existence. But she is fully aware of the futility of making such a request even if it were granted: '[S]he knew very well that she could not return to her people. Once a woman was married she swore to stay with her husband's people for better or for worse, and no one would have her back at her home' (20).

She also soon realizes that marriage has deprived her of agency. As a single woman, she possessed a measure of freedom, having chosen Ochola for her husband over the objections of her relatives. As a married woman she is a mere instrument of her husband's will, as Ochola makes clear when he is asked if he intends to take her with him to Tanganyika. 'Can a hunter go to the wilderness without his spear . . . ?', he asks. 'Can you go to cut wood without an axe? I cannot go to Tanganyika empty-handed' (31). When she realizes that she has no option but to emigrate with Ochola, Nyapol, distressed at the prospect of even greater alienation, compares marriage to imprisonment:

> She thought of her mother and sisters who were, perhaps, even now enjoying the tales of old times in the village where they had lived for so many years. She wished she had not married. Marriage was a form of imprisonment in which the master could lead you where he wished. (46)

It is not, then, as Charles Larson claims, the end of the novel that 'destroys the mood of what could have been an idyllic memoir of African agrarian life', but its very beginning which focuses on a distressed and unhappy woman who resents the basis of male–female relations in her 'agrarian' society. Lloyd Brown sees Ochola and Nyapol as 'sexual archetypes':

> Ochola is the conventionally masculine figure – dominant and jealous of his male prerogatives as head of the family. . . . On the other hand, Nyapol is the model of the traditional wife – obedient, subservient to her husband, and performing without question all the duties that custom has assigned to women only. (26)

Nyapol is, however, considerably less docile than Brown suggests. When Ochola first informs her that 'we're moving to Tanganyika', she flatly rejects the proposition. She also transgresses the norms of the sexual code by 'threatening [Ochola] with her fingers, a thing she had been told never to do to husband' (26), and by speaking to him in a way no man ever had, 'even those who thought they were stronger than he was' (47). Enraged by her audacity, Ochola responds first with verbal and then with physical abuse, slapping her so that she will 'learn that it was not correct to speak to a husband in that way'. But she only provokes him further by being unrepentant and refusing to weep: 'She sat where she was as stubborn as a mule, as though nothing had happened' (47–8).

Nyapol, in fact, has a whole array of tactics which she uses in an attempt to combat male domination. As part of her campaign to dissuade Ochola first from migrating to and then from staying in Tanganyika, she enlists the support of his relatives, withdraws some of her services, '[sings] sad songs so that Ochola could hear her' (187), pleads, cries, and maintains a stony silence. But because he is 'the master', because society invests men with authority, Ochola is able to resist Nyapol's efforts. 'When I married you, you promised to obey me', he tells her (27).

Nyapol does, however, conform in certain respects to 'the model of the traditional wife'. At the same time, Ogot disassociates her heroine from tradition, most explicitly through the proposal Nyapol makes to a horrified Ochola shortly after they arrive in Tanganyika: that they should dispense with a particular cultural practice – one that valorizes patriarchal ideology by making the man the first occupant of a couple's new house – 'now we're not in our own country' (81). Furthermore, Nyapol's efforts to conform appear to be motivated less by a commitment to the model than by a desire to enhance her position by projecting the 'right' image. In other words, conformity for Nyapol is a strategy for survival. Thus while they are still in Kenya, she ingratiates herself with Ochola's family by being attentive and obliging. She is thus able to enlist her father-in-law's support in her dispute with Ochola over emigrating. And once they have emigrated, Nyapol's performance of her role earns her the commendation of Ochola and of their Luo neighbours:

> Nyapol was a good wife! Many people in this new land had remarked how strong she was in the fields and how well she cultivated the land. Her hands were light during weeding time, she had also proven herself fertile by giving birth to a son. If she was able to brew beer, then her qualities as an ideal wife would be complete. (101)

Nyapol's immaculate character gains her an enormous moral advantage over Ochola. For as 'an ideal wife', she cannot be held responsible by him or by anyone else for the disasters that meet the family.

Nyapol does eventually revolt against Ochola's authority, siding with the healer Magungu who, having treated Ochola for the mysterious illness he contracts after his Tanganyikan neighbour places a curse on him, insists that the family return to Kenya. Although Ochola is 'wild with rage' that she has decided 'to leave without consulting him' (201), he is forced to comply with her decision as he cannot remain in Tanganyika 'empty-handed'. In the end, then, with the assistance of Magungu, a man who has more influence than Ochola, Nyapol manages to undermine her husband's authority. In fact she succeeds in reversing the terms of the marriage contract, for it is now Ochola for whom 'marriage [is] a form of imprisonment' and she is 'the master' who can 'lead [him] where [she] wish[es]'. Furthermore, it seems unlikely that Ochola will ever regain total mastery. For although he makes a complete physical recovery under Magungu's treatment, his mental condition continues to deteriorate.

Ochola is, as Brown claims, 'the conventionally masculine figure', which appears to be the point of the portraiture, as is suggested by a dialogical reading of the novel. The text that Ogot most obviously seems to interrogate is *Things Fall Apart*. Ochola and Okonkwo share a similar personal history and a number of characteristics. Like Okonkwo, Ochola is obsessed with wealth and status: 'Ochola's ambition in life was to be rich, richer than those whom he had known in his youth' (87). Like Okonkwo, too, he spends his childhood years in poverty, then rises to considerable prominence, and finally loses everything he has struggled to obtain. More crucially, in his repression of his feelings and his engagement in acts of aggression, he can be seen to suffer from the same emotional disorders as Okonkwo. As is the case with Achebe's hero, Ocholo's manhood is the basis of his identity and he can brook no challenge to it, especially from a woman. As we have seen, he becomes abusive when Nyapol raises objections to his plan to immigrate. He even sees her decision to return to Kenya as an affront to his manhood – 'Was he not the father of the family?', he asks himself. 'Was he not the owner of the village?' (201) – although it is evident that he will die if he remains in Tanganyika. He also conceals his fears and anxieties from Nyapol as revealing them would 'betray the secret of manhood in the eyes of a woman' (84).

Ochola's status in Ogot's narrative is, however, very different from Okonkwo's in Achebe's. For one thing, he is no nationalist hero. Nyapol, in fact, has a more legitimate claim to the title of national subject than does Ochola. For her faith is in Seme, the area of Kenya where she and Ochola were born, whereas in his eyes Tanganyika is 'the promised land'. Furthermore, although he tells his father that once he has emigrated 'all the money troubles' of the whole clan 'will vanish' (35), he makes no effort to send money home during his period of prosperity, despite Nyapol's frequent urging.

Ogot further discredits Ochola by representing Luo migration as a form of colonization analogous to the British form in its underlying ideology and in the consequences it has for the people indigenous to the place of settlement. That Ochola is himself at least subconsciously aware that in claiming land in Tanganyika he is as guilty of ethnocentrism and as responsible for the displacement of another people as are British settlers in Kenya is indicated by the dream he has, just before he falls ill, of his Tanganyikan neighbour hurling accusations at him:

'You Luo people, you Luo people,
What kind of people are you?
I hate all of you.
You cheat yourselves that you were born to rule others.
You cheat yourselves that you are the only good farmers,
That you know how to make money and keep cattle.
You let your land fall into the hands of white men.
The white men will steal away all your land from you. . . .
Return to your land all of you!' (128)

Ochola is also not, which is Moore's complaint, a 'tragic figure'. In his greed, he becomes like Tekayo – a man who consumes his own children. For by refusing to leave Tanganyika, he endangers not only his own life but the lives of his children. Ultimately he emerges as a pathetic, if not a patently ridiculous figure. Intertextual echoes are, in this context, quite revealing. For while Okonkwo's tragedy is, in the words of Obierika, that he, 'one of the greatest men in Umuofia . . . will be buried like a dog' (187), Ochola's story ends with him looking forward to being reunited in death with a mad dog. But contrary to Moore's claim, Ogot's story does not lose its 'force and point' as a result of Ochola's diminished status. Rather it is from it that the novel acquires much of its meaning.

As I have already suggested, regional migration is compared not only to European-style colonization but also to marriage in terms of the conditions the latter imposes on women. The parallels between the two situations are made quite apparent in the narrative. When, for example, Ochola and Nyapol first arrive in Tanganyika, even though Ochola knows they will be living in a Luo settlement, he feels as alienated and displaced as Nyapol initially did in his village: 'he felt he was a complete stranger going to live in an unknown country amongst unknown people' (64); and his thoughts turn, as hers had done, to home. He is also, as Nyapol had been in his village, 'almost paralysed . . . with fear' when he is left to spend the night alone in their new hut (82). But in contrast to Nyapol who, despite her double alienation, remains sound in body and mind, Ochola falls apart both physically and mentally under the strain of expatriation.

The nature of Ochola's illness is revealing. First he develops 'thorn-like

71

warts' all over his body (134) which make him look like 'a human porcupine' (145) or a creature which is 'half–man–half–animal' (168). Later, he becomes obsessed with his dog. When both it and his children fall ill, he weeps over the dog and prays for its recovery but is almost indifferent to the fate of his children. When he is finally forced to leave Tanganyika, he wants more than anything else to take 'his dog, his brother, his friend' with him (203). And although the dog is now as mad as he is and tries to bite him, his parting thoughts (and the closing lines of the novel) are that he 'would never forget his dog. He believed he would meet him in the next world' (205).

The equation of Ochola to various animals reduces him to a non–human category. Thus Ogot represents 'the conventionally masculine figure' as being unfit to be a hero. The degradation of the male subject and the inversion of gender stereotypes are manifestations of the influence of patriarchal ideology on Ogot's fiction. At the same time, they are the strategies she employs in her attempt to undermine the manichean allegory of gender. By discrediting the male subject Ogot creates new narrative space for the representation of women. Ochola's failure as a settler vindicates Nyapol in her commitment to Seme. Her values prevail over his and her voice is granted authority.

The Graduate is almost identical in structure to *The Promised Land*. It, too, opens on a scene which privileges the female voice. The male subject is then discredited in the main narrative, and the novel closes with a scene which celebrates women's capabilities. The central issue of the novel is the political marginalization of women in 'post-colonial' Kenya – a theme which has itself been marginalized in the African literary tradition. It is set in the months immediately following Kenya's independence in 1963, and its main protagonist, Juanina Karungaru, is the first and only woman to be named to the cabinet of the new government, a position which she acquires only by default when the originally-appointed male minister dies in a road accident. For much to the consternation of Kenyan women, the original 'long list' of ministerial appointments 'turn[s] out an all male cabinet' even though there are ten women parliamentarians from amongst whom at least one female appointee might have been chosen. Furthermore, when the lists are read out, women discover that all the top-ranking civil service posts have also gone to men:

> The women went on hoping that there might be something in store for them, even a consolation prize. Those women waited patiently as the list of Permanent Secretaries was read. Chairmen of all the Statutory Boards, and all the Ambassadors and High Commissioners were still to come. Still there was nothing offered to women. They

waited until all the Provincial Commissioners and all the District
Commissioners Grade I had been read out aloud. (12)

To appreciate *The Graduate* fully, it is necessary to consider it in relation
to the particular socio-political context in which it was produced and
received. In the period 1975–9, the years immediately preceding the novel's
publication in 1980, there were no women ministers and only one female
assistant minister in the Kenyan parliament. By setting her novel fifteen
years prior to the time of its writing, Ogot incorporates into it a double
time frame which enables her to remind her readers that no progress has
been made toward establishing political equality between men and women
since independence. More significantly, perhaps, Jomo Kenyatta, Kenya's
first head of state and the leader of the ruling KANU party from 1963 to
the time of his death in 1978, never did appoint a woman minister, not in
1963–4 when Ogot sets her story nor at any time after that.[7] In *The
Graduate*, then, Ogot tampers with history. What she produces can be
classified as speculative fiction, for it addresses the question of the difference
the participation of women in national affairs might have made to the
formulation and implementation of national policies in those crucial years
immediately following independence.

In 1983, Ogot was herself appointed by President Moi as a nominated
member of parliament. But as the issue of *The Weekly Review* that covers
her nomination states: 'Kenya's women still have far to go' ('Women in
Parliament' 17). For that parliament, Kenya's fifth, had only one elected
woman member. Nor has life imitated fiction with regard to ministerial
appointments. For, to date, no woman has been made a full minister,
although Ogot had the honour of becoming 'the second woman since
Independence to be appointed to the cabinet' when she was named the
Assistant Minister for Culture and Social Services in 1986 ('Cabinet: second
woman' 8).

The opening scene of *The Graduate* examines some of the contradictions
of women's exclusion from the power hierarchy of national politics, as well
as some of the problems encountered by women who work outside the
home. Juanina is talking to her young daughter, Nyokabi, who feels she is
being neglected now her mother is a minister. Juanina is, herself, guiltily
aware that she has been sacrificing family to professional interests since she
took up her appointment three weeks earlier. She also realizes that her
husband, Ireri, might be resentful of the change in marital sex-role relations
that her appointment has occasioned:

Suddenly it seemed the tables were turned on [Ireri]. She had
overheard a friend warning him to be tough with a woman minister,

who might soon be drunk with power, and might forget that she was still a wife. She was the one who was given the free house, the free car, and a handsome allowance. Besides, all the doors that were closed to Ireri were yawning to receive her – with security escort, and all. (10)

Juanina has no intention of subordinating her public role to her private duties, but at the same time she does not wish to alienate her husband or her children or to jeopardize her marriage. She therefore proposes to resolve her dilemma by pushing herself harder. She will get up earlier so that she can spend more time with the children and she will be especially attentive to the requirements of 'the sensitive Ireri' (10).

As in *The Promised Land*, cross-gender comparisons are a structural component of *The Graduate*. Thus, later in the novel, when the main male protagonist, Jacoyo, 'the graduate' of the novel's title, is introduced, the question of domestic responsibility, in this case that of men, is returned to. Jacoyo, too, has taken time out from family life – and not just a few weeks but a full seven years – in order to devote himself to his professional interests. He has gone to America to study, leaving his wife and children behind in Kenya. And although he misses them, he does not feel anxious or guilty about having abandoned them until he arrives back in Nairobi when he is suddenly shaken by the thought that his wife might not have remained celibate during his long absence:

> It had happened to students who were his close associates. The news had been hidden from them until their return home. The bomb shell was then dropped at their feet with terrible consequence. The thought humbled him! One married a woman to live with, and yet he had gone away and abandoned [his wife] for seven long years. (40)

However, no such news awaits Jacoyo and he is greeted warmly by a loving and (presumably) faithful wife. For Jacoyo, then, for a man, there is no conflict between family and professional responsibilities and no double (or triple) burden of work.

Juanina's discussion with Nyokabe proves to be a consciousness-raising experience for both mother and daughter. On the one hand, Nyokabi learns why it is important for women to hold top-level positions in government. Women and women's issues, Juanina indicates, have been discounted by male politicians. As a result, it is the women of Kenya whom she considers to be her constituency and she intends to lead a women's delegation to the president to demand further representation and to fight for the placement of issues that are of particular concern to women on the national agenda:

the provision of 'good nursery schools, health clinics, and little shops where [women] can market their farm produce and handicraft' and of pipe-borne water to villages 'to relieve the women from the back breaking job' of carrying water long distances (7). She also explains to Nyokabi the relationship between poor educational opportunities and women's political subordination, setting for herself the additional task of waging a campaign against sexism in education. She will, she says,

> help educate our people to understand that little girls are just as clever and important as little boys. That no one should discriminate against girls and think that they should only take courses in home economics, nursing, nursery teaching, and secretarial work; while boys are encouraged to study engineering, medicine, and architecture.

'[B]oth boys and girls', she concludes, are needed 'to build a strong nation' (7).

At the same time, Nyokabi's observation that 'it would be good . . . if more men ministers died' for then '[t]he President could appoint [more] women ministers' (8) shocks her mother into a fuller realization of the extent of the ruling male elite's betrayal of Kenyan women. Juanina recalls the contribution women made to the liberation struggle by carrying food and ammunition to the freedom fighters:

> [They] strapped the guns tightly on their bodies along their bellies; then put their simple clothes on top of the weapons, and held the babies tightly. . . . They had learnt from experience that as soon as a Mzungu officer approached for inspection, you quickly pulled your breast out and pushed it in the mouth of the child until the Mzungu officer was out of the way. (11)

Forced by 'the ugly face of Nyokabi's questions', as she terms it (10), to countenance the bitter fact that had her predecessor not died she would not have been appointed and Kenyan women would have had no cabinet representation, Juanina determines to fight for the substantive equality to which Kenyan women have earned the right. She takes as her political goal the creation of a society in which 'only ability would count, and not sex'. She considers her appointment as a minister to be in itself a victory against sexism in that it 'shattered forever the myth of a woman's place being in the kitchen' (8). But she believes she can actively contribute to the establishment of sexual egalitarianism by demonstrating to the male elite that women too can be of service to the state – thus would she 'pave the way for many Kenyan women to move to the top, and stay there' – and by providing a role model for 'the many young women still at school' (14).

Juanina's first ministerial assignment is to persuade Kenyan students who have been studying in America to return home to take up posts currently held by expatriates in the civil service and the professions. As an agent of decolonization, Juanina, a mere woman with no university qualifications, succeeds 'where many [male] degree-holding politicians had failed' (29). The students are at first cynical and come to the meeting expecting only 'a tinful of slogans and empty promises' (24). And they are hostile toward Juanina not only because she is a politician but also because she is a woman. However, they are soon 'humbled into accepting their woman leader who had by magic words resuscitated their fainting hearts' (28). Juanina succeeds in implementing the government's Africanization policy where highly qualified men had failed because she embarks on her mission 'armed with honesty, hope and love' (14). And the students are quickly able to discern that 'this woman who stood before them [was] different. There was something genuine in her immaculate outlook which pulled one towards her' (24). As a result, a number of them respond to her plea that they help 'remove . . . the yoke of colonial domination from [the nation's] shoulders' by returning to Kenya (26).

Ogot's view seems to be that women make more effective politicians than men because they are more committed to promoting national interests. The problem with men, she implies, is that they have been corrupted by their natural accession to patriarchal power. Addressing the question of the difference the involvement of women in national affairs would have made to the nation's development, Ogot claims that more progress would have been made toward decolonization, at least in terms of dispensing with the services of the foreign 'expert'. Thus 'the white man', whom Juanina features in her speech to the students as 'sitting in his rocking chair laughing at my people' for thinking they are prepared for 'weaning . . . from Britain' (26), would have been proved wrong.

Juanina's appointment is itself celebrated as a victory over the colonialists. The argument here is that by excluding women from political power the Kenyan male ruling elite perpetuated a colonial practice, that the root cause of much of the current inequality is the gender dimorphism produced by colonialism. Thus Juanina points to 'the big rift' that was created 'between brother and sister, husband and wife, girl and lover' by the colonial educational policy of providing schools only for boys. She also locates in colonial taxation and labour laws the origin of the disabling myth 'that a woman's place was in the home, in the kitchen', the same myth that Amadiume cites in her discussion of the erosion of Igbo women's power under colonialism. In Ogot's analysis, Africans were coerced into the labour market by taxation. At the same time, women were excluded from employment in the cash economy of the burgeoning urban areas by colonial labour policies. As Juanina puts it: 'When the colonizer came, he recruited men to help him build his towns and cities'. Furthermore, the colonizer provided no accommodation for families in the new towns, but only 'tiny tin huts which adult men shared'. Thus, Juanina concludes, women came to be regarded as 'custodians of the land and home' (16–17). The women students whom Juanina encounters therefore hail her appointment as providing 'tangible proof that the colonizer . . . was dead in Kenya' (16). More generally, it is viewed as a sign of Kenya's progressiveness. For it 'humiliated the colonialists who in their own country had refused women the vote for well over one hundred years' (8) and it made 'Kenya's star [stand] shining bright among African nations' (17).

The rest of the narrative is concerned with the experiences of Jacoyo, one of the students Juanina recruits, when he returns to Kenya to take up the post she has offered him in her ministry. Although Jacoyo sports a 'bushy nationalist beard' (41), he is not cast as a nationalist hero, the beard being, on Ogot's part, an ironic designation. He does not, in fact, emerge as a hero of any sort. His function in the novel is to enhance the stature of the female protagonists, Juanina and her secretary Anabell Chepkwony. In appointing him, in choosing a man for the post, Juanina asserts her integrity, proving that she is more genuinely committed to serving national interests than are male politicians. For she does not respond to her colleagues' discriminatory practices with reverse sexism, but acts in accordance with the principle that it is 'ability' (and Jacoyo is eminently qualified for the post) and 'not sex' that counts.

Furthermore, Jacoyo's experiences underscore the importance for national development of Juanina's successful implementation of the Africanization policy. For they point to the consequences of a failure to remove 'the yoke of colonial domination'. When Jacoyo returns to Kenya, a group of British 'experts' hatch a plot to block his appointment and reserve the position for another candidate – a less-qualified expatriate. The expatriates are manipulative, devious, and self-seeking. They have already succeeded in foisting off a set of defective textbooks on Kenya's educational system.

As migration is in *The Promised Land*, so exclusion on the basis of social factors is the main motif of *The Graduate*. For as a result of the expatriates' plot, Jacoyo finds himself, just as Ochola does when he emigrates, in precisely the same position as Kenyan women: he is denied access to the public life of the nation. By situating Jacoyo in this plot, Ogot is able to comment indirectly on Kenyan (male) politicians, in their practice of a parallel exclusivity, one based on gender, rather than race. Prevented from seeing Juanina in her office and unable to reach her on the phone, Jacoyo experiences – just as Kenyan women did when the president named his 'all male cabinet' – acute frustration.

But more than anything else, Jacoyo is introduced into the narrative in order to be dismissed, to be designated 'not a hero', to underscore the fact that in this novel it is women who command the action. For in contrast to Kenyan women who, when they find themselves excluded from political power, begin to lobby and demonstrate for substantive representation, Jacoyo falls apart when his hopes and aspirations are frustrated. Paralysed, incapable of purposeful action, he first threatens to 'kick the hell' out of Juanina's private secretary (49), who, quite predictably, has him expelled from her office by security guards. Then he develops a fever and shakes and shivers on the streets of Nairobi. Finally, he resorts to whisky 'to soothe [his] nerves and drown [his] sorrow' (56) and ends up vomiting on the floor of a bar lavatory.

Jacoyo is saved from further humiliation by the quick action taken by Anabell, who discovers the plot and risks being fired and even imprisoned in order to expose it, not because she expects to benefit in any way from helping Jacoyo – he is, to her, 'a mere job seeker' (71) – but because it is her 'national duty' (68). As she sees it: 'Even if it cost her her job it was her duty to expose this plot to fool the minister into pushing a fellow Kenyan into the cold, while the expatriate and his family kept warm and cosy within' (66). As Juanina recognizes, Anabell has acted heroically, and she commends her for her courage and resourcefulness and gives her a promotion.

In *The Graduate*, then, as in *The Promised Land*, the debasement of the male protagonist takes place in circumstances that are analogous to those which the female protagonists have met without disgrace. More completely, however, than in the earlier novel, the male subject in *The Graduate* is displaced. For it is Juanina and Anabell who command the action and determine its meaning. Immediately after his disgrace and well before the novel's conclusion, Jacoyo is simply driven out of the story, although he does make a brief appearance in the final scene where he is presented sitting in Juanina's office receiving his letter of appointment. The narrator then brings the story to an end with the observation: 'This was the job he would have missed if it were not for the sharp eye of Anabell Chepkwony!' (71). Thus Ogot underscores the fact that in this novel the subject position, the role of national actor, is reserved for women.

Following Ogot, a number of writers have attempted to deal with the question of how to create female national subjects. This is a vexed issue, the problem being the construction of nationalism as a patriarchal ideology.

One of Ogot's solutions is to represent women's anti-national experience, but she also attempts to reconstruct nationalism so as to include women's aspirations. The inscription of women as national subjects is one of the distinguishing features of her fiction.

If we accept that literature and politics fight for the same territory, then Ngũgĩ's disparaging reference to Ogot while delivering his paper, 'Writing against neo-colonialism', at the 1986 Stockholm African Writer's Conference seems to provide a fitting starting point for a final assessment of Ogot's literary strategies. With specific reference to Ogot's entry into politics, Ngũgĩ spoke of 'becoming a state functionary' as one of the options open to a writer in a neo-colonial society (Petersen 11). Such a writer, he says, ceases to serve 'the people'. The choice he himself has made – living in exile – is also problematic in that the writer 'is driven from the very source of his inspiration'. But it is quite clearly, in Ngũgĩ's view, the better option, for it does not involve a betrayal of 'the people', the oppressed peasants and workers of Kenya (101).

As we have already seen, in his naming of canonical authors in his essay, Ngũgĩ does not mention a single woman; and his periodization of contemporary African literature operates to exclude women's literary expression. Ignoring gender as a social as well as an analytic category, he constructs the African writer as male. As we have also seen, in *Petals of Blood* he defines 'the people' from a male perspective, which is also the case in his more recent fiction, as I hope to demonstrate in my last chapter.

'Writing against neo-colonialism' is also one of Ogot's undertakings. But the primary target of her attack is Kenyan male domination. The literary strategies she employs operate to undermine institutional forms of exclusion, forms such as the 'all male cabinet'. And entering parliament is as much in accordance with Ogot's textual practices as living in exile is with Ngũgĩ's. In writing against patriarchal power, Ogot also writes against representations of women such as Ngũgĩ's. Portraying women as subjects of national aspiration, she constructs an alternative form of subjectivity. Ogot's male characters are also revisions. Men fall apart in her fiction in order to make room for women.

4

FLORA NWAPA AND THE FEMALE NOVEL OF DEVELOPMENT

Achebe's *Things Fall Apart* is the first title in Heinemann's African Writers Series. His Igbo compatriot Flora Nwapa's *Efuru*, the first novel in the series by a woman, is the twenty-sixth. Because Heinemann was the major English publisher of African literature between 1958 and 1986, such figures are significant: the gap of eight years and of twenty-five titles between the appearance of Achebe's canonical text and the publication of the first female-authored work in the series. Furthermore, the next work in the series by a woman, *Idu*, also by Nwapa, did not appear until 1970, thirty male-authored texts later. How can these gaps be explained? What are the factors to which the relatively small number of women authors can be attributed?

Male bias in education is clearly one such factor. As we have already seen, colonial policy in Africa favoured the education of boys over girls and hence operated to cut women off from the written word. The same male bias is evident in education in 'post-colonial' Nigeria. Speaking in 1984 at the Third Annual Conference of Women in Nigeria, Ayesha Imam referred to the notion of equality of opportunity in education as a 'myth'. 'Not only are there more boys than girls in schools', she says, 'but also there are more schools (and school places) for boys'. Citing a study that shows that 76 per cent of families 'would educate their sons but not their daughters, if finances were limited', Imam also points to the role of 'social prejudice' in limiting girls' access to education (99).

Critical devaluation of women's writing is another factor. Although Nwapa has recently been hailed as 'the mother' of an African female tradition in fiction, when *Efuru* was first published, its critical reception was, like that of Ogot's *The Promised Land*, mainly hostile. One notable exception was a review by Ogot which appeared in *East Africa Journal* in 1966. 'Of the many novels that are coming out of Nigeria', she writes approvingly, '*Efuru* is one of the few that portrays vividly the woman's world, giving only peripheral treatment to the affairs of men' ('Women's world' 38). Much more influential, however, were the reviews produced by the male critical establishment, in this case represented by Eldred Jones and Eustace Palmer, both of whom rebuke Nwapa for focusing on 'the women's world'. Jones, to whom Achebe once referred as 'our finest literary scholar, a man of great sensitivity and perception' (*Morning* 52),[1] was the most pre-eminent African critic of the period, and both reviews were published in prestigious journals. Jones's appeared in 1967 in *The Journal of Commonwealth Literature*, while Palmer's was published twice in 1968, first in the inaugural issue of *African Literature Today* and then in *The Journal of Commonwealth Literature*.

Jones and Palmer both compare *Efuru* to Elechi Amadi's *The Concubine*, also published by Heinemann in 1966, on the grounds that both texts have an Igbo setting and a female protagonist who is associated with a water deity. In each case, the comparison is derogatory, the key critical term in both assessments being 'deficiencies'. In Jones's view, 'these make *Efuru* a very minor work beside *The Concubine*' (130), while for Palmer they decree that 'if Elechi Amadi's effort is rated a beta plus, Miss Nwapa's must surely rank beta double minus' (Review 58).

Nwapa's reputation as a writer is only just beginning to recover from Jones's and Palmer's assault, despite the early efforts of Ernest N. Emenyonu who has from the outset defended her.[2] And she has suffered from critical neglect – she ranks twenty-fourth on Lindfors's scale ('Famous Authors' ' 142) – despite the fact that she has published four more novels – *Idu* (1970), *Never Again* (1975), *One is Enough* (1981), and *Women are Different* (1986) – as well as two collections of short stories – *This is Lagos and Other Stories* (1971) and *Wives at War and Other Stories* (1980).

The comparative aspect of the Jones and Palmer reviews provides an excellent opportunity for investigating the claim to objectivity of New Criticism. In his by now well known exchange with Adeola James in 1975, Palmer himself makes 'a plea for objectivity' in criticism. Responding to James's claim in her review of his *An Introduction to the African Novel* that because 'the African people are the most oppressed and the most dehumanised in the world' African criticism should 'be subjective, ie looking at African literature not from any vague or glib universal criteria . . . but from the definite historical reality which gives birth to our literature' (Review 150–1), Palmer asks:

> [B]ut what has [the oppression of African people] got to do with the criticism of works like *The Radiance of the King*, *The Concubine* or *The African Child*? . . . . This is the enunciation of a critical doctrine which I find both dangerous and irresponsible, and which totally disregards

the educational needs of readers. I will never accept that the critic should allow his commitment to influence his criticism. On the contrary, I will maintain that the African critic, like other critics, has to strive to be as objective as possible, or his criticism will be valueless. He must approach the work in question with an open mind, honestly prepared to evaluate and illuminate what he finds there. It is dangerous for any critic to try to read his ideological prejudices and preconceptions into a work.

('Plea' 126)

The question is, then, are Jones's and Palmer's valoration of *The Concubine* over *Efuru* and their effective dismissal of the female-authored novel free of the 'ideological prejudices and preconceptions' of patriarchal culture? Or are these damaging reviews instances of what Mary Ellmann has named 'phallic criticism' (27–54)?

That Jones and Palmer were consciously aware of gender while they were writing their reviews is quite evident. For like Moore, Larson, and Killam in their discussions of *The Promised Land*, they employ the convention of gendered naming. Nwapa is always 'Flora Nwapa' or 'Miss Nwapa', while Amadi is always 'Elechi Amadi' or simply 'Amadi'. Thus they inscribe authorial sexual difference in their critical texts.

Jones and Palmer charge *Efuru* with a whole litany of 'deficiencies': theme, character, plot, setting, language – all are mishandled by 'Miss Nwapa'. But as I hope to show, patriarchal thought patterns underlie a number of these charges. For example, of the thematic scope of Nwapa's and Amadi's novels, Jones writes:

Flora Nwapa's novel informs about Ibo village life while Amadi's informs about human nature. The gap is wide indeed. What Flora Nwapa's novel lacks is a strong overall conception apart from the obvious urge to show how Ibos live. (129)

But it is evident that for Jones 'human nature' is synonymous with 'male nature'. For it is Amadi's presentation of his hero, Ekwueme, that he praises. It is, he says, 'a penetrating study . . . of a man with a mother fixation, forced by circumstances to marry . . . an emotionally immature girl'. Further, the 'psychology governing the relationship between Ekwe, his mother and his "concubine"', he asserts, is 'totally' and 'universally acceptable'. 'Ibo village life', on the other hand, or what in another passage Jones calls 'the trivia of everyday existence', clearly belongs to what he classifies as 'the woman's world'. 'Flora Nwapa's world is predominantly a feminine world', he writes. And later: '[*Efuru*] reads like a manual on how young brides are treated in an Ibo village' (127–30). Unlike the 'study . . . of a man with a mother fixation', such subjects do not inform about 'human nature'. They are by definition trivial – unimportant, irrelevant, trifling, frivolous – in other words 'feminine'. As such, they are not fit subjects for literature. This privileging of a certain type of experience as worthy of literature denies value to women's experience and discourages women writers from engaging that experience.

Jones's critique of Nwapa's handling of language falls into the same class of criticism. Amadi, he says, succeeds in conveying 'the feel of the Ibo community . . . by a judicious selection of proverbs and idioms', while Nwapa fails because her 'novel is full of small talk'. Unlike proverbs, he claims, '[t]he ordinary items of small talk do not fare so well' in translation (129). Nwapa does, in fact, use proverbs, fewer than Amadi according to Austin J. Shelton's count in his discussion of Igbo writers' use of orature, but nonetheless a significant number: 18 to Amadi's 26 (38). Is Nwapa's selection not as 'judicious' as Amadi's? Or are the proverbs she uses rendered invisible by her gender – by a system which classifies proverbs as belonging to the male linguistic domain in African literature and criticism? Such a system certainly operates in *Things Fall Apart*, which provides Jones with his standard of success in the translation of Igbo into English.

Jones's labelling of the language of *Efuru* as 'small talk' raises similar kinds of issues. For 'small talk' is just one of the many code words for the talk of women. What Jones is really saying is that *Efuru* is nothing more than the idle chatter, chit-chat, prittle-prattle, gossip of a woman. Such derogatory remarks about women's speech have been a staple of African (male) literature and criticism. Amadi's narrator in *The Concubine* provides one example when, with no hint of irony, he makes the same kind of distinction as Jones: 'As [the men] crunched their kola nuts slowly they talked to each other with a dignified buzz, an octave lower than the high-pitched, piping, market-chatter of the women' (34). It is mainly the voices of women that are heard in *Efuru*, a representational strategy that counters the portrayal of African women as 'voiceless' in both colonial and African male literature. But men as well as women engage in 'small talk' in Nwapa's novel. More crucially, such talk has literary significance in the novel in that it performs what Patricia Meyer Spacks refers to in her anatomy of gossip as 'its symbolic function as voice of "the world" – the amorphous social organization that enforces its own standards and disciplines those who go astray' (7).

Both Jones and Palmer are critical of the handling of plot in *Efuru*. Jones considers a number of the work's episodes 'gratuitous' (129). In Palmer's view, 'Flora Nwapa . . . does not show any awareness of plot as the sum-total of events causally related to each other'. 'Efuru is', he says, 'made up of a string of episodes some of which could have been usefully omitted' (58). Palmer also finds that, whereas in *The Concubine* the 'sociological informa- tion . . . is always relevant, necessary and functional', in *Efuru* 'the bulk of it' is 'unnecessary'. 'The novel could quite conveniently have been half [its] length', he asserts, if such elements as 'an unnecessary description of a cure for convulsions, a lengthy story by the town's professional story-teller and numerous Nigerian songs' had been omitted (57). *Efuru* is about the same length as *The Concubine*, and certainly the 'lengthy story' that Palmer refers to is, as I hope to show, as integral to the novel's thematic structure as the folktale Achebe's Ekwefi tells is to that of *Things Fall Apart*. Furthermore, whether or not Nwapa violates the standards of New Criticism by including in her novel 'unnecessary sociological information' and 'gratuitous' episodes as the critics claim, *The Concubine*, when judged by those very same standards, can be seen to have its fair share of 'irrelevancies'. The following exchange between Ekwueme's father and his second wife is one such example:

> 'My lord, your meal is ready.'
> Wagbura looked up. Aleruchi his second wife was at the door.
> 'I'm coming,' he said.
> 'Please come soon, my lord, or the foo-foo may get hardened. You know the harmattan is on.'
> 'I wonder what the world is coming to. It is rather late in the year for the harmattan.'
> 'They say the king of the Wakanchis is dead and that they are producing the harmattan to preserve the corpse until human heads are procured for the burial.'
> 'Ha-ha, I've heard this silly story. I am sure that fool Wakiri the wag of Omokachi is behind it all.' (100)

This discussion continues for another three-quarters of a page neither advancing plot nor elucidating theme or character and there are several other passages like it.[3]

Palmer also claims that 'Miss Nwapa seems to be incapable of creating credible masculine characters' (57), thus raising the issue of women writers' representation of men. This is an issue which is repeatedly taken up by (male) critics and one which, as we shall see in the following chapters, the next generation of women writers, in response to such criticism as Palmer's, and also in an attempt to transcend, rather than merely reverse the manichean allegory of gender, have addressed. What is of interest here, however, are the double standards Palmer employs in his assessment of

Nwapa's and Amadi's characters. For although Amadi's main female protagonist, Ihuoma, is for Palmer 'a beautiful, elegant and almost perfect
women', he does not accuse Amadi of being incapable of creating credible
female characters. What Palmer is really saying is that he finds portrayals of
men as feckless and philandering, as Efuru's two husbands are, incredible.
At the same time, he commends Nwapa for her depiction of Ajanupu, 'the
bitchy but good-natured aunt of Efuru's first husband'. Ajanupu, he says, is
the work's 'one perfect feminine character', being 'obviously based on Flora
Nwapa's accurate observation of the idiosyncrasies of certain Nigerian
women' (56–7). Flora Nwapa's observation of the 'idiosyncrasies' of certain
men is obviously inaccurate. Such are the double standards of phallic
criticism.

In their reading as well as in their valorization of *The Concubine*, Jones
and Palmer endorse the values and attitudes to which it gives expression.
The Concubine is a thoroughly misogynistic novel, its ideological function
being to legitimate and reinforce patriarchal ideology. Like *Things Fall
Apart*, it is concerned with the gender balance in Igbo society. But in
Amadi's rendering of this theme, it is not the over-valuation of masculine
values but rather the pernicious influence of female sexuality that threatens
to destroy the social order. In a non-literary work published in 1982, a work
which appears to be attacking sexual discrimination but which, in fact,
justifies its practice, Amadi makes clear his views on female sexuality:

> If men are so sure of their powers, why do they go to such lengths
> to discriminate against women, who are their life-long and insepa-
> rable companions? . . . It must be . . . that men fear women. Why?
> Fear is generated only by the realization that the feared object has
> more power than one can cope with. It is suggested here that men
> discriminate against women because they believe women have a
> power which they cannot match or control. This power is obviously
> sexual power. Every woman has it, and every normal man is suscep-
> tible to it. The power is awesome because women cannot be deprived
> of it. Moreover, it operates all the time. Man cannot – indeed, is not
> inclined to – design any armour against it. Yet it irks him to think
> that a companion who is otherwise so weak can dominate him
> completely with this naturally endowed power.
> Because man recognizes instinctively that feminine sexual powers
> are overwhelming, he is reluctant to concede any further powers and
> privileges to women. More than that, he actively seeks to reduce her
> powers by discrimination and other forms of unethical treatment.
> (*Ethics* 78–9)

In *The Concubine*, too, Amadi projects on to women a rabid, dangerous, and ever-present sexuality. As Jones says, Ekwueme is 'a man with a mother fixation'. His first wife, a young woman selected for him according to tradition, attempts, with her mother's assistance, to capture his interest by administering a love potion to him. Ekwueme first suffers from muscular pains, next dysentery, and then in rapid succession rashes, joint pains, and boils. Finally he goes insane. The motherly Ihuoma, Ekwueme's personal choice for a wife, is a death-snare for men. For although she has no actual power in society, she exercises a formidable influence through her sexuality. Her first husband, next a suitor, and finally Ekwueme – the cream of village manhood – all die because they love her. Amadi provides an explanation for these deaths by introducing a myth: Ihuoma is the wife of a god, the powerful Sea King, who has sworn vengeance on any man who is attracted to her. Palmer finds this water deity myth, or 'supernatural element' as he terms it, 'credible, convincing and acceptable' – a myth which perpetuates the myth of the danger female sexuality poses to men. '[Amadi's] tragic vision', he says approvingly, 'recalls that of the English novelist Thomas Hardy' (56–7). But Amadi's 'tragic vision' is of a world in which men are under the malign influence of women. Women in this novel are like a contagious disease and gynophobia is the psychology which fuels the plot – a psychology which, in Jones's words, is 'totally' and 'universally acceptable'. [4]

By contrast, Jones's and Palmer's reading of *Efuru* denies the values to which it gives expression. Like Moore's and Larson's reading of *The Promised Land*, theirs is a misreading. *Efuru* is not a tragedy, as Palmer claims (58). Rather it is a novel of successful development, of a woman's successful development – a female *bildungsroman*. Nor is Efuru 'a patient Ibo Griselda' as Jones claims (127). Instead, she is a self-assertive, self-authenticating women. Jones's and Palmer's difficulty seems to be that Efuru's developmental trajectory runs so counter to literary stereotypes and societal norms of female development that Nwapa's novel is incomprehensible to them. For Efuru does not find her fulfilment in either of the conventional ideals of African womanhood: neither in the much vaunted glory of motherhood, nor in the silently-assenting-to-her-subservience contentment of wifehood.

In this chapter, I will examine three of Nwapa's novels: *Efuru* and the more recently published *One is Enough* and *Women are Different*. Each of these works is a novel of development, as also is *Idu*. And I shall conclude the chapter with a brief discussion of the significance of the female *bildungsroman* in the context of the contemporary African literary tradition. In my treatment of Nwapa's novels, I follow in the footsteps of Lloyd

Brown, Susan Andrade, and Jane Bryce[5] who have undertaken the task begun by Ernest Emenyonu of recovering Nwapa's reputation. I am particularly indebted to Brown who, as well as acknowledging the contribution Nwapa has made to genre development by her efforts 'to integrate oral forms with the literate design of the novel' ('Inventing' 4), was the first critic I have encountered to recognize that *Efuru* is a novel of development. Andrade's recognition of Nwapa's place in a female literary tradition is also important, but I take issue at several points with her reading of *Efuru*.

In Andrade's view, '[t]he male text which Nwapa appears most obviously to interrogate' in *Efuru* is Ekwensi's 'novel of a middle-aged prostitute, *Jagua Nana*' (98). As I hope to show, one of Nwapa's later novels benefits much more from a reading which juxtaposes it to Ekwensi's novel than does *Efuru* which profits more from a reading which places it in primary opposition to Achebe's first novel. Andrade does identify *Things Fall Apart* as one of *Efuru*'s male predecessors, but only in order to illustrate Nwapa's 'more gradual and subtle representation of the insidious ways in which European violence permeated traditional Igbo culture' (102). But Nwapa's interrogation of *Things Fall Apart* is much more stringent than Andrade acknowledges.

Like *Things Fall Apart*, *Efuru* is set in rural Igboland in a town Nwapa calls Ugwuta.[6] The time of the novel is the late 1940s and early 1950s, about half a century later than that of Achebe's novel.[7] However, Ugwuta has not as yet felt the full impact of colonial occupation, but it is on the verge of rapid social and cultural transformation. Remarks such as 'Things are changing fast these days' (11) serve as a refrain in the novel. The broader concerns of *Efuru* coincide with those of *Things Fall Apart*: to recreate Igbo social, political, and religious life; and to portray the effects of colonialism on Igbo society. But Nwapa's focus is quite different from Achebe's. It is on 'the women's world', as Ogot puts it.

In her reconstruction of Igbo history, Nwapa writes into *Efuru* what Achebe left out of *Things Fall Apart*. Repeated reference to the British banning of local gin production,[8] an industry controlled by women, serves as a reminder of Igbo women's resistance to colonial domination. For rather than passively submitting to their economic marginalization, Nwapa's gin distillers defy the colonial authorities and devise ways to carry on their trade undetected. As one of them says: 'We shall continue cooking our gin. I don't see the difference between it and the gin sold in special bottles in the shop' (13).

By contrast, Nwapa casts men in the role of collaborators. When Efuru's father dies, the manner in which he has acquired his wealth is with great irony revealed in the narrative – an aspect of the past that the people of Ugwuta have forgotten in their construction of history:

> It was the death of a great man. No poor man could afford to fire seven rounds of a cannon in a day. . . . The booming of the cannons was announcing the departure of a great son, the last of the generation that had direct contact with the white people who exchanged their cannons, hot drinks and cheap ornaments for black slaves. (200, 203)

Like Ogot's Ochola, Nwashike Ogene bears a striking resemblance to Okonkwo, having been in his youth not only a successful yam farmer but also a famous wrestler and warrior. But like Ochola, Nwashike Ogene is no nationalist hero. For rather than fighting the forces of imperial conquest, this 'great son' has co-operated with them, acquiring, as a result, great wealth and power, as well as the right to honourable burial. It would seem that at the beginning of their writing careers, both Ogot and Nwapa felt the need to refute the Okonkwo-type hero.

Nwapa also introduces the theme of women and western education in *Efuru*, a theme which she treats much more fully in her later novels. Through her dramatization of the Ugwuta debate on female education, she characterizes one of the dilemmas colonialism created for the gendered 'native'. For if she is, as a result of indigenous attitudes, denied access to education, then she is excluded from the burgeoning professional and bureaucratic sectors of the economy. If, on the other hand, she gains access to education, she is exposed to damaging western views of women.

Majority opinion in Ugwuta is that boys should be given preference over girls for school attendance. Efuru's second husband, Gilbert, himself a man of some education, articulates the argument which is reiterated elsewhere in the novel. '[I]t is a waste sending [girls] to school', he says. 'They get married before the end of their training and the money is wasted' (191–2).

The argument that education debilitates women by socializing them into an acceptance of western gender norms is most vividly represented in a scene in which two women engage in 'small talk'. Omirima is complaining to Amede about her daughter-in-law's behaviour:

> 'She went to school and so she thinks she knows everything. She is so lazy. Have you ever known a woman, brought up in our town who sleeps until the sun is up?'
>
> 'No, impossible. Who sleeps until the sun is up?' Amede asked unbelievingly.
>
> 'My daughter-in-law, Amede, my daughter-in-law. I have talked and talked, my son does not want to listen to me. Please help me to

talk. Go there now, and you will be told by one of the numerous servants that she is in bed sleeping.'

'This is bad. She is unlike our women. Where did she learn this foreign bad behaviour? I thank God my daughter-in-law does not sleep till sunrise.'

'She learnt it from the white woman. That's what I told her. I said to her, you are not an idle white woman. Women of our town are very industrious. They rise when the cock crows. Husbands of white women are rich, so their wives can afford to be lazy. An idle woman is dangerous, so I told her to her face.'

'Yes, an idle woman is dangerous. I pity these white women you know. How can one sit down in a big house all by oneself and do nothing? It must be a difficult life,' Amede said. (193–4)

In Omirima and Amede's view, western education is domesticating 'our women', imprisoning them in the gender definitions of an overwhelmingly patriarchal society, one much harsher and stricter than their own – one which condemns women to confinement in houses owned by men where they 'sit down . . . all by [themselves] and do nothing'. The 'foreign bad behaviour' of Omirima's 'lazy' and 'idle' daughter-in-law contradicts Amede and Omirima's definition of what it means to be a woman. And they insist on the right to and on the superiority of their own definition: 'Women in our town are very industrious'. It is from this definition that they derive their sense of self-worth, as Amede clearly recognizes as she estimates the cost of a life of dependency.

Significantly, this conversation takes place on Orie day, 'a day', Omirima tells us, 'when our women must not be disturbed' because it is dedicated to the worship of the goddess Uhamiri (195). But despite Omirima and Amede's confident assertions, it is evident that 'our women' are being 'disturbed', though not by the sexual demands of their own menfolk, which is what Uhamiri specifically prohibits, but by the demands of a colonizing patriarchal culture. The story of imperial conquest and of the colonization of women is, however, written on the margins of *Efuru*. It provides the background against which Efuru's story is told: a time of radical change when women's position in society is threatened. At the centre of the novel is the myth of Uhamiri, the goddess of an ancient matriarchal religion. For Efuru's development is defined by her relationship to Uhamiri.

Like Amadi's story of Ihuoma and the Sea King, the myth of Uhamiri is a water deity myth. Such myths feature prominently in the literature of Eastern Nigeria. As we have already seen, the river goddess Idemili, in the guise of a male deity, figures in *Things Fall Apart*. In the same guise, she plays a more central role in Achebe's *Arrow of God* (1964), as the god of Ezeulu's main rival for authority over the clan. Reading *Efuru* dialogically through Achebe's novels highlights the strategies of resistance that are inscribed in Nwapa's novel. Nwapa's act of writing the myth of Uhamiri into her narrative draws attention to Achebe's error in gender ascription. For not only are Uhamiri and Idemili both water deities, but in the characteristics attributed to her, Uhamiri closely resembles Idemili as Amadiume describes her: a goddess who is associated with 'female industriousness' and 'prosperity' (*Male Daughters* 27).[9] '[N]early all the storey buildings' in Ugwuta, we are told, have been built by women who worship Uhamiri (153). The myth of Uhamiri also challenges the ideology of motherhood that Achebe fails to examine in *Things Fall Apart*, the notion that 'Mother is Supreme'. For Uhamiri is not only 'beautiful' and 'wealthy', she is also 'happy' even though she has 'never experienced the joy of motherhood' (221).

More crucially, Nwapa's narration of the myth places Achebe's characterization of Igbo society as strictly patriarchal and excessively masculinist under revision. For the myth of Uhamiri embraces both matriarchal and patriarchal principles. Upholding the principle of gender equality, it gives cultural legitimacy to female power:

> Uhamiri, the owner of the lake, and Okita, the owner of the Great River . . . were supposed to be husband and wife, but they governed different domains and nearly always quarrelled. Nobody knew the cause or nature of their constant quarrels. (201)

Furthermore, through the myth Nwapa articulates a feminist ideology and celebrates a matriarchal heritage.

Although Andrade does not mention it, Ekwensi's *Jagua Nana* also alludes to the myth of a water deity. No details are given (the deity is not even gendered), but the myth occupies a privileged position in the narrative. For reference to it occurs at the climax of Jagua's story – during her affair with 'a vanished father' (190), an affair which symbolically takes place in 'a shed by the river, a stone's throw from the shrine' (181). Jagua, who has been longing to be a mother, conceives by the shrine of the river deity. But Ekwensi punishes her for the profligate life she has led in Lagos before returning to her village, and the baby dies in infancy. Nevertheless, as Ernest Emenyonu points out, conception itself fulfils Jagua, for it represents her 'absolution by the land she had so long rejected and fled from', her 'final loyalty to her heritage [assuring] her fecundity' (*Cyprian Ekwensi* 90–1). Jagua, then, discovers her true identity by performing the customary, biologically based roles of womanhood. By contrast, Efuru finds hers when, under the influence of Uhamiri, she is freed from such conventional definitions of her gender.

But to be thoroughly appreciated, *Efuru* also needs to be examined in relation to the treatment of water deity myths by other Nigerian writers. The Igbo poet Christopher Okigbo's *Labyrinths* (published originally between 1962 and 1965 as separate poems) is also one of *Efuru's* male precursors, as is Soyinka's *The Interpreters* (1965). Okigbo opens his poem with an invocation to the water goddess Idoto: 'BEFORE YOU mother Idoto, / naked I stand; / before your watery presence, / a prodigal' (3). A recurring figure, Idoto performs a number of roles in the poem. She is the poet's muse, not a creative artist herself but the source of *his* creative inspiration. She is also, as the opening lines suggest, a Mother Earth/Africa figure – an embodiment, in the Negritude mode, of the African cultural traditions which the prodigal poet has abandoned in favour of western values and practices. In addition, she encompasses, as Obiora Udechukwu suggests, the attributes of Mammy Watta, another mythological female figure, in this case one who lures men to their death through her irresistible charms (82). In the words of Elaine Savory Fido, 'fear of women can . . . be clearly perceived' in Okigbo's poetry (226). Idoto merges with the Lioness whose 'armpit dazzle' (11) is a fatal attraction, and with the destructive female figure who celebrates the poet's homecoming amidst 'the dismembered / joints' and 'entrails of [her] ministrants' (55). When at last he achieves union with Idoto, the poet discovers that he must seek his identity 'among [her] variegated teeth' (60).

In *The Interpreters*, Soyinka explicitly associates the courtesan Simi with Mammy Watta (51). Infatuated by Simi, Egbo, one of 'the interpreters', sees his desire 'like a choice of drowning' (253), and he likens her impact on him to 'the wanton strike of a snake'. '[H]e welcomed the poison through his veins' (51–2).

Nwapa's treatment of myth offers a sharp departure from that of Okigbo and Soyinka, as well as of Amadi, who, in their association of female sexuality with death and destruction, reproduce and reaffirm the manichean allegory of gender. For in *Efuru* it is male sexuality which is represented in negative terms as corrupting or polluting:

> [Efuru] was sleeping alone in her bed. It was Orie night, and she was in white. She had to keep Orie days holy for the woman of the lake whom she worshipped. She was therefore forbidden to sleep with her husband. (165)

Furthermore, in the male-authored texts, it is the effect of the goddess figure on the male subject which is the focus of the narrative. The emphasis in

Efuru, on the other hand, is not, as Brown notes, on 'the male's desire or need', but rather on 'the woman's, Efuru's needs' (22). For the goddess figure, rather than being an object of male desire, is a symbol of freedom and independence for women.

According to Andrade, the dialogic tension within *Efuru* is between 'the discourse of tradition' and '[the discourse] of modernity'. Further, she claims that '*Efuru*'s insistence on the virtue of its protagonist and on the importance of Igbo custom indicates Nwapa's privileging of the discourse of tradition over that of modernity' (97), as does the novel's 'elision of indigenous patriarchy and the colonial oppression of Igbo women' (105). As we have already seen, *Efuru* does offer an account of the colonial oppression of Igbo women, a marginalized account to be sure, but one which provides the historical context for the events of the main narrative. Nor does the novel elide indigenous patriarchy. In fact, the discourse of patriarchy has considerable status in the novel.

Andrade's categories are problematic and they lead her into making contradictory assertions. Paradoxically, implicit in her own analysis is a construction of Igbo culture as patriarchal. 'The discourse of tradition' is, in other words, patriarchal discourse. 'The discourse of modernity', on the other hand, is constituted by the myth of Uhamiri in Andrade's analysis. Andrade acknowledges Nwapa's inscription of an 'indigenous feminism' (99). At the same time, she is critical of the novel's 'blind adherence to Igbo tradition' (104). 'Efuru's desire to be traditional (here inscribed as mother-hood)', she writes, 'threatens to subvert the text's manifest assertion of female independence' (105). As her labels imply, then, the assumption underlying Andrade's categories is that feminism is external to 'Igbo tradition'. Thus in her construction of Igbo culture and of feminism, Andrade falls prey to the same kind of 'gross generalizations' that she condemns western feminist critics for making (92–3).

As Brown observes, 'Efuru achieves independence within the community, not outside it', such independence being, as he says, 'sanctioned by one set of the community's traditions (enshrined by [Uhamiri's] presence) despite the fact that it departs from another set of traditions (centred on the woman's more conventional roles as wife and mother)' (144). As Brown's analysis suggests, *Efuru*'s dialogism can be less problematically designated as comprising the competing discourses of feminism/matriarchy and patri-archy, each of which is, in Andrade's terms, both traditional or indigenous and modern or contemporary. For the goddess of the lake, Uhamiri, and the god of the river, Okita, are both ancient deities – Uhamiri, we are told, is 'as old as the lake itself' (221). Each is also a vital force in contemporary culture. The discourse of patriarchy, however, circulates much more freely and openly in Ugwuta society than does that of feminism or matriarchy which tends to be confined, at least until near the end of the novel, to a more private or personal form of communication.

The suppression of the discourse of matriarchy is symbolically related to the theme of the missing mother that runs through *Efuru* and Nwapa's other novels. Nwapa's fiction places considerable emphasis on mother–daughter relationships as the means of keeping alive the set of traditions Uhamiri embodies by passing them down through the female line from one generation to another. The folktale embedded in *Efuru*, which Palmer pronounces 'unnecessary', provides an example of Nwapa's treatment of the mother–daughter relationship. The girl in the story fails to follow her mother's instructions. As a consequence, she is forced to marry a maggot-eating spirit.[10]

The absence of a mother in Nwapa's novels signifies a break in the line of succession to female power. Like several other Nwapa heroines – the eponymous Idu of the second novel and both Rose and Agnes of *Women are Different* – Efuru is a motherless girl, her mother having died when her daughter was in childhood. Efuru misses her mother: 'the time her mother died' is her first point of reference when, made miserable by her inability to find fulfilment in marriage or motherhood, she reviews her life in an attempt to locate her error (52). More crucially, Efuru's development is delayed until she is well on in her adult years because she has no mother. Abandoned in the world of the fathers, she has only her own intuition to rely on as a guide. Her first act is to flout patriarchal authority by marrying a poor farmer without her father's permission and without the bride price being paid to him before the marriage. But what Efuru does not yet know is that, in choosing to be Adizua's wife rather than her father's daughter, she has merely exchanged one inhibiting role for another. Although she has flashes of recognition, it is not until she begins to dream of Uhamiri that she becomes consciously aware of the choices that are available to her and of a matriarchal tradition that is her rightful inheritance. For it is only then that her father remembers to tell his daughter what her mother, had she lived, would have told her long ago – that she, too, dreamed of Uhamiri:

> 'You see, your mother had similar dreams. Now that you are here, I recall these dreams of your mother. Your mother prospered in her trade. She was so good that whatever she put her hand to money flowed in. . . . She was so rich that she became the head of her age-group. She spent a lot of money for her age-group. Then she took titles. She was about to take the title of "Ogbue-efi" when she died.' (149–50)

Reading *Efuru* from the vantage of Nwapa's later novels suggests that the death of Efuru's mother is also linked to the colonial oppression of women, that it is symbolic of the decline in Igbo women's power under colonialism's patriarchal order. *Idu*, too, has a colonial setting and *Women are Different* focuses on the damaging effects of a colonial education on women. And even when, as in *One is Enough*, the daughter has a mother, the relationship is invalidated by the daughter who values what she has learned in school from the missionaries over what her mother tells her.

Efuru's story tells of a daughter's search for a lost mother. It begins when Efuru is on the verge of entering adult life, having decided to leave her father's house and get married, and it concludes about ten years later when she returns to her father's house for the second time, a divorced woman. As Brown states, her experience is 'both cyclical and progressive' (148), for by the end she has grown from a dependence for her identity on the conventional female roles of wife and mother into a self-authenticating woman. In the course of her experience, she encounters several women who act as substitute mothers, but she does not find a replacement for her lost mother until she begins to dream of Uhamiri whose worshipper she becomes. For it is Uhamiri, the symbol of matriarchy, who enables Efuru to develop into an independent woman.

Efuru's formal education is marked by a series of ceremonies designed, as Brown notes, to prepare 'a young woman for the usual roles of mother and wife' (144): the rites of clitoridectomy through which she is initiated into womanhood; fertility rites when she fails to become pregnant during the first year of marriage; post-natal ceremonies when she gives birth to a daughter; and purification rites when the child dies in infancy. The rites of clitoridectomy are treated most fully, their function as a mode of patriarchal indoctrination made quite evident. The main lesson to be learned by the initiates is that women are primarily for reproduction and eroticism. Thus Efuru is told that clitoral excision is necessary for the safe delivery of a baby and that the pain of the operation is 'what every woman undergoes' (15). Efuru does accept the pain as a woman's lot, but she is much less tolerant of the mandatory period of confinement which follows the operation, her refusal to remain secluded and be fattened, as is customary, foreshadowing her ultimate revolt against her confinement in sexual roles. Longing 'to be up and doing', she insists that '[o]ne month of confinement is enough' and she returns to her trading (17).

The lessons learned in these schools are reinforced by the wider community. Thus when Adizua deserts her for another woman, Efuru is enjoined to patience not only by her father and long-suffering mother-in-law but even by the strong-willed Ajanupu. It is, however, 'small talk' or gossip that is the main vehicle of patriarchal discourse in *Efuru*. This is gossip's primary role in the novel: performing what Spacks terms 'its symbolic function as voice of "the world"'. In this guise, gossip is an instrument of social control, a repressive and punitive force which insists on the maintenance of patriarchal norms. Thus when Efuru fails to produce a child after a year of marriage to Adizua, gossip punishes her for deviating from the standard definition of her gender:

> Neighbours talked as they were bound to talk. They did not see the reason why Adizua should not marry another woman since, according to them, two men did not live together. To them Efuru was a man since she could not reproduce. (24)

When she again fails to conceive after marrying Gilbert, the treatment is repeated:

> One day [Efuru and Gilbert] went to the stream, and while they were swimming the people in the stream began to gossip.
> 'Husband and wife, they are swimming together,' one woman began. . . .
> 'Seeing them together is not the important thing,' another said. 'The important thing is that nothing has happened since the happy marriage. We are not going to eat happy marriage. Marriage must be fruitful. Of what use is it if it is not fruitful. Of what use is it if your husband licks your body, worships you and buys everything in the market for you and you are not productive?' . . .
> 'Did you look at her body when she was changing?' one of the women asked.
> 'So you looked at her body. I watched her too. Nothing has happened. You can be sure of that, nothing has happened. . . . A woman, a wife for that matter, should not look glamorous all the time, and not fulfil the important function she is made to fulfil.' (137–8)

Efuru, herself, exhibits a healthy disregard for gossip. 'Who can please the world?' she asks dismissively on one occasion (19). But she is unable to escape indoctrination into an acceptance of the conventional definitions of womanhood that are in such wide circulation in Ugwuta. When she fails to conceive, gossip strips her of her sexual identity by defining her as 'not a woman'. Efuru falls into gossip's trap of objectification, for in her eyes, too, it is only motherhood that can confirm her identity as a woman. Thus, wishing desperately to experience 'the joy of motherhood' (24), she spends many sleepless nights worrying and weeping over her apparent sterility.

Thus, too, when she does give birth, she rejoices in the knowledge that 'I am a woman after all' (31), and when the child dies she feels that '[m]y only child has killed me' (73).

Efuru's dreams provide an alternative discourse to that which gossip embodies. It is a discourse that enables Efuru to react against and transgress the patriarchal discourse that entraps her. For she dreams of a beneficent goddess who gives women beauty and wealth but does not give them children. In contrast to so many male-authored works, beauty does not in this novel signify the sexual objectification of women. Rather, it is the biologically-based definitions of womanhood constructed by the discourse of patriarchy – 'Efuru was a man since she could not reproduce' – that objectify women in *Efuru*. Liberated by her dreams from the self-definition of the Ugwuta patriarchy, Efuru now knows that her beauty, her female physiology, confirms her sexual identity. She is a woman after all, even if she is not a mother.

As Brown points out, of the various ceremonies in which Efuru participates, the rites of Uhamiri worship are the only ones which are not 'physically oriented' (146). Significantly, it is on an Orie night shortly after her initiation as a worshipper of Uhamiri that Efuru has her last bout of insomnia. But rather than grieving over her reproductive shortcomings, she uses this period of freedom from conjugal obligations to puzzle out an answer to the vexing question of why Uhamiri does not give women children. Having worked out a solution, she concludes that she is 'growing logical in her reasoning'. The answer she poses – 'because [Uhamiri] has not got children herself' (165) – confirms her assessment, for it indicates that Efuru has arrived at a more mature understanding of her own experience. It is important to note that Uhamiri prohibits neither marriage nor motherhood. It is simply that women who worship the goddess acquire great wealth but have very few children. What Efuru realizes, then, is that 'infertility' is a form of resistance to male domination which, however unconsciously, is practised by some women.

Efuru's conduct during her marriage to Adizua suggests that she herself has employed such a strategy. For many of the decisions she takes indicate that she is intuitively, if not consciously, aware that motherhood can interfere with a woman's attainment of social and economic power. She is, for example, resolute in her decision to take up trading as her vocation rather than join Adizua in farming. As a result, husband and wife live apart during the first few months of marriage. Then, when she does become pregnant, she insists on continuing to trade almost up to the time of delivery. Furthermore, much to Adizua's annoyance, she spends what turns out to be the night she gives birth at an age-group celebration. Finally, contrary to the advice she is given, she returns to her work almost immediately after the birth of the baby. The same strategy, it would seem, was also adopted by Efuru's mother, for although she became wealthy and took titles, she gave birth only to Efuru. Thus, not only is Achebe's mythic notion of supreme motherhood interrogated in *Efuru*, but female 'infertility' is reconceptualized as a feminist strategy.

Nwapa's portrayal of Efuru's surrogate mothers, her mother-in-law, Ossai, and Ossai's sister, Ajanupu, also challenges conventional male representations of women. More importantly, it introduces into contemporary African fiction a literary convention that, following Nwapa, successive generations of women writers – from Buchi Emecheta through Mariama Bâ to even more recent novelists like Tsitsi Dangarembga[11] – have adopted. Like the Mother Africa trope, the convention has more than one mode, the defining feature of the form, as Nwapa introduces it, being the familial or social juxtaposition of two female characters (sisters, cousins, co-wives, best friends) who, in their response to male domination, are the antithesis of each other, one passively submitting, the other actively resisting. I have called this device the convention of the paired women. It is a recurring feature of the African female tradition in fiction and one that runs counter to a number of the trends in the male literary tradition, including the tendency to identify women with tradition and to resolve narrative tension with such themes as redemption through marriage and/or motherhood or through repatriation to the village. It acts as a corrective to the image of women which men writers valorize, for it is the radical not the conservative sister or friend, the one that challenges patriarchal authority, who is rewarded in the narrative.

The sisters Ossai and Ajanupu are complementary characters, one serving as a negative, the other as a positive role model for Efuru. Each offers motherly advice on marital matters to the motherless Efuru. 'It pays to be patient' is Ossai's motto as well as the counsel she gives when Adizua deserts Efuru for another woman (59). Her own story has a quite different moral. It is a cautionary tale of a woman enfeebled by her own submissiveness. Set on being a model wife, she wastes her younger years awaiting the return of a truant husband. Economically and emotionally dependent on her only son Adizua, she is devastated when, on abandoning Efuru, he also severs his ties with her. Losing her will to live, she sickens and almost dies, confined in her smoke-filled hut just as she is in the roles of wife and mother. An emblem of suffering, she is a warning that a strict adherence to conventional roles can be suicidal for a woman. Efuru heeds this warning. '[S]elf-imposed suffering . . . does not appeal to me' is her response to Ossai's story (61), and she divorces Adizua and goes back to live with her father.

In contrast to her sister, Ajanupu is energetic and self-assertive. A successful business woman as well as a wife and mother, she attempts to teach Efuru how to manipulate the conventions of marriage so that they serve her purposes too, recommending polygyny as a means of liberating an ambitious woman from the burdensome obligations of a monogynous union. And she comes to Efuru's defence when Gilbert accuses her of adultery, knocking him unconscious by administering a blow with a mortar pestle. Efuru acknowledges her debt to Ajanupu near the end of the novel, telling her in gratitude, 'You have been a mother to me' (208). But despite her aggressive tactics, Ajanupu, too, as we have already seen, counsels patience in marital matters. While she comes close to providing a self-authenticating model for Efuru, it is only Uhamiri who truly responds to Efuru's innermost needs and wishes.

Andrade finds Nwapa's negotiation of closure to her narrative problematic. In her view, the last paragraph of *Efuru* manifests an 'ambivalence about happiness without children': 'Although Uhamiri appears to have everything she needs, the narrative suggests that motherhood is necessary to completely fulfil her – and, by extension, her disciple, Efuru' (100). But Andrade overlooks the changes that have occurred in Efuru's circumstances, changes that provide the narrative context for the passage. More crucially, she ignores Nwapa's disruption of established narrative patterns in the closing lines of the novel.

As we have already seen, Efuru's initiation and experience as a worshipper of Uhamiri emphasize physical separation and mental development. Furthermore, although she returns once again to her father's house when she leaves Gilbert, it is under different circumstances. As she herself says: 'I have ended where I began – in my father's house. The difference is that now my father is dead' (220). With neither a husband nor a father to exert his authority over her, she is quite literally a free and independent woman.

The last paragraph of the novel begins: 'Efuru slept soundly that night'. It breaks the pattern of sleepless nights that has been established in the narrative and implies contentment and peace of mind on the part of Efuru. On this night, Efuru dreams once again of Uhamiri, as usual of the goddess's great wealth and beauty and of the gifts she gives to women, but also of her happiness and longevity, characteristics which have not previously been attributed to Uhamiri. While the first confirms Efuru's own happiness, the second acknowledges her growing awareness of the matriarchal heritage Uhamiri embodies. The final lines of the novel – 'but [Uhamiri] had no child. She had never experienced the joy of motherhood. Why then did the women worship her?' (221) – are not a qualification. The question at the end is ironic and rhetorical. It has been answered by Efuru's story.

In *Efuru*, Nwapa can be seen to have undertaken the task Achebe failed to perform in *Things Fall Apart*: that of helping African women regain the 'dignity and self-respect' they lost during the colonial period. Nwapa's version of Igbo society is very different from Achebe's. Whereas in Umuofia, women have almost no social or political significance, in Ugwuta they have status and power. Ugwuta women also actively resist Igbo male and colonial domination. In contrast to *Things Fall Apart*, *Efuru* also promotes a positive image of female power. Efuru uses the power she acquires to succour the members of her community, taking the ill to hospital, paying medical bills, and lending, even giving money to those in financial difficulty. The beauty Uhamiri bestows on women affirms the beneficence of female power. By contrast it is the cannon which celebrates Nwashike Ogene's greatness that symbolizes the nature of male power.

Nwapa's treatment of Efuru is also quite different from Achebe's handling of his female characters. Hers is a realistic portrayal, for Efuru is a complex character, one who learns from her experience and changes in response to her social circumstances, rejecting orthodox definitions of her gender. Nwapa's male characters, on the other hand, Efuru's two husbands and her father Nwashike Ogene, conform to their assigned gender characteristics. Double-dealing, irresponsible, and unfaithful, Adizua is just like his father, and Gilbert, too, conforms to the model. These characterizations can be seen as a retaliatory act, tit for tat. They can also be seen as evidence of the influence of patriarchal structures on Nwapa's writing. What they accomplish is a reversal of the manichean allegory of gender.

Efuru was written in the years immediately following Nigeria's independence, a period which was marked by power struggles between different groupings of a male elite. The primary ideological function of the novel is to challenge the legitimacy of the 'post-colonial' male hegemony. In this, Nwapa's character portrayals and her valorization of female power are both significant, but the myth of Uhamiri is of prime importance. For the meaning of the myth is the affirmation of the cultural legitimacy of female power. *Efuru* also challenges male idealizations of motherhood and it refutes Achebe's portrayal of Igbo women by bestowing subjectivity on its heroine. It also refutes Achebe's portrayal of Igbo society through its celebration of a matriarchal heritage. By providing a symbol of female transcendence and empowerment, the novel furnishes a basis for resistance to images that render women powerless. Recognizing its efficacy, at least one other woman writer has, as we shall see, incorporated the symbol into one of her novels.

Efuru also provided a model for Nwapa's later novels. The main difference between *Efuru* and *One is Enough* is that the latter has a more contemporary setting. For *One is Enough* is essentially a retelling of Efuru's story in a 'post-colonial' setting. The years after independence are represented in the novel as a time of opportunity for women – a time for regaining the ground that was lost under colonialism. 'Post-colonial' urban migration provides the framework for the heroine's story. The novel opens in the Eastern Nigerian town of Onitsha where Amaka lives with her husband. Made miserable by her marriage, she goes to Lagos where, by the end of the novel, she has made her fortune as a contractor and found happiness as a single woman. In contrast to her male predecessors, then, Nwapa indicates that cities are good for women. The Nigerian Civil War is portrayed in a similar light. For although, as *Never Again* makes evident, Nwapa clearly deplored the war, in *One is Enough* it is the opportunity it afforded to women for economic advancement that is emphasized. It is with her participation in the 'attack trade' during the war – purchasing commodities from Nigerian soldiers and selling them to fellow Biafrans – that Amaka's development commences. For the experience alters her self-perception, making her aware of her capacity for self-reliance: '[I]n the "attack trade", she rediscovered herself. She was amazed at what she was able to do and to accomplish' (4).

Like Efuru, Amaka grows significantly only after she has attempted to find fulfilment in conventional roles:

> Amaka had always wanted to be married. She envied married people, and when at last Obiora decided to marry her, she was on top of the world. She was going to show everybody that a woman's ambition was marriage, a home that she could call her own, a man she would love and cherish, and children to crown the marriage. (1)

But Amaka soon discovers that a woman has no 'home she [can] call her own' unless she builds a house for herself, and that loving and cherishing a man means subjugation, self-abnegation, and humiliation. When, in his view, Amaka becomes unruly, Obiora beats her or 'point[s] an accusing finger at her and call[s] her a whore' (23). And when she fails to produce children, he labels her 'barren' and takes another wife, making it clear to Amaka that she no longer has any rights in his house. Because she is childless, she must not, he says, 'raise [her] voice in this house' (19). '[I]f you step out of this house in protest', he adds, 'you stay out forever' (20). Stripped of her identity and denied her rights, Amaka finally awakens to the limitations of the roles she has chosen and begins to consider the possibility of finding fulfilment in other roles: 'Was a woman nothing because she was unmarried or barren? Was there no other fulfilment for her? Could she not be happy, in the real sense of the word, just by having men friends who were not husbands?' (22). Shortly after she determines to break with marital authority for ever:

> She would leave and set up house somewhere. She would live a single and respected life. . . . She would find fulfilment, she would find pleasure, even happiness in being a single woman. The erroneous belief that without a husband a woman was nothing must be disproved. (23–4)

And so at the age of 30 Amaka sets off for Lagos 'to start life again' (38).

Amaka's development is delayed until she is well on in adulthood for the same reason as Efuru's: an inadequate education in the ways of the mothers. The discourse of matriarchy is even more marginalized in Amaka's Nigeria than it was in Efuru's Ugwuta. There is no longer a goddess religion to give it official status, making it completely dependent on the mother–daughter relationship for its transmission from one generation to another. By contrast, the discourse of patriarchy in which Amaka becomes entrapped has institutional status. An imported rather than an indigenous product, it transmits the gender ideology transported by the British through the colonial education system. The product of a mission school education, Amaka is one of its victims.

Like the girl in the folktale told in *Efuru*, Amaka pays no heed to what her mother tells her, following instead the dictates of '[t]he good missionaries [who] had emphasized chastity, marriage and the home' (11). By contrast, Amaka's mother stresses the importance of 'self-determination and motherhood' (23). The essence of her teaching is that female sexuality is a resource which a woman must exploit if she is to get what she wants in a male-dominated society. Hence, for her, marriage is of secondary importance and 'virtues' such as chastity and faithfulness are worthless. Thus when Amaka is disappointed by a number of suitors, her mother advises her to 'make men friends and start thinking of having children' (11). And when Amaka refuses to listen, she tells her in disgust to 'go ahead and eat virtue' (32). She also holds up to her as a model for emulation her sister who 'got herself "kept" by a Permanent Secretary', a married man from whom she gains not only children but a house in her own name (33). However, although Amaka wonders when she is unhappy whether there was not 'something traditional which she did not know because she went to school and was taught the tradition of the white missionaries' (11), it is not until she sets off to start life afresh in Lagos that she determines to put into practice 'all that her mother taught her' (74).

According to Katherine Frank, the role of Amaka's mother in the novel is to 'embody traditional African values', by which she means 'patriarchal values' ('Women' 16). *One is Enough* is among the texts Frank discusses in order to give substance to her views on what she calls 'African feminist novels' (16). In defining the narrative tension in such novels, Frank constructs the same categories as Andrade does in her analysis of *Efuru*. The question posed by novels such as *One is Enough*, she states, is 'how can the contemporary African woman negotiate her way between the claims of tradition and modernization . . . ?' (18). Implicit in her discussion is an identification of feminism as a western phenomenon. '[A]ll of [the novels] have', she says, 'educated, highly Westernized heroines.' But Frank is much more explicit than Andrade in her identification of 'traditional African values' as the source of African women's oppression. Mothers like Amaka's, she asserts, 'reinforce the patriarchal values of African society' (16).

Using tactics she has learned from her mother, Amaka does, indeed, disprove the belief that 'without a husband a woman is nothing'. By sleeping with an Alhaji and a Catholic priest, she makes useful contacts and gains lucrative contracts. Soon she is able to return the dowry Obiora paid for her and to build houses in Onitsha and Lagos. Reflecting on the miserable years she spent in Onitsha as a wife, she realizes that she had not known 'how hurt she was until her eyes were opened in Lagos and she began to see what she could do as a woman, using her bottom power' (120–1).

In time, Amaka also becomes the mother of twin boys the priest has fathered. But when Father Mclaid decides to leave the priesthood and marry her, she is adamant in her refusal:

> 'I don't want to be a wife any more, a mistress yes, with a lover, yes of course, but not a wife. There is something in that word that does not suit me. As a wife, I am never free. I am shadow of myself. As a wife I am almost impotent. I am in prison, unable to advance in body and soul. Something gets hold of me as wife and destroys me. When I rid myself of Obiora, things started working for me. I don't want to go back to my "wifely" days. No, I am through with husbands. I said farewell to husbands the first day I came to Lagos.' (127)

In rejecting marriage, Amaka makes a deliberate choice for independence and freedom. She has found, as she purposed, when she left Obiora 'fulfilment, . . . pleasure, even happiness in being a single women'.

Frank sees Amaka's life in Lagos in terms of moral laxity, and the freedom she negotiates as a false freedom. '"Bottom power"', she says, 'is really just a shrewd kind of prostitution.' '[T]he means by which Amaka gets ahead are questionable to say the least, and undermine the validity of her success' (21). But Frank's perception of the kinds of transaction in which Amaka engages is clearly much closer to that of an Ekwensi or Ngũgĩ than it is to

Nwapa's. For Nwapa, who, as we shall see in the next chapter, takes her cue from Emecheta, revises the topos of the prostitute, subverting the authority of figures like Jagua and Wanja. As Patricia Ruddy indicates in her discussion of One is Enough, it is necessity, not moral laxity, that causes Amaka to trade in sex (12). 'You know Lagos', Amaka says to her good friend Adaobi. 'No man can do anything for a woman . . . without asking her for her most precious possession – herself' (67–8). In Nwapa's conception, then, it is men who are the agents of social corruption. Prostitution, on the other hand, is for her a strategy women have adopted for confronting male domination. The narrative also emphasizes the relative beneficence of female power. Amaka takes her friend Adaobi along with her on her journey to independence, negotiating contracts for her which Adaobi cannot negotiate herself because she is married. While men make war and stage coups (the coup that toppled General Gowon in 1975 is reported near the end of the novel), women empower other women.

Furthermore, sexual negotiation plays a minor role in both Amaka's life and Nwapa's novel. Nwapa's concern is with women seeking independence. It is men writers who look at 'prostitutes'. As Amaka herself reflects: 'She had not come to Lagos to be a whore' but 'to look for her identity' (45). This she discovers in her success as a business woman.

That the freedom Amaka negotiates is real is clearly seen in her refusal to remarry. Added evidence is provided by the fact that, unlike Ekwensi and Ngũgĩ, Nwapa does not punish her heroine for trading in sex, but instead rewards her, bestowing on her not only wealth but children. Significantly, it is during her ' "wifely" days' when, as she says, she was 'in prison', that Amaka is barren. Furthermore, Nwapa does not invoke the theme of redemption through repatriation to the village. She does not, in other words, send Amaka back to Onitsha for moral reformation. Rather, she resolves the good women/whore, rural/urban dichotomies with a counter-theme: what we might call the theme of empowerment through urban migration. 'Lagos was good for her, Lagos was kind to her' is Amaka's thinking (45) and her author agrees with her.

In One is Enough, then, Nwapa interrogates such male texts as Ekwensi's Jagua Nana and Ngũgĩ's Petals of Blood, the main ideological function of the novel being to refute the prostitute topos. Necessity replaces moral laxity in Nwapa's depiction of women's engagement in prostitution, and the freedom which is negotiated through that engagement is represented as real freedom. By resolving narrative tension with the theme of empowerment through urban migration, Nwapa also undermines the notion embedded in much male fiction, as well as in other types of discourse, that cities are male territory. The novel thus functions as a means of reclaiming urban space for women through the challenge it offers to patriarchal ideology.

One is Enough also seeks to valorize indigenous over foreign or imported gender ideologies through its portrayal of Amaka's mother and its account of Amaka's colonial education. It is this function which is primarily served by Nwapa's most recent novel, which is also, as Jane Bryce states, her 'most recognisably autobiographical' work ('Inventing autobiography' 6). *Women are Different* tells the stories of four women, starting from their school days in the 1940s at a mission school named after the one Nwapa herself attended,[12] to the time they reach their mid-forties in the 1970s. A *bildungsroman*, this novel conforms less closely than *One is Enough* to the model provided by *Efuru*. For one thing, it has multiple heroines. For another, the development of the main protagonists is not merely delayed, it is arrested. The intertwining stories of the three friends, Rose, Agnes, and Doris, are at the centre of the novel. They are stories of women who are unable to break out of the definitions of womanhood they internalized in the course of their missionary education, and they tell of defeat and humiliation. The story of their schoolmate Comfort, on the other hand, significantly, a girl whom the others excluded from their circle 'because of her "loud mouth"' (9), tells of determined resistance to western gender definitions.

The theme of the missing mother is particularly strong in this novel. Of the four girls, only Comfort has a mother who provides a positive role model. Rose and Agnes have both lost their mothers and each suffers from a lack of maternal support and guidance. Menstruation comes as a shock to Rose '[b]ecause she had no mother' (11); and when her mother dies, Agnes is forced into a marriage her mother had opposed. Doris, the only one of the trio who had a mother during her adolescence, points to a more general failing. 'Our . . . mothers', she says, 'did not prepare us for the kind of life we would be called upon to live in Nigeria of the seventies' (100). The discourse of matriarchy, it would seem, has been almost totally suppressed, the mother–daughter line of succession to inherited female power broken.

In search of maternal guidance, the girls turn to the missionaries who seek to socialize them into an acceptance of 'good Christian norms' (35): love, honour, duty, selflessness. And although the girls eventually recognize that they were as ill-prepared for adult life by 'the good missionaries' as they were by their mothers (100), they continue to be guided in their behaviour by the Christian values they have internalized.

The primary concern of the novel, however, is with 'True Romances' as a particularly pernicious form of patriarchal discourse in the effect it has on female psychological development. The girls' favourite author is Marie Corelli, a turn-of-the-century writer of romantic fiction. In his study of the relationship between literature and society in West Africa, Emmanuel Obiechina identifies Corelli as one of the writers whose works led to 'the emergence of romantic love as a vital factor' in the area (40). Her novels were, he says, 'very popular in West Africa in the nineteen-forties and fifties, and made a great impression on the minds of the young grammar school students who read them with excitement' (38). Romantic fiction continues to be popular in Nigeria with authors like Barbara Cartland and series such as Mills & Boon being readily available.[13]

'Rose, Agnes and Dora got more and more interested in True Romances and therefore in boys' (11). So the three friends are presented as they stand on the brink of adult life, their ideas about male–female relationships having been shaped by 'True Romances'. Nwapa interrogates the conventions of romantic fiction, undercutting them with irony and parody. Contrary to the girls' expectations, there are no 'happily-ever-after' endings to their own stories. She is also critical of the romantic plot as a paradigm for female development – a plot which enjoins women to sacrifice their personal and material interests to male requirements.

Initially, 'life' imitates fiction in Nwapa's narrative. Girls meet boys and '[w]hat the girls read in "True Romances" [acquired] meaning. . . . The girls sang, the boys sang, they held hands, they kissed. It was heaven' (16). Soon Rose is exchanging love letters with Ernest as is Dora with Chris and Agnes with Sam. 'As far as [the girls] were concerned, they had found their future life partners' (27). But it is not long before these romantic plots begin to unravel. Ernest's letters to Rose become less and less frequent and then, when he goes to Britain to study, they cease altogether. Eventually Rose learns that he has married another woman. Years later he reappears and begs her to marry him. The next time Rose hears of him he has been arrested for smuggling cocaine with Agnes's daughter. In the meantime, Rose falls in love with Mark who stages a fake marriage, dupes her out of her life-savings, and then disappears for ever. But still Rose persists in her quest for romance and when her last dream turns to ashes, she collapses inwardly:

> Rose was on her own as always. Since leaving school, she has always been on her own. Ernest was beyond her reach, in jail or in protective custody, she did not know. Mark duped her and deserted her. Dora has come to terms with Chris and has her children; Agnes lost her lover but she has her husband and children. . . . But Rose, what had she? (138)

From Rose's perspective, the answer to the final question is 'nothing'. For even though she has friends and material success, what really matters to her is having a man in her life. Unlike either Efuru or Amaka, Rose does not learn from her experience. There is no progression, no awakening, only a lapsing into despair and self-pity.

Dora doesn't fare much better, although she and Chris marry and have five children before he deserts her after selling the house they have built with her money. But despite his behaviour, when he reappears many years later, Dora welcomes him. She has been 'sad' she says, 'because my marriage failed' (101) and she needs a husband to preside over the business she has established. Agnes, too, in the end, takes back a husband who has deceived and maltreated her.

Romantic love, Nwapa indicates, serves the interests of male domination. It makes women act in ways that contradict their own material interests, and it thwarts visions of authentic selfhood and genuine liberation. Love and marriage remain the primary source of the three friends' identification. For they are unable to transcend the limitations of their miseducation.

In contrast to her schoolmates, Comfort resists indoctrination into western categories of womanhood from the outset. She intends, she says, 'to live life fully', which means marrying, not for love, but for money as 'my mother did' (30). Comfort herself assumes the role of enabling mother figure. Even as a young girl, she warns Rose not to 'be taken in by what you read in "True Romances"' (30); and years later she attempts once again to disabuse Rose of her 'missionary way of thinking' (116).

But it is to the next generation of women that Comfort is really of service, supporting them in what she terms their 'defiance' (117). When Doris's daughter Chinwe becomes a prosperous business woman, after having divorced two husbands in quick succession, it is from Comfort that she receives support. For Dora and Rose, Chinwe's business is 'a cover up for prostitution' (115), and they are scandalized by her success as an independent woman: '[They] did not approve of a society where it is possible for young women of twenty-four or twenty-five to boast of possessing a Mercedes Benz, . . . credit cards and so on, without a husband' (118). That Chinwe has her author's wholehearted approval is made quite explicit in the narrative:

> Chinwe had done the right thing. Her generation was doing better than her mother's own. Her generation was telling men, that there are different ways of living one's life fully and fruitfully. They are saying that women have options. . . . Marriage is not THE only way. (118–19)

This passage not only celebrates the achievements of Chinwe's generation

of women, it also conveys Nwapa's dismay at the failure of women of her
own generation to challenge male domination and maintain the tradition
of feminism which is their cultural inheritance. What Rose, Agnes, and
Dora's experience emphasizes is women's need for a liberating developmental model. Nwapa's novels themselves provides such a model in the
stories they tell of successful female development.

Following *Efuru*, the novel of development has proven to be a popular
form among women writers. With the exception of *Never Again*, all of
Nwapa's own novels can be read as *bildungsromane*, as can a number of
Emecheta's, including *The Bride Price* (1976), *The Slave Girl* (1977), and *The
Joys of Motherhood* (1979). Nafissatou Diallo's *A Dakar Childhood* (1975),
Miriam K. Were's *Your Heart is My Altar* (1980), and Tsitsi Dangarembga's
Nervous Conditions (1988) provide other examples. It was, of course, men
writers like Camara Laye in *The African Child* (1953) and Ngũgĩ in *Weep
Not, Child* (1964) who originally redefined the form in African terms, using
it mainly as a vehicle for representing the processes of acculturation as
experienced by colonized male subjects. In redefining this tradition, women
writers tend to thematize not only race but also gender as a developmental
issue. Thus, for example, Nwapa provides a critique both of colonialism and
of Igbo patriarchy through her depiction of the forces that inhibit female
development.

In certain important respects, the female *bildungsroman* stands in opposition to the entire African male literary tradition – a tradition to which
the very notion of female development is alien. For it is a form which, by
its very definition, characterizes women as active and dynamic – as
developing. Women are, in other words, conceptualized not as the Other
but as self-defining. Furthermore, their status as historical subjects is given
due recognition. This, then, is the form which Nwapa introduces into the
female literary tradition: a form which seeks to subvert the manichean
allegory of gender by putting female subjectivity in process.

5

'THEIR NEW SISTER'

Buchi Emecheta and the contemporary African literary tradition

Buchi Emecheta's first novel, *In the Ditch*, was published in 1972, six years after Ogot's *The Promised Land* and Nwapa's *Efuru*. Asked in an interview about her relationship 'to other female writers, such as Flora Nwapa, Grace Ogot, Christina Aidoo and Bessie Head', Emecheta described herself as 'their new sister' (Umeh and Umeh 25), thus acknowledging her debt to the women writers who have preceded her and placing herself within the literary tradition that has emerged with their writing. In her fiction, too, Emecheta pays tribute to her female predecessors, especially to her Igbo compatriot Flora Nwapa whom she identifies as a role model. Sometimes the acknowledgement of indebtedness is quite explicit, as in her second novel, *Second-Class Citizen* (1974), where the heroine Adah points to Nwapa's success as a writer when her husband, prior to burning the manuscript of Adah's first novel, ridicules the very idea of a black woman becoming a writer (184). Emecheta's awareness of her membership in a literary sisterhood marks the emergence of a self-conscious female literary tradition. One of my aims in this chapter will be to highlight some of the features of this tradition.

Emecheta has had more success as a writer than any of her female predecessors. She has written eleven novels, more, in fact, than most of the men writers I examine. Her first two novels, semi-autobiographical works set mainly in London where Emecheta herself has lived since 1962, have been followed by the publication at regular intervals of nine others which are set mainly in Nigeria: *The Bride Price* (1976), *The Slave Girl* (1977), *The Joys of Motherhood* (1979), *Destination Biafra* (1982), *Double Yoke* (1982), *Naira Power* (1982), *The Rape of Shavi* (1983), *A Kind of Marriage* (1986), and *Gwendolen* (1989).[1] She has, in addition, written an autobiography, *Head Above Water* (1986), as well as children's stories and plays for television.

Emecheta is also one of the few women writers who, along with Bessie Head and Mariama Bâ, has gained any degree of recognition for her writing.

She has won a number of awards[2] and received considerable critical attention. As a result, she is one of the writers who, as we have already seen, has in recent years displayed 'upward mobility' in Lindfors's ranking of authors ('Famous Authors'' 142). Emecheta is also probably the most widely read African woman writer. She has, she reports, been able to support herself from the proceeds of her writing since the late 1970s (Head 241–3).

Emecheta's literary upward mobility has been due largely to the attention she has received from feminist critics. As I noted in my Introduction, the prevailing trend in feminist criticism of African women's writing has been to adopt a western feminist perspective. As Chandra Mohanty points out, there is 'a coherence of *effects*' resulting from the assumption of 'the west' as 'the primary referent in theory and praxis' (61–2). These effects include the privileging of the concerns of western feminism, the denial of social and historical agency to women of other cultures, and the obliteration of cultural and historical difference. They are evident in feminist criticism of Emecheta, particularly so in Katherine Frank's and Marie Umeh's essays.

Both Frank and Umeh read Emecheta in order to foreground a particular type of western feminism. Such a reading demands the suppression of the anti-colonial discourse of Emecheta's texts. Thus, for example, according to Umeh, had the heroine of *The Slave Girl* married anyone other than the westernized (Christian, literate, urbanized) Jacob, 'the marriage would have been another type of slavery' ('African women' 198). But as Emecheta makes clear, this is precisely what the marriage is, her whole point being that under colonialism women are subjected to interlocking forms of oppression:

> One does not ask whether [Jacob and Ojebeta] loved and cared for each other ever after. . . . There was certainly a kind of eternal bond between husband and wife, a bond produced maybe by centuries of traditions, taboos and, latterly, Christian dogma. Slave, obey your master. Wife, honour your husband, who is your father, your head, your heart, your soul. (173)

Frank's reading in her 'Women without men' of Emecheta's *Destination Biafra* as a narrative of separatist feminism provides another example. According to Frank, the novel's heroine, Debbie Ogedemgbe, is 'the apotheosis of the African New Woman' (25): 'She embodies a liberating ideal of potentiality, of a rich, active, and fulfilling future for African women, and it is an autonomous future, she embraces, a future without men' (29). But it is Frank who has embraced Debbie's future by imposing on her the perspective of a particular type of western feminism. For it is not *men* that Debbie repudiates at the end of the novel, but her *white* lover on the very specific grounds that she is 'not ready yet to become the wife of an exploiter of my nation' (258). Thus in her reading of Emecheta's novel, Frank enlists the anti-colonial struggle into the service of western separatist feminism.

In another 'colonialist move', as Mohanty characterizes such discursive practices (78), Frank and Umeh dichotomize 'traditional African culture' (Frank, 'Death' 478) and feminism, while at the same time constructing 'the African woman' as a unitary and monolithic subject. For them, a feminist self and an African self are mutually exclusive categories of subjectivity. As Frank puts it – and Umeh reiterates her view, citing Frank approvingly ('Reintegration' 175): 'There is an irredeemable antagonism between the African woman's identity as an African and as a woman' ('Death' 492):

> In order to be free and fulfilled as a woman she must renounce her African identity because of the inherent sexism of traditional African culture. Or, if she wishes to cherish and affirm her 'Africanness', she must renounce her claims to feminine independence and self-determination. (478)

Thus, like many male writers and critics, Frank and Umeh elide indigenous African feminism, as well as African women's acts of resistance to their oppression both as women and as Africans.

More crucially, while Frank and Umeh ignore race as a category, they valorize the racial allegory in their criticism and read Emecheta's narratives as parables of western civilization and African barbarism. Thus, for Frank 'sexism' is 'inherent' to 'traditional African culture', the latter being the sole source of 'the African woman's' oppression, while for Umeh Emecheta's 'theme [is] that Igbo women are enslaved to Igbo traditions' ('Reintegration' 174). Their readings of *The Bride Price*, which are almost identical, are particularly illuminating of their vilification of 'African culture'. For even though the events that lead to the heroine's death are precipitated by the death of her father from injuries he received while fighting *as a conscripted soldier in the British army in Burma*, Umeh claims that '[a]ccording to the author, Aku-naa's life becomes complicated by traditional African attitudes toward women' ('African women' 195). Frank, too, elides the precipitating event: '*The Bride Price* explores the enslavement of women by traditional society and its rules and taboos' ('Death' 483).

Conversely, both critics designate 'the west' as the source of liberating values and modalities, although Frank is more blunt than Umeh in her ascription: 'Education . . . is the crucial liberating force in the lives of Emecheta's heroines, and in fact their degree of servitude is inversely proportional to the amount of education they receive' ('Death' 481). In fact, for Frank 'the African woman's' degree of servitude would seem to be directly proportional to her proximity to ('darkest') Africa. For if she seeks independence, Frank says, 'she will almost certainly have to turn her back on her homeland and go, as the heroine of Emecheta's first two novels does, to England or some other Western country' (492).

Like the critical studies JanMohamed cites at the beginning of *Manichean Aesthetics*, Frank's and Umeh's essays demonstrate a 'refusal' on the part of a particular type of critic 'to come to terms with the colonial situation' (1). What is at stake for these critics is a view of western feminism as universal. As I have already indicated, Emecheta has made a point of distancing herself from western feminism. And, as if in response to such claims as Frank's of 'an irremediable antagonism between the African woman's identity as an African and as a woman', she recently declared: 'if I am now a feminist then I am an African feminist' ('Feminism' 175).

In this chapter I will examine the interaction between the literary symbolism of three of Emecheta's novels and particular social structures: those of Igbo patriarchy and of colonialism as well as neo-colonialism. I will, however, be primarily concerned with the intertextual relation of Emecheta's novels to African men's writing and to their female precursors. I have chosen *The Joys of Motherhood* in part because it is Emecheta's best-known novel. But it is also a work which is clearly influenced by Emecheta's reading of other African authors. So, too, are *Destination Biafra* and *Double Yoke* which I have also selected.

Through its intertextuality with *Efuru*, *The Joys of Motherhood* confirms the existence of a female tradition in fiction. Deriving its title from the final lines of *Efuru*, it constitutes a response to the question with which Nwapa ends her novel: '[Uhamiri] had never experienced the joy of motherhood. Why then did the women worship her?' (221). Like Nwapa's question, Emecheta's title is ironic as is demonstrated in each case by the protagonist's story. As Andrade observes, Nnu Ego's 'personal and family history' is very similar to Efuru's (97). Like Efuru, she is from an Igbo village – from Emecheta's hometown of Ibuza. Like Efuru, too, she loses her mother at an early age which leaves her dependent on her father for guidance. Nnu Ego also marries twice, returning to her father's house on the failure of each marriage, and for a time she, too, is held in disrepute by her inability to bear children. But Emecheta underscores the irony of Nwapa's question by departing from Nwapa's narrative. Nnu Ego spends most of her adult life in Lagos and she eventually experiences 'the joy(s) of motherhood' many times over. As a result, her life becomes a cumulation of miseries.

Emecheta also acknowledges her debt to *Efuru* through the similarity of the protagonists' psychological experience. The story of a slave woman who is buried alive with her master's dead wife is central to *The Joys of Motherhood*,

111

performing the same kind of function in the novel as the myth of Uhamiri does in *Efuru*. This story seems to have taken a strong hold on Emecheta's imagination, for she tells it also in *The Bride Price* and *The Slave Girl*. But it occupies a more privileged position in *The Joys of Motherhood* where Emecheta integrates it into the main narrative. Nnu Ego is the daughter of the slave woman's master, Agbadi, the great chief of Ibuza. Because the circumstances of her conception lead to the slave woman's death and because she is born with a lump on her head on the precise spot where the slave woman was hit, the slave woman is declared to be Nnu Ego's *chi*.[3]

Just as Efuru dreams of Uhamiri, so Nnu Ego dreams of her *chi*. But what the slave woman offers her is not beauty or wealth but the one gift that Uhamiri withholds from her worshippers: children. Emecheta intensifies the irony by making the offer subject to certain economic conditions. Thus, while as yet financially secure, the apparently barren Nnu Ego dreams of her *chi* taunting her by holding out a beautiful baby boy and then vanishing. Shortly afterwards, Nnu Ego gives birth to a son who dies in infancy. Some time later when she and her husband are experiencing privation, Nnu Ego has a similar dream. On this occasion the baby is extremely dirty, and her *chi*, mocking Nnu Ego with laughter, tells her she can have as many babies of this kind as she wants. Soon Nnu Ego, who has repeatedly implored her *chi* to allow her to conceive, is encumbered with a bevy of children that she cannot afford to feed, clothe, or educate.

Like *Efuru*, then, *The Joys of Motherhood* defines its heroine's experience through her psychic identification with a deity. But while the myth of Uhamiri specifies a paradigm of female transcendence, the slave woman's story tells of entrapment and defeat. Of the difference between her own and Nwapa's perspective, Emecheta suggests in an interview that it may be due to the presence of a tradition of female independence in the culture of eastern Igboland (where both Nwapa and Achebe were born), which is lacking in the culture of Igbo settlements, such as Ibuza, that are located west of the Niger (Umeh and Umeh 23 and 25).

It is, then, quite possibly, in an effort to provide a more positive role model that Emecheta modifies the version of the slave woman's story told in *The Joys of Motherhood*, incorporating into it, in further acknowledgement of her own debt to Nwapa, aspects of the myth of Uhamiri. Thus Nnu Ego learns that the reason 'the slave woman . . . would not give her a child' is 'because she had been *dedicated to a river goddess* before Agbadi took her away in slavery' (31, emphasis added). The slave woman is, then, in this revised version of her story, an avatar of both Efuru and Uhamiri. This allows Emecheta to give to Nnu Ego what is denied the heroines of *The Bride Price* and *The Slave Girl*: final victory over the forces that oppress her.

The intertextual relation of *The Joys of Motherhood* to the male tradition is most evident in the challenge Emecheta offers to conventional male views of motherhood. Using chapter headings to highlight her purpose, she is blatantly critical of the privileging of motherhood in such works as *Things Fall Apart, Jagua Nana*, and *Petals of Blood*. The first chapter of the novel is called 'The Mother'. It tells of Nnu Ego's attempted suicide following the death of her first baby. The second chapter, 'The Mother's Mother', concludes by relating the death of Nnu Ego's mother, Ona, in childbirth, while the circumstances of Nnu Ego's own death are recounted in the final chapter, ironically entitled 'The Canonised Mother': '[O]ne night, Nnu Ego lay down by the roadside, thinking that she had arrived home. She died quietly there, with no child to hold her hand and no friend to talk to her' (224). Nnu Ego has three sons and four daughters, yet she dies childless.

Critics generally view Emecheta's novels as providing an authentic representation of African women. Thus, according to Umeh, '*The Joys of Motherhood* stands as a model for other African women writers who wish to portray the actual condition of women and their response to their condition' ('*Joys*' 46).[4] But the essence of Emecheta's realism lies, as JanMohamed argues is the case with Achebe, in her portrayal of 'the inseparability of [her] protagonists' existence from their social and historical context' (162). In *The Joys of Motherhood*, this contextualization of the female characters' experience constitutes Emecheta's strongest statement in response to male idealizations of motherhood. It is a statement that addresses such questions as the one Ngũgĩ suppresses in *Petals of Blood* as to how Wanja, having renounced prostitution, supports herself and her baby. Realism is also Emecheta's response to the stereotypical representations of women.

Nnu Ego's life begins in Ibuza in 1909 and spans almost the entire colonial period. As Andrade states, '*The Joys of Motherhood* affirms *Efuru*'s claim that pre-colonial Igbo women had more independence than their colonized descendants' (101). For even though Ona's life too is circumscribed by the prescriptions and taboos of Ibuza patriarchy, she enjoys far more freedom than her daughter Nnu Ego. As the novel's narrator observes: 'To regard a woman who is quiet and timid as desirable was something that came after [Agbadi's] time, with Christianity and other changes' (10). Nnu Ego is, then, in contrast to her female forebears, subject to two forms of oppression, to the definitions imposed on her by colonial society as well as by Ibuza patriarchy.

The contradictions that overwhelm Nnu Ego in the end arise from her stubborn loyalty to values cherished in Ibuza at a time when her society is, as a result of colonialism, experiencing rapid transformation. Too timid to flout patriarchal authority, Nnu Ego accepts without question until her later years that there is no 'greater honour . . . for a woman than to be a mother' (119). But because her society is changing rapidly, she receives none of the rewards conventionally conferred on a fertile woman. Assessing her own situation, she eventually concludes 'that all she had inherited from her agrarian background was the responsibility and none of the booty' (137). Eventually she becomes alienated from society.

When, as a result of her failure to produce children, her first marriage breaks down, Nnu Ego moves to Lagos in order to marry Nnaife in the hope that he will remove the stigma of barrenness from her and make her into 'a real woman' (53). But her children, raised in an urban colonial environment, rather than bringing her the anticipated 'joys', become 'her chain of slavery' (186), binding her to the feckless Nnaife and to the back-breaking drudgery of abject poverty. '[F]aced with the harsh reality of making ends meet on a pittance' (137), she engages none too successfully in petty trading, suppressing her anxiety and discontent by 'remind[ing] herself of the old saying that money and children don't go together: if you spent all your time making money and getting rich, the gods wouldn't give you any children; if you wanted children, you had to forget money, and be content to be poor' (80). Caught in this double-bind that Ibuza patriarchy has created for her, she clings to motherhood as her ideal even in the face of starvation:

> If you made the mistake of pitying her, she would tell you what her two sons were going to be when they grew up; for anybody who had no 'two sons', or who had only daughters, or who had no children at all . . . it was better to keep quiet. (105)

And despite her jealousy and her concern over the further sharing of scarce resources, Nnu Ego is unable to raise an effective protest when Nnaife takes a second wife, schooling herself instead 'to play the role of the mature senior wife' (123–4), a role that has been stripped of its meaning by the exigencies of Lagos life.

While the grim poverty that characterizes Nnu Ego's life in Lagos is partly due to her adherence to values that are no longer appropriate, it is also the result of the manichean structure of colonial society. As Nnu Ego herself observes: '[We are] all slaves to the white man . . . If they permit us to eat, then we will eat. If they say we will not, then where will we get the food?' (117). Nnaife's income on which the family depends for its survival is irregular, subject to the whims and requirements of his colonial masters. And when he is conscripted into the British army and shipped off to Burma, Nnu Ego and the children are made destitute.

As a result of her experience, Nnu Ego arrives at an understanding not only of race relations of power but also of those of gender, the impassioned plea that she makes in desperation to her god constituting the novel's strongest feminist statement:

'God, when will you create a woman who will be fulfilled in herself, a full human being, not anybody's appendage? . . . What have I gained from all this? Yes, I have many children, but what do I have to feed them on? On my life. I have to work myself to the bone to look after them, I have to give them my all. . . .

The men make it look as if we must aspire for children or die. That's why when I lost my first son I wanted to die, because I failed to live up to the standard expected of me by the males in my life, my father and my husband – and now I have to include my sons. But who made the law that we should not hope in our daughters? We women subscribe to that law more than anyone. Until we change all this, it is still a man's world, which women will always help to build.' (186–7)

But despite her insight, Nnu Ego continues to conduct her life according to the patterns laid down for her by Ibuza patriarchy, 'taking comfort' in all her travails 'in the fact that one day her boys would be men' (161), and conspiring through her child-rearing practices to consign her daughters to the same miserable existence she so desperately needs to escape herself.

Nnu Ego's adherence to Ibuza values leads to the event that marks her complete social alienation: her lonely death by the roadside. Her devotion to her children has left her with no time for friends. And 'her boys', now university-educated men, repudiate the values she has sacrificed herself for in favour of the western-style individualism they have imbibed in Lagos. Blamed by Nnaife for the children's defection, she returns for the second time in disgrace to Ibuza where, when she receives no word from her sons, she suffers a mental breakdown and dies unattended.

Nnu Ego's co-wife, Adaku, is, by contrast, flexible and adaptable in her attempt to define her identity in a rapidly changing society, although she, too, comes to Lagos in the first instance with the hope that relations with Nnaife will produce the issue that will confirm her worth. For although Adaku has a daughter from a previous marriage, she has no son and hence no standing in Ibuza society. Of the difference between the two women, Nnu Ego surmises that it is due to their different class backgrounds, to the fact that 'Adaku came from a low family where people were not tied to pleasing the rest of their members, as she Nnu Ego had to please her titled father Agbadi all the time' (127).

Initially Adaku bears the humiliation of having failed to produce male progeny with fortitude, devoting her considerable energy to petty trading in which she is much more successful than Nnu Ego. But when her reproductive shortcomings are invoked to place her in the wrong in a quarrel Nnu Ego has initiated, she revolts against the standards of Ibuza patriarchy, damning her *chi*, which the men called to settle the dispute have advised her to consult 'to find out why male offspring have been denied [her]' (166), and declaring that she is 'going to be a prostitute' (168).

The freedom Adaku negotiates through her rebellion, unlike the independence achieved by Nwapa's Efuru, is not sanctioned by the traditions of her community. But in keeping with Emecheta's irony and realism, Adaku is not, in the end, alienated from the society whose laws she transgresses. For despite her nonconformity, she is able to create a place for herself in Ibuza society, at least as that society exists in Lagos. Adaku remains a loyal member of the Oluwum family, attending its important gatherings and offering moral and financial support to Nnu Ego in times of crisis. Her daughters are, after all, she asserts, still sisters of Nnu Ego's children.

Emecheta's female characters are, then, portrayed realistically. They are complex social beings whose personalities are defined and destinies determined by their interaction with their environment. Adaku adapts to the changes brought about by colonial occupation, while Nnu Ego, though increasingly aware of the inappropriateness of her behaviour in her new context, remains static. As a result, she becomes more and more isolated from the social community, while Adaku maintains her ties with it. '[H]ow was she to know', Nnu Ego asks, reflecting on the choice she made as a young woman, 'that by the time her children grew up the values of her country, her people and her tribe would have changed so drastically, to the extent where a woman with many children could face a lonely old age, and maybe a miserable death all alone, just like a barren woman?' (219).

These portrayals are the basis of Emecheta's realism. Through them, as Nwapa does through her portrayals of women, she counters the tendency toward gender romance in works like *Things Fall Apart*. Realism is also Emecheta's response to male idealizations of motherhood. As Andrade notes, Emecheta 'does not argue against the state of motherhood as such' (108). What is at issue in *The Joys of Motherhood* is its romanticization and the status accorded to it as the sole route to female fulfilment. Nnu Ego believes in the supremacy of motherhood. Emecheta mocks this notion as romantic by juxtaposing Nnu Ego's expectations with her actual experience as a mother: her dire poverty, endless toil, and miserable death. Such notions are outmoded, Emecheta insists, while at the same time casting doubt on their verity in pre-colonial Igbo society through the death of Ona in childbirth.

While Emecheta portrays her female characters realistically, her male characters tend toward stereotypes. Nnu Ego's father, her two husbands, and her three sons are cast in a similar mould. All are egotistical, callous and irresponsible. Like both Ogot and Nwapa, then, she initiates a reverse discourse as a means of subverting the sexual allegory. Several male critics have objected to Emecheta's derogatory portrayal of their gender. As Eustace Palmer expresses it: '[T]he author's determination to show up the males as irresponsible and unreasonable interferes somewhat with her characterization of them. Their irresponsibility is exaggerated to the point of unrealism' ('Feminine point of view' 44).[5] The issue of 'unrealism' in women writers' portrayal of male characters is one which, as we shall see, Emecheta addresses in *Double Yoke* through her representation of the pressures and dilemmas experienced by the novel's male protagonist.

As the discussion of realism has perhaps suggested, Emecheta also, following Nwapa, adopts the convention of the paired women in her characterization of Nnu Ego and Adaku. The convention occupies a much more central position in *The Joys of Motherhood* than it does in *Efuru*, but it serves the same intertextual function, the pairing operating to challenge some of the orthodoxies of male literary representation. Like the two sisters, Ossai and Ajanupu, the co-wives, Nnu Ego and Adaku are the antithesis of each other in their response to their patriarchal society, Nnu Ego choosing to conform to its role definitions and Adaku revolting against them. Emecheta punishes her conservative heroine and rewards Adaku for her radical action. While Nnu Ego sinks further and further into poverty and remains dependent, Adaku prospers and achieves independence, the freedom she finds corresponding to that enjoyed by the pre-colonial Ona, a woman so stubborn and arrogant, we are told, 'that she refused to live with Agbadi' (11). Adaku is quite explicit about her intentions: 'I want to be a dignified single woman', she tells Nnu Ego. 'I shall work to educate my daughters, though I shall not do so without male companionship' (170–1). Reinvesting her profits from prostitution in the cloth-vending business and sending her daughters to the best schools in the land, she enacts what Nnu Ego can only wish for. She becomes a woman 'fulfilled in herself' and one who has 'hope in our daughters'.

Again following Nwapa, but elaborating the technique considerably, Emecheta uses images of physical confinement to represent her conservative heroine's entrapment in conventional roles and to highlight the consequences of adhering to such roles. Thus Nnu Ego is presented nursing her third pregnancy and fretting over the condition of her malnourished son in 'the one room that served [the Oluwum family] as bedroom, playroom and sitting-room' (101). It is a 'cramped room' (167), a room 'choked with sleeping mats and utensils' (130) to which Nnu Ego is confined by her conventionality. Emecheta also represents Adaku's transcendence of orthodox roles through spatial images, ones which in this case connote freedom and well-being. Thus, having walked out of what she refers to as that 'stuffy' and 'stinking room' (168), Adaku enters 'a separate room of her own, much bigger than the one they all shared before' (171).

Through the convention of the paired women, then, Emecheta, like Nwapa, interrogates the male practice of identifying women with tradition, pointing to its underlying ideological function as a means of perpetuating women's subordination. She also refigures the topos both of the mother and of the prostitute. In Bakhtinean terms, she can be said to 'dialogize' the discourse of motherhood and of prostitution and hence to relativize and deprivilege them (*Dialogic Imagination* 427). At the same time, Emecheta seeks to subvert the good woman/whore, rural/urban dichotomies upheld by writers like Ngũgĩ and Ekwensi, constructions which, as we have seen, serve to legitimate and perpetuate women's marginalization in society. For their authors, both Wanja and Jagua have to be redeemed from their profligate life in the city by a devotion to motherhood and to village life. By contrast, Adaku is redeemed when she decides to remain in the city and be a prostitute. Valorizing the theme of empowerment through urban migration in her treatment of Adaku, Emecheta also ridicules the notion of redemption through repatriation to the village in her treatment of Nnu Ego. For poverty, loneliness, and mental deterioration characterize Nnu Ego's final years which she spends in Ibuza. It is, however, the related notion of redemption through devotion to motherhood that is the main target of Emecheta's attack, such a devotion causing Nnu Ego misery throughout her life.

While *The Joys of Motherhood* looks back to *Efuru*, it also looks forward to *One is Enough* which was published three years after Emecheta's classic narrative of maternity. In this case, Nwapa acknowledges her debt to Emecheta through the similarity of her protagonist's story to Adaku's.[6] For as we have already seen, both Adaku and Amaka migrate to and settle in Lagos. Both also leave their husbands and trade in sex. But in neither case does the negotiation of sex play a major role in the protagonist's life. Furthermore, both women are pragmatic about their sexual transactions, using them as a means to an end, to gain access to a more lucrative kind of market. Finally neither plans to remarry, Adaku's statement of her intentions, quoted above, anticipating Amaka's declaration of independence which begins, 'I don't want to be a wife any more' (127). There is, then, an on-going dialogic relation between Nwapa's and Emecheta's novels, one in which the authorial roles of precursor and successor are not fixed but are interchangeable.

Once again invoking the myth of Uhamiri, Emecheta pays a final tribute to Nwapa in the concluding lines of *The Joys of Motherhood*. Nnu Ego is given a grand funeral by her sons who have neglected her during her lifetime, and a shrine is built in her name so that appeals can be made to her for fertility:

> Stories afterwards, however, said that Nnu Ego was a wicked woman even in death because, however many people appealed to her to make women fertile, she never did. Poor Nnu Ego, even in death she had no peace! Still, many agreed that she had given all to her children. The joy of being a mother was the joy of giving all to your children, they said.
>
> And her reward? Did she not have the greatest funeral Ibuza had ever seen? . . . That was why people failed to understand why she did not answer their prayers, for what else could a woman want but to have sons who would give her a decent burial?
>
> Nnu Ego had it all, yet still did not answer prayers for children.
> (224)

In her refusal to answer prayers for children, Nnu Ego becomes after death, as the slave woman, her *chi*, had before her, like Uhamiri.

By invoking the myth of Uhamiri, Emecheta intensifies the irony of her narrative and gives Nnu Ego final victory over the forces that have oppressed her. She also creates an intertextual celebration of the feminist tradition Nwapa memorializes in *Efuru*, symbolically passing on that tradition to the women of Ibuza. Moreover, by repeatedly acknowledging her debt to Nwapa, Emecheta writes into *The Joys of Motherhood* what the critical establishment has written out of African literary history: she hails Nwapa as the mother of a female tradition in fiction.

The Joys of Motherhood has two major ideological functions: to valorize the emergence of a female literary tradition and to refute conventional images of women. Secondary functions include challenging the construction of motherhood and prostitution in patriarchal ideology and highlighting various aspects of colonial experience. The novel's intertextual relation with Nwapa's novels is confirmatory. While *The Joys of Motherhood* extends *Efuru*'s critique of colonialism and Igbo patriarchy, and elaborates the argument against the privileging of motherhood, *One is Enough* follows the model provided in *The Joys of Motherhood* in refiguring the prostitute topos. The relationship between *The Joys of Motherhood* and the male tradition, on the other hand, is characterized mainly by antagonism. For although there is intertextual agreement on the damaging effects of colonialism on African societies, Emecheta's focus is, like Nwapa's, on its impact on women. More importantly, her major concern is to challenge patriarchal ideology.

Even more clearly than *The Joys of Motherhood*, *Destination Biafra* invites an intertextual reading. As its title suggests, the novel belongs to the body of literature generated by the Nigerian Civil War, a relative latecomer to the tradition. According to Chidi Amuta, this literature occupies a position of special prominence not only in Nigerian but also in African literary history:

> To be familiar with Nigerian literature in the period between 1970 and the present is to be conversant with one dominant and recurrent area of social concern: the Nigerian Civil War (1967–1970). This dominance is so pronounced that it can safely be said that in the growing body of Nigerian national literature, works directly based on or indirectly deriving from the war experience constitute the largest number of literary products on any single aspect of Nigerian history to date. . . . And given the statistical dominance of Nigerian literary works in African literature, the Nigerian Civil War could well be said to be the single most imaginatively recreated historical experience in Africa so far.
>
> ('Literature' 85)

This body of works has been produced mainly by men. In her foreword to her novel as well as in the narrative itself, Emecheta quite explicitly relates *Destination Biafra* to these works. In the foreword she tells of how Soyinka influenced the characterization of her heroine through his account in *The Man Died* of his imprisonment during the war by the Federal authorities. '[It] gave me the idea', she says, 'that some non-Ibos suffered with us. From that I developed my heroine "Debbie Ogedemgbe" who is neither Ibo nor Yoruba nor Hausa, but simply a Nigerian' (viii). In the main narrative Emecheta invites the reader to compare her version of the war to that of her male predecessors. 'Destination Biafra', we learn, is the title Debbie gives to the book she is writing about her own experience during the war (246). What would be lost if Debbie should be killed, we are told, is 'the entire story of the women's experience of the war' (223).

Through her prefatory remarks and the self-referentiality of the narrative, then, Emecheta specifies an intertextual approach to her novel. By these same means, she also quite clearly points to the nature of the relationship between *Destination Biafra* and its male precursors. As her acknowledgement of her indebtedness to Soyinka's *The Man Died* suggests, the relationship is in part confirmatory. For as we shall see, Emecheta affirms some of Soyinka's views as well as those of other men writers. The relationship is, however, also marked by antagonism. For as the passage concerning the consequences of Debbie's journal not reaching publication indicates, Emecheta proposes to write the story that has been suppressed in the dominant version of the war, 'the entire story of the women's experience'.

In the discussion that follows I shall examine in more detail the nature of the relationship between Emecheta's civil war novel and the dominant tradition. Chidi Amuta's essays in which he attempts to define both the thematic and the formal characteristics of literature based on the conflict provide a useful starting point for my discussion.

According to Amuta, in terms of theme one of the concerns of Nigerian Civil War literature is to raise questions about 'external involvement in the war' ('Literature' 87). *Destination Biafra* conforms to this characteristic. For like her male colleagues – John Munonye in *A Wreath for the Maidens* (1973), for example, or Cyprian Ekwensi in *Survive the Peace* (1976) – Emecheta adopts a critical stance toward western nations for their role in promoting the conflict. In the novel's opening scene, 'post-colonial' ethnic tension is linked to colonial policies and practices through the portrayal of the last colonial governor of Nigeria. Considering the Hausa to be the most tractable ethnic group, Governor Macdonald is biased toward the Northern party in his handling of the first general elections, his sole concern being to ensure 'that the right man was elected . . . the man who would offer the least resistance to British trade' (1–2).

Debbie's lover, Alan Grey, is likewise motivated in his dealings with Nigerian leaders by the desire to promote British interests. Supplying arms to both the Federal and the Biafran forces, as well as looting Nigeria of its art treasures, Alan personifies neo-colonialist attitudes and practices. As we have already seen, Debbie ultimately rejects Alan's offer of marriage in words which reveal her own growing national consciousness.

In Amuta's analysis, most writings on the war also 'share a critical, even a condemnatory stance toward the quality of leadership provided by the national elite in the pre-war time periods' ('Literature' 87). Emecheta adopts a similar stance as is particularly evident in the portrayal of Debbie's father. A minister in the cabinet of the first post-independence government, Ogedemgbe uses his position to make money and live extravagantly. Self-serving and corrupt, he is shown to be more interested in the balance of his Swiss bank account than in the welfare of the nation. Like Soyinka and others, Emecheta is also critical of the quality of leadership provided by both sides at the time of the war. Gowon, represented by the character

Saka Momoh, is portrayed as vacillating and ineffectual, while the Ojukwu-like Abosi, whom Debbie initially admires, turns out to be as unprincipled as her father.

There is, however, a difference between the analysis of leadership in *Destination Biafra* and that in the works Amuta examines: Soyinka's *Madmen and Specialists* (1971), Eddie Iroh's *Forty-Eight Guns for the General* (1976), and Munonye's *A Wreath for the Maidens*. While the men writers focus on class, on the failure of elite leadership, Emecheta emphasizes gender, the failure of male leadership. What made the war inevitable, she suggests, was as much the patriarchal structure and values of 'post-colonial' Nigerian society as its class structure. As Uzoma, one of the women Debbie meets while trying to reach Biafra, says:

> 'Our men! A few years ago it was "Independence, freedom for you, freedom for me." We were always in the background. Now that freedom has turned into freedom to kill each other, and our men have left us to bury them and bring up their children; and maybe by the time these ones grow up there will be another reason for them to start killing one another.' (214)

Debbie's friend, Babs, makes a similar comment:

> 'Any fool of a woman [can see that the East will lose in a war with the rest of the country], but not men, least of all army men turned politicians. The women and children who would be killed by bombs and guns would simply be statistics, war casualties. But for the soldier-politicians, the traders in arms, who only think of personal gain, it would be the chance of a lifetime.' (109)

Through such passages, Emecheta points to the failure of patriarchal historiography to include gender as a category of analysis.

Conventional war narratives also come under attack in those scenes in *Destination Biafra* that relate to what Amuta terms 'the familiar fact that war enthrones an anarchic ethos in which social morality suffers a major dislocation' ('Literature' 89). Like the authors Amuta discusses, Emecheta, too, is concerned with the effects of war on social morality. But she approaches the theme from a different perspective, correcting a bias by telling stories that have been suppressed in the dominant tradition. The works Amuta cites as examples tell, in his words, of 'the moral predicament of the Nigerian womenfolk in the war situation' (89). Faced with material hardship, Gladys in Achebe's 'Girls at war' (1972) and Aku in Isidore Okpewho's *The Last Duty* (1976) both relinquish their principles and trade in sex in order to gain essential commodities. Such stories are quite common fare in Nigerian Civil War literature.[7] Lurking within them is the manichean allegory of gender. For while women are portrayed as lacking in moral resolution, there is always a male character who, like Achebe's maimed soldier or Okpewho's Mukoro Oshevire, maintains his integrity.

Emecheta seeks to subvert the allegory by highlighting in her narrative incidents of male sexual assault on women. Even before war breaks out, the soldiers who come to kill Debbie's father take 'liberties', ordering her mother to undress and fondling Debbie's breasts. Travelling to Biafra after the outbreak of hostilities, Debbie, along with other women, is subjected to the same kind of treatment by Federal soldiers manning road blocks. One of Debbie's companions, a pregnant woman, is killed by the soldiers. A witness to the event, Debbie's mother is unable to forget 'how they had pushed the butt of the gun into her, how they had cut her open, how the unborn baby's head had been cut off' (136). Soldiers also rape and kill the nuns from whom Debbie seeks medical help for the sick children who have come under her care. And she learns from women she meets of how young girls have been raped by both Federal and Biafran soldiers. Debbie herself is gang-raped by marauding Federal soldiers despite her protestations that she is an officer of the very army in which they are serving. When her anguished mother reports the incident to the authorities, the commanding officer asserts: 'It's war, madam. . . . Hundreds of women have been raped – so what? It's war' (135).

Glossed over in historical as well as in literary discourse,[8] rape is one of the hidden facts of the Nigerian conflict. Recording the conflict from the point of view of women, Emecheta breaks through this conspiracy of silence, a silence that protects male interests. Acts of sexual violence against women, she insists, are part of the record.

At the level of form, Amuta concentrates on what he sees as the evolution of the heroic figure in Nigerian fiction in response to socio-historical determinants. Writers, he says in one of his essays, have been 'grappling' since the early 1960s 'with the problem of creating characters who, although deeply rooted in their respective ethnic cultures, are striving to become national characters' ('Nigerian' 88). As we have already seen, Emecheta claims to have been inspired by Soyinka's *The Man Died* to create a protagonist whose character is defined by national rather than ethnic considerations. One of the ways in which she handles the problem of giving her heroine a national identity is to make Debbie the member of an ethnic minority: rather than being Igbo or Yoruba or Hausa, she is Itsekiri. Debbie is also a firm believer in national unity. Evidence of Soyinka's influence on Emecheta's narrative is most clearly seen in the way in which Debbie translates this belief into action. For as Soyinka did just prior to his imprisonment, Debbie travels to the East, her assignment being to persuade Abosi that Biafran succession is in nobody's interest.

Through Debbie's experience while on this assignment, Emecheta interrogates conventional views of women as well as conventional interpretations of national identity. Such views and interpretations are, she shows, mutually confirming and they do not permit women to express their national aspirations. An Oxford graduate, Debbie enlists in the army for a number of reasons, one of which is that she wants to serve her country. While attempting to carry out her orders, she is raped not only by ordinary soldiers but also by one of her fellow officers, a sergeant who has been informed of her mission. His intention, he asserts, is to show Debbie that she is 'nothing but a woman' (175). Even Saka Momoh exploits Debbie's sexuality. She is, he charges, on giving her her assignment, to 'use [her] feminine charms' to convince Abosi that the country should remain united (123). On his part, Abosi dismisses Debbie as an emissary for precisely the same reason as Momoh chooses her. 'You are not a man', he says derisively (239). In the male perception, then, the national subject is by definition male and Debbie remains inescapably female despite her attempt to lay claim to the status of national subject.

Debbie's experience also raises the question of how writers are to create female characters who, as Amuta puts it, 'are striving to become national characters'. How, in other words, given the patriarchal cast of nationalism, are writers to create female national subjects? It is a question with which, as we have seen, Ogot attempts to deal, and one with which, as we shall see in Chapter 7, Ngũgĩ also struggles. Emecheta's answer is, like Ogot's, to rewrite nationalism, but the revision she undertakes is much more thoroughgoing. She begins by examining the dilemma patriarchal constructions of social roles pose for women. Debbie's choice of a conventionally male vocation as a profession is unorthodox, but from her own perspective, a career in the army is an attractive alternative to the stereotypically female roles of wife and mother which her society prescribes for her:

> She wanted to do something more than child breeding and rearing and being a good passive wife to a man whose ego she must boost all her days, while making sure to submerge every impulse that made her a full human. Before long she would have no image at all, she would be as colourless as her poor mother. Surely every person should have the right to live as he or she wished, however different that life might seem to another? . . . Yes, she would join the army. (45)

In joining the army, however, Debbie casts herself in a stereotypically male role and she soon takes on masculine values and attitudes. As a demonstration of her patriotism, she volunteers to carry out Momoh's order that all Igbo officers in the army be arrested. As she realizes later, this makes her responsible for many deaths and for an increase in ethnic tension in the country. In the end, she opts for a different kind of heroism. Her plans for the future are, she says, to help bring up children orphaned by the war, using the money her father left her.

This decision by Debbie marks Emecheta's attempt to recast nationalism by incorporating feminine values into it, a move that initiates a much more thoroughgoing revision than does Ogot's inclusion of women's aspirations. The new role Debbie intends to take on is as conventionally female as the roles she initially rejected. In a chapter entitled 'Women's War', Emecheta presents her heroine hiding from Federal soldiers in the bush with other women and foraging for food for the children who are with them. From this experience, which is quite different from that of participating in the 'men's war', Debbie learns to appreciate feminine values. Thus she decides to serve her nation in a traditionally female way – through mothering.

Nwapa's war memoir, *Never Again*, also expresses what Jane Bryce refers to in her discussion of women's Civil War fiction as 'dissent from officially sanctioned "patriotism"' ('Conflict' 35). As Bryce observes, the sole concern of Kate, the work's narrator, is survival, which means ensuring her children don't suffer from malnutrition and fleeing from town to town with her family in advance of the Federal forces. As Kate says to her mother who wants to know exactly who is to blame for all the suffering:

> You and I don't understand. All that is left now, is to keep alive. This is not the time to apportion blame. Let's keep alive first. Perhaps at the end of this calamity, this tragedy, if we are alive, we shall be able to find answers to these questions. (28)

There is, then, general agreement between Nwapa and Emecheta on what constitutes heroism in a war situation. It is not militaristic acts but rather ones that affirm and promote life.

In another essay, Amuta characterizes the heroes of the novels he examines as 'repudiations of a specific phase of bourgeois hegemony in Nigerian history' ('History' 69). In his analysis, such heroes embody both the class view of their authors and a critique of the values of that class view. Bryce, who also attempts to assess Emecheta's characterization of Debbie in terms of Amuta's class analysis of war novel heroes, finds the portrayal unsatisfactory. In her view, Debbie is uncritical of bourgeois values and hence 'remains a product of her class' ('Conflict' 40). But Bryce overlooks aspects of Emecheta's portrayal of her heroine.

Like the heroes of the novels Amuta discusses – Iroh's *Forty-Eight Guns for the General*, Munonye's *A Wreath for the Maidens*, and Chukwuemeka Ike's *Sunset at Dawn* (1976) – Debbie reflects the class position of her author in that, on the basis of her status as a university graduate, she can be viewed as a 'transposition[ ] of the world view and class role(s) of the bourgeoisie in the war milieu' (Amuta, 'History' 61). At the same time, one of Debbie's challenges as a heroine is, quite clearly, to transcend the values of her class. Critical of her parents for flaunting their wealth, she sees a career in the army as a way of distancing herself from and rebelling against their extravagant lifestyle. But, as Debbie discovers, military leaders are no better than politicians: both are corrupt and self-serving. Watching a fleet of luxury cars being loaded on to the plane in which Abosi is making his escape from Biafra, Debbie is outraged: 'A hot uncontrollable anger enveloped her, making her sweat and shiver at the same time. To be so betrayed, by the very symbol of Biafra!' (257). Debbie is also aware that class divides her from the women she travels with to Biafra and she does her best to bridge the gap. More crucially, in deciding to use her father's money to raise orphans, she subverts the values of her class.

Debbie can thus be seen to conform to the characteristics of the hero as Amuta defines them. But what Amuta does not mention is that the heroes of Iroh's, Munonye's, and Ike's novels also reflect the position of their authors in the gender hierarchy. It is not simply that these heroes are men but that they are not critical of male domination as a form of oppression with its own system of values. The characterization of the hero in each of the novels in fact serves to legitimate the status quo of male domination. For example, the two protagonists of Munonye's novel, Biere and Medo, 'symbolic rebels against the values of their class' as Amuta describes them ('History' 67), have little use and no time for women. The same is true of the novel as a whole, despite its title. For in *A Wreath for the Maidens* women are cast either as nagging mothers or as unfaithful girlfriends.

Through her portrayal of Debbie, Emecheta interrogates the characterization of the hero in such works as *A Wreath for the Maidens*. For in addition to criticizing the values of her class, Debbie also faces the challenge as heroine of exposing the fact and the consequences of male domination. Thus her retort when she is first asked to make the trip to Biafra to see Abosi: 'You men make all the mess and then call on us women to clear it up' (114–15). Thus, too, the question she poses to Abosi when he dismisses her as a peace emissary: 'Tell me, if I were a man, a man born almost thirty years ago, a graduate of politics, sociology and philosophy . . . would you have dismissed my mission?' (239). And in deciding to care for orphans, she offers a vision of a society that has undergone radical transformation, one in which patriarchal values have been transcended.

Nigerian Civil War literature has been almost exclusively the property of men writers. Nevertheless, by the time Amuta's essays were published, several works of fiction based on the war had been written by women: Nwapa's *This is Lagos* and *Wives at War*, both of which contain stories about the conflict, as well as her *Never Again*, and Emecheta's *Destination Biafra*. Amuta does make reference to *Never Again* in two of his essays, but his concern is not with examining Nwapa's themes or her construction of heroism, but with what he sees as the artistic failings of her novel ('Literature' 90, 'Nigerian' 90). Like the critics I discuss in my Introduction, Amuta elides gender both as a social and an analytic category. As a result, in characterizing the literature of the Nigerian Civil War, he defines only the male tradition of that literature. Furthermore, his essays function to valorize male domination in both literature and society.

Destination Biafra is a response to a question Debbie asks in the novel: 'When the history of the civil war was written, would the part played by her and women like Babs, Uzoma and the nuns in Biafra be mentioned at all?' (195). The novel has two main ideological functions: to bring to consciousness women's experience of the war and to challenge conventional constructions of nationalism and heroism. Its relationship with the male tradition of war literature is marked by both agreement and antagonism. For while Emecheta affirms some of the views of her male predecessors, her account of the war is written from a perspective which is diametrically opposed to that of the dominant gender.

Like *Destination Biafra*, *Double Yoke* is a self-reflexive novel, a narrative about narratives, a meta-narrative that sets out some of the characteristics of contemporary African fiction. The primary concern of the novel is to highlight a dialogue on gender as one of the defining features of the contemporary literary tradition. The work's main male protagonist, Ete Kamba, is an aspiring writer who is learning his craft from 'the most talked about female writer in Nigeria, and maybe in the whole of Africa' (6). That is how Ete refers to his teacher Miss Bulewao, a lecturer in creative writing at a Nigerian university much like the University of Calabar where Emecheta herself taught in 1981. But his words are almost as meaningless as Lindfors's designation of Ogot as 'Kenya's best-known female writer'. Ete himself looks to Ngũgĩ for inspiration. 'He is one of our greatest writers if not the greatest', he tells his friends, and in his estimation *Petals of Blood* is the work most likely to bring literary recognition to Africa (72–3). Ete is also completely disgusted with himself when he realizes he has taken Miss Bulewao as a role model. 'How low could one sink!' he exclaims. 'He was wishing to be as successful as a woman: he was wishing to adopt the method being adopted by an ordinary woman in the field of Arts!' (9). This is, however, one of the main points of the novel: that men writers have much to learn from their female counterparts.

Double Yoke is structured around Miss Bulewao's creative writing classes, its main narrative framed by two scenes which take place during these classes. In the opening frame, Miss Bulewao gives the students an assignment: to write 'an imaginary story of how you would like your ideal Nigeria to be' (5); and in the closing frame she discusses their work with them. The intervening narrative is comprised in part of the story Ete writes for Miss Bulewao, a story which tells of his relationship with his childhood sweetheart, Nko, from the time of their first meeting up to the time they are both at university. What this story reveals is that in the 'ideal Nigeria' of Ete's imagination the status quo of male domination would be perpetuated. For Ete produces a conventional male narrative. But the same story is also told by the novel's narrator from Nko's perspective. Counter-discursive in its strategies, this version of the story displays some of the characteristics of women's writing. Repeatedly interrupting Ete's story, the narrator subverts the codes of the conventional male narrative and engages the text of the novel's would-be male author in a dialogue on gender.

To acquire heroic stature in Emecheta's novel, Ete must come to terms with 'the new woman' (37) or the 'modern African woman' (61), as he designates women like Nko who are getting a university education. His privileged status as a male threatened, he tries to resolve the problem of 'the new woman' by shaping her character and plotting her story so as to reserve the position of dominance for himself. Thus when he first meets Nko, he expresses a number of wishes:

> [H]e would like her to be younger than he was and to be in a lower grade at school. . . . [H]e would like to live . . . with a woman who would be like his mother, but with this difference, she must be well educated. Yes that was the type he would like. A very quiet and submissive woman, a good cook, a good listener, a good worker, a good mother with a good education to match. But her education must be a little less than his own, otherwise they would start talking on the same level. (26)

Conforming to his specifications, Nko obliges him – at least initially.

Ete's norms are conventionally masculinist, his concern with superiority and dominance being particularly evident in his fantasies of sexual conquest: 'He . . . imagined himself the first of all men, taking possession, hurting, conquering his bleeding partner whose blood would have washed them both almost like a living sacrifice' (61). But when he translates his dream into action and assaults Nko, he is terribly disappointed, for there is no sea of blood to proclaim his victory over her. His masculinity threatened, he resorts to verbal abuse, calling Nko '[a] whore, a shameless prostitute' (57) before beating her up.

Promoting a derogatory image of women, Ete's narrative valorizes the manichean allegory of gender. Untroubled by the double standards he employs, Ete portrays Nko as the moral antithesis of his virtuous (though not so virginal) hero, himself. Representing himself as the innocent victim of female perfidy, he fixes her in the status of prostitute. Soon we find him placing all women in the same category: 'you can get any of them with a few naira' becomes his motto (125). Ete also produces a version of the redemption through repatriation to the village theme in his wish that Nko had never come to university, that she had remained 'just a simple village girl' (124). In his present view, women are corrupted by university life, though he had once wanted 'an educated virgin' as a wife (54). Thus he places women in a double bind: whereas female virtue is situated in the village, economic opportunities for women are linked to the university.

In his anxiety, Ete also offers 'nostalgic praise to the African Mother', conforming in this respect to Mariama Bâ's classic description of the African male author. Ete would if he could marry his mother who represents for him 'the epitome of womanhood':

the type whose price was above biblical rubies. The type who took pride not in herself but in her man. The type who would always obey her man, no matter what, even if he commanded her to walk through fire, the type that never questioned. (37)

Thus he champions the stereotype of the docile 'traditional' African woman who passively surrenders to the dictates of 'her man'.

The version of the story told from Nko's perspective constitutes an alternative discourse. Offering a portrayal of women that counters Ete's stereotypes, and exposing the double standards underlying his judgements, it subverts the authority of the conventional male narrative. 'To hell with your mother', Nko tells a shocked Ete Kamba when he instructs her to take his mother as a role model (59). And she reminds him when he brands her a whore that 'it takes two people at least to make any woman a prostitute' (58).

In this version of the story, Nko acquires heroic stature while Ete becomes a marginal figure. For although Nko hopes to marry him, her main concern is to get a good degree so that she can help her parents. Nko's challenge as a heroine is to transcend the patriarchal values of her society.

In her younger years she is content to conform to conventional definitions of her gender, her sole ambition being, as she says, 'to be a good wife and mother' (159). But in contrast to Ete who adheres to outmoded values and remains static, Nko changes and develops. Taking her mother into her confidence, she explains the addition of a university education to her agenda:

'Oh mother, I want to have both worlds, I want to be an academician and I want to be a quiet, nice and obedient wife, the type you all want me to be. . . . I know I can be of more use to you and my brothers if I had these two worlds.' (94)

As her mother observes, this means subjecting herself to a double oppression, placing herself under 'a double yoke' (94).

At university Nko must deal not only with Ete's definition of her gender but also with the exploitation of women's sexuality within the structure of the university. For in order to get her degree, she must trade in sex. But despite the warnings she receives from Ete and others that her aims are irreconcilable, her determination to combine conventional female roles with academic success remains unabated:

Oh blast it all. She was going to have both. She was going to manoeuvre these men to give her both. They thought they could always call the tune and women like her must dance to it. With her, they were going to be wrong. (135)

And so she agrees to have sex with the repulsive and hypocritical Professor Ikot after he has indicated that she won't graduate if she refuses. Then she coerces him with the threat of exposure into promising her a first class degree. Nko is pragmatic about her sexual transactions. As she and her room-mates agree: 'It is easier to get a good degree using one's brain power than bottom power' (155). But if their professors 'reduced them to using their sex to get their certificates, then that was what they were going to do' (154).

The main narrative concludes with Nko's discovery that she is pregnant with Ikot's baby. Still determined to achieve her aims, she refuses either to have an abortion or to abandon her studies. Instead, she will have her baby in her village and then return to the university to complete her degree. Looking back on her own earlier ambitions, Nko wonders what has happened to 'that girl whose only dream was to be a good wife and a mother. Has she gone forever?' she asks one of her room-mates, an older woman who has married and had children before coming to university. 'No she has not', Mrs Nwaizu assures her. 'She has simply just grown because she is going to be a sure academician and a mother' (159). And while Ete wishes 'she would go away and hide her shame', Nko acquires 'a kind of independence' through her refusal to submit to his categories (160).

Challenging the definitions of womanhood that Ete's narrative inscribes, Nko's version of the story engages the conventional male narrative in a dialogue on gender. Subversive in its relation to Ete's narrative, it defines one of the characteristics of women's writing. It also adopts the perspective of that writing on a number of issues. Most notably, sexual negotiation or 'prostitution' is viewed as a means of confronting male domination. Like Adaku and Amaka before her, Nko negotiates sex out of necessity – in order to fulfil her ambitions. Nko is also, like Nwapa's heroines, provided with a supportive female community. As well as encouraging her to achieve her goals, her mother and room-mates help her to understand her situation.

Double Yoke, however, breaks with one of the strongest traditions in female fiction: that of derogatory portrayals of men. It can be classed as a *bildungsroman*, a novel of, in this case, male development. For Ete is its central character and in the end he, too, acquires heroic stature within the terms Emecheta sets for him by changing or developing. Ete's challenge as a hero is spelt out for him by Miss Bulewao who, although she is impressed with his writing ability, is critical of the blatant sexism of his essay. '[A]re you strong enough to be a modern African man?' she asks him. 'Nko', she adds, 'is already a modern African lady, but you are still lagging . . . oh, so far, far behind' (162). Ete takes up this challenge, for although he has sworn that he will never again have anything to do with the shameless Nko, when her father dies he accompanies her to her village. Miss Bulewao commends Ete for his action. 'It's nice to know', she tells the men in her class, 'that many of you are bearing your double burdens or yokes . . . heroically' (163).

The main ideological function of *Double Yoke* is to promote gender equality. Through her portrayal of Ete, Emecheta provides her male readership with a positive role model. The portrayal of Ete can also be seen as Emecheta's response to male critics' complaints about negative portrayals of their gender and as her attempt to reduce the level of antagonism in the literary dialogue on gender. In contrast to such male characters as Adizua and Gilbert in Nwapa's *Efuru*, or Nnaife in Emecheta's own *The Joys of Motherhood*, Ete is not confined in a stereotypically reduced characterization of manhood. His is a realistic portrayal, for, like Nko, he changes in response to his social circumstances. Miss Bulewao, 'the most talked about female writer in Nigeria', is the catalyst in bringing about the transformation. The portrayal thus serves as a reminder to women writers that men, too, face problems of adjustment in a rapidly changing society, that they, too, as Miss Bulewao indicates, labour under 'a double yoke'.

Through her depiction of Ete in his relationship with Miss Bulewao, Emecheta also makes the point that men writers can learn much from women writers. As a result of his conversation with the teacher he originally deprecated because of her gender, Ete acquires the confidence to tackle the obstacles he faces in making writing his vocation. Furthermore, the transformation in character that Ete has also undergone under the influence of Miss Bulewao is an indication that his next story will not be a conventional male narrative.

Double Yoke is a novel that is about the effects of patriarchal social structures on the African literary tradition. The dialogic tension within the novel is between the discourse of male domination constituted by Ete's narrative and the discourse of gender equality that Nko's version of the story comprises, the same kind of tension that defines the relationship between men's and women's writing. It is also a novel that looks forward to an improvement in both social and literary relations between the sexes, a reduction in present tension. Emecheta herself attempts to effect such a reduction by placing women writers' portrayal of men under revision.

Buchi Emecheta is, then, both a disruptive and a cohesive force within the contemporary African literary tradition. She situates herself quite firmly within a specifically female tradition which she celebrates, and from the position of which she launches an attack on the male tradition. But she also displays some affinities with the male tradition, sharing, for example, similar views on colonialism and on Nigerian politicians. And in *Double Yoke*, she can be seen to be quite consciously working to reduce the friction between men's and women's writing. As we shall see in Chapter 7 several men writers have undertaken this same task of reducing the level of antagonism in the dialogue on gender.

6

'LITERATURE AS A . . . WEAPON'
The novels of Mariama Bâ

Mariama Bâ's first novel, *Une si longue lettre* (1979), brought its author immediate worldwide recognition when it won the first Noma Award for Publishing in Africa shortly after its publication. The novel was soon available in 'sixteen different editions or translations' (Zell *et al.*, *New Reader's Guide* 357), including the English version, *So Long a Letter* (1981). As Lindfors's data shows, the novel also quite quickly gained a place in the syllabuses of Anglophone African universities where in 1986 it ranked eighteenth in a list of books which, in Lindfors's words, 'teachers of African literature . . . evidently regard as worthiest of their students' attention' ('Teaching' 50). As a result of the award, critics, too, have given Bâ considerable attention. This criticism, as it has appeared in English-language journals, has not always been favourable, and it brings to the fore some of the trends we have noted in the commentary on African women's writing, indicating that these are negative trends and not isolated instances of perversity. It also makes evident that Bâ's novel has become one of the sites of critical controversy over the issue of gender.

Interestingly, Eldred Jones chaired the committee that chose Bâ as the recipient of the first Noma Award. In announcing the Committee's decision, Jones stated:

> Mariama Bâ's novel offers a testimony of the female condition in Africa while at the same time giving that testimony true imaginative depth. The distinguishing feature of this novel is the poise of its narrative style which reveals a maturity of vision and feeling. As a first novel, it represents a remarkable achievement to which the Committee, with this Award, is giving recognition.
>
> (Zell, 'First Noma Award' 199)

But the awarding of a prestigious literary prize to a woman seems to have provoked a male critical backlash. Frederick Ivor Case and Abiola Irele use the occasion of their reviews of Bâ's novel to launch a broad-based attack on women writers. In Case's view, 'So Long a Letter reminds us of the worst elements of Flora Nwapa's literary production' (539). Irele is much more complimentary to Bâ, whose novel he sees in almost the same terms as Jones does. But he is also much more sweeping in his deprecation of Bâ's predecessors:

> It is true that the novels of writers like Flora Nwapa, Bessie Head and Ama Ata Aidoo . . . touch upon the situation of women in African society, and more lately, Buchi Emecheta has devoted her writing to a lively defence of the cause of the African woman. Not one of these writers, however, displays the depth of insight of John Munonye in his novel, The Only Son, into the situation of the African woman. (661)

Irele's choice of The Only Son (1966) as a model for the portrayal of 'the situation of the African woman' is revealing of his own view of women. The novel belongs to that class of narratives Jameson labels 'national allegories'. A story about colonization, it tells of a son's abandonment of his mother, the embodiment of his African heritage, and his acceptance of western culture. Munonye quite explicitly identifies women with tradition, the self-defined role of the mother, Chiaku, being to safeguard the family inheritance following her husband's death so that one day her son can 'continue the lineage' and 'build up the homestead' (14). Devoting herself to nurturing Nnanna, Chiaku is the epitome of the self-sacrificing mother. And although she is vastly disappointed by the defection of Nnanna who, unlike his mother, recognizes the social and material benefits that will accrue from adapting to the new order, she is not defeated. Rather she is rewarded for her orthodoxy by her author with marriage to a man of property and of 'striking masculinity' who almost immediately makes her pregnant. 'Who knew if it would be a boy!' she thinks hopefully (183–4).

The derogatory comparison of female- to male-authored texts seems to have acquired the status of a convention in the annals of African (male) literary criticism – a convention which functions to exclude women writers from the canon. Following Jones, Irele, and others, Case makes the same kind of comparison. Referring to '[t]he literary accomplishments' of such (male) writers as Abdoulaye Sadji and Ousmane Sembène, he states that '[n]ovels which have as their focus the condition of women in Senegal have tended to be significant works dependent on a well-defined symbolic structure' (538). As, in his view, So Long a Letter lacks such a structure, it is 'of limited value' which, he concludes, 'leads to speculation about the [policies of Bâ's publishers] as well as about the criteria used for judging texts for the Norma [sic] Award' (540).

For Case, *So Long a Letter* has no redeeming features. In his view, Bâ fails to integrate 'sociological . . . details' – 'one is tempted to say anthropological', he adds snidely – into the novel's framework or to make the plot plausible. These are the same charges that Jones and Palmer level against *Efuru*, a coincidence which suggests that what the critics elaborate are not the qualities of either novel but the modes and maxims of masculinist criticism. Case also finds Bâ's 'piece of work . . . difficult to define as a novel'. This, too, makes him 'wonder at the literary prize . . . that the text was awarded' (538). Case's definition of genre seems to have been derived from a reading of authors like Sadji and Sembène and it operates to bind women writers to literary conventions which serve the purposes of the dominant gender.

So Long a Letter also provoked the first of Femi Ojo-Ade's two attacks on women writers which appeared in *African Literature Today*: 'Still a victim? Mariama Bâ's *Une si longue lettre*'.[1] In a blatant display of hostility, Ojo-Ade concludes his discussion of Bâ's novel by threatening to 'tear . . . up and throw . . . into the dustbin' any other such 'letter', should one be written (86). Ojo-Ade's project is to discredit feminism and women writers who, in his view, advocate women's liberation. 'Feminism', he declares, is 'an occidental phenomenon' (72). Thus what it offers African women is 'a fake freedom' (85). He divides women writers into two classes. There are those who 'constitute the "old guard"': Grace Ogot, Efua Sutherland, Ama Ata Aidoo, Flora Nwapa. These authors have his approval, for they are 'steeped in the traditions of the land, complaining of their sufferings as subjects of the male master, but seeking solace in a society that has proclaimed woman the mother'. Then there are those who are 'crying out for the liberation of women' (72). These he characterizes as victims and purveyors of 'social and psychological alienation; cultural bastardization; a destiny of death' (86). Bâ (along with Emecheta and Nafissatou Diallo) falls into this second category. Her feminism, Ojo-Ade asserts, 'smacks of Beauvoirism', an ideology of 'liberation' which 'engulfs the erstwhile victim in another abyss, solitude'. What he offers in place of this 'facile, sham solution' is an ideology which, he claims, promotes 'true freedom': 'Solidarity, human, man-woman (couple), man-child-woman (family) solidarity, this is the essence of life' (84).

Ojo-Ade positions himself in this essay as an African nationalist, a stance which, he emphasizes, is authorized by the historical experience of colonialism. But his nationalism is quite clearly a gendered ideology, for the 'true freedom' he offers elides the historical reality of male domination. His reading of Bâ also suppresses her celebration of female solidarity. For in his perspective there is only one type of solidarity. Female friendships obviously 'engulf' women in 'solitude'. Furthermore, in his division of women writers into two categories, he negates the notion of a female literary tradition and brings into play a divide and rule strategy, one which functions to maintain the status quo of a male-defined literary tradition.

In Ojo-Ade's essay, there is a convergence of male critical and literary discourse. For the essay replicates the features of the conventional male narrative. As we have seen, Ojo-Ade valorizes and idealizes motherhood and prescribes conventional roles for women. In designating feminism as 'an occidental phenomenon', he also denies agency to African women and characterizes them as passive in their response to male domination. More crucially, perhaps, he constructs a good woman/whore dichotomy on the texts of the female literary tradition. The 'good woman' – writers like Ogot and Nwapa – is identified with tradition; the 'whore' – writers like Bâ and Emecheta – is accused of 'cultural bastardization'. Thus the woman writer is placed in a double bind. If, in order to win the male critic's approval, she chooses to place her art in the service of 'the traditions of the land', she ends up writing gender romances – or, in Ojo-Ade's words, 'seeking solace in a society that has proclaimed woman the mother'. If, on the other hand, she chooses to place her art in the service of the struggle for women's liberation, she becomes the object of the male critic's hostility.

One of the tasks of feminist criticism is to subvert the categories of masculinist criticism. Ironically, however, there is also a convergence between the terms of Ojo-Ade's essay and those of a certain type of feminist criticism. As has already been suggested, Ojo-Ade (falsely) ascribes to Bâ the view that African traditions are the sole source of African women's oppression, and western values and practices their means of liberation. So, too, does Katherine Frank in what has almost become a conventional ascription. The main difference between the perspectives of the two critics is that while Ojo-Ade is critical of the views he imputes to Bâ, Frank endorses them. According to Frank, Bâ's novel depicts 'the painful, faltering, but ultimately successful movement of a woman from a traditional African world to a very different, Westernized urban life'. What impedes the heroine's progress initially is that she 'assumes the posture of the traditional, obedient African wife', but she is eventually able to find 'Westernized, feminist fulfilment' ('Women' 18–19). However, as we shall see, Bâ does not write the racial allegories that the critics attribute to her any more than the writers Ojo-Ade designates 'the old guard' write gender romances.

As we saw in Chapter 2, Bâ urges women writers to politicize their art, to 'use literature as a non-violent but effective weapon' in the struggle to 'overthrow the status quo which harms [them]' (Schipper 47). In this chapter, I will investigate the strategic value of Bâ's own writing in relation to the social and ideological conditions in which it was produced and to the conventions of representation of the male literary tradition. Bâ wrote only two novels, *So Long a Letter* and *Scarlet Song* (1985), published originally as *Un chant écarlate* (1981) shortly after her death.

So Long a Letter is set in Dakar about twenty years after Senegal's independence from France. Its world is that of Dakar's professional middle class, the members of which, in their student days, were in the vanguard of the nationalist and feminist movements of the 1950s. Bâ evaluates the outcome of these movements from a contemporary perspective, revealing the betrayal of the hopes and aspirations of both by this same privileged elite: the undermining of the nationalists' socialist ideals by bourgeois materialism, and the compromising of the feminist ideal of gender equality through adherence to imported western and indigenous Islamic patriarchal values and practices.

The male text which Bâ appears most obviously to interrogate is Ousmane Sembène's *Xala* (1973), the story of a middle-aged Senegalese businessman who becomes impotent when, at the height of his fortunes, he takes a beautiful young girl as his third wife. *Xala* is one of the novels Jameson selects to illustrate his theory of 'third-world' texts as national allegories. As Jameson states, Sembène's satiric treatment of Senegal's ruling classes 'is explicitly marked as the failure of the independence movement to develop into a general social revolution' ('Third-world literature' 81).[2] The relationship between *So Long a Letter* and *Xala* is partly confirmatory, for Bâ, too, is critical of the Senegal's bourgeoisie. There is, in fact, on the level of character portrayal, a striking similarity between the two novels. In both his professional and his private life, Modou Fall, a lawyer and the husband of Bâ's main protagonist, Ramatoulaye, follows in the footsteps of Sembène's El Haji. In his youth Modou was a trade union activist, as was El Haji. But after independence he, too, betrays the movement, leading the unions 'into collaboration with the government' (25) in return for a top post in the civil service. Modou also takes to himself a beautiful young (though, in his case, second) wife once he becomes affluent. In both cases, too, the new wife has little say in the matter, for she comes from a poor family, the members of which promote the marriage in anticipation of social advancement and material enrichment. And while El Haji becomes impotent as soon as he marries, Modou dies of a heart attack not too long after. Sembène is not, however, interested in the problems created by polygyny for either men or women. Rather, he exploits them for their metaphorical potential in elaborating his theme of the bankruptcy of Senegal as a neo-colonial nation. Bâ deals with the issues that Sembène suppresses, giving polygyny thematic status in her novel and treating it as a form of marriage that degrades women.

Bâ also challenges the orthodoxies of male literary representation through her use of the convention of the paired women. Occupying a much more prominent position than it does in either *Efuru* or *The Joys of Motherhood*, the convention provides *So Long a Letter* with its narrative framework. The story is told in the first person by Ramatoulaye in the form of a letter-diary that she addresses to her friend Aissatou and writes following the death of Modou. A character in her own story, Ramatoulaye conforms to both the literary and social definitions of her gender. By contrast, Aissatou refuses to submit to pre(in)scribed categories. While Bâ treats her conservative heroine ironically, having her tell her story with subconscious evasion and revelation, she quite explicitly identifies with her radical heroine who is not only a divorced woman (as Bâ herself was) but also shares Bâ's last name.

More closely than Nwapa does the two sisters Ossai and Ajanupu, or Emecheta the co-wives Nnu Ego and Adaku, Bâ pairs the two friends Ramatoulaye and Aissatou. 'We walked the same paths from adolescence to maturity', Ramatoulaye writes at the beginning of her letter (1), and later, 'Our lives developed in parallel' (19). Friends from childhood, they attend the same schools, graduate from the same college, choose the same profession, and even marry essentially the same man. For in the final analysis, there is little or nothing to distinguish the lawyer Ramatoulaye marries from his doctor friend, Aissatou's husband, Mawdo. They also espouse the same principles. 'We were true sisters, destined for the same mission of emancipation', Ramatoulaye writes in her letter (15). But confronted with the same dilemma, they opt for different solutions, Aissatou to resist the imposition of patriarchal standards and Ramatoulaye to submit and reap the rewards of conformity.

As Ramatoulaye's narrative reveals, the crisis in her life came not with the death of Modou but with his acquisition five years earlier, after twenty-five years of marriage to Ramatoulaye, of a second wife, a teenage friend of one of their twelve children. It is on this moment that Ramatoulaye dwells in her letter, endeavouring to come to terms with the choice she herself made, 'a choice that [her] reason rejected' and one made against the wishes of her children: to remain within the marriage and live 'according to the precepts of Islam concerning polygamic life' (45–6). For Ramatoulaye, Aissatou serves not as a correspondent – she already knows the story and in any case the letter is never sent – but as an alter ego. Ramatoulaye writes to herself in an attempt to locate the source of her disequilibrium.

Like Nwapa and Emecheta, Bâ uses physical confinement in domestic space as a metaphor for her conservative heroine's psychological state. The metaphor is, however, more pervasive in *So Long a Letter* than it is in either *Efuru* or *The Joys of Motherhood*, for it is provided by the narrative setting created for the telling of the story. Ramatoulaye writes her letter during the four months and ten days of secluded mourning prescribed by Islam for widows. As we shall see, her physical confinement during this period of mourning in the house she once shared with Modou replicates her psychological confinement in debilitating stereotypical definitions of womanhood.

As Mbye Baboucar Cham points out, Bâ also makes use of the Islamic concept of *mirasse*, combining it with the novel's epistolary form to create the framework for Ramatoulaye's narrative. *Mirasse*, he explains, is a 'religious as well as juridical principle . . . of inheritance' which 'implies disclosure of all known and unknown or secret material possessions of a deceased for division among the survivors'. Bâ's skill as a novelist, according to Cham, is evident in her extension of 'the notion of disclosure . . . to encompass material possessions as well as non-material attributes and history of the individual'. For this adaptation enables her to provide Ramatoulaye with the 'framework within which to undertake a comprehensive exposition . . . of intimate secrets of married life with Modou Fall, particularly the latter's weaknesses as a human being and the effect of such on their relationship' (32–3).

Equally important is Bâ's use of the concept of *mirasse* to underscore her ironic treatment of her conservative heroine. As a devout Muslim, Ramatoulaye considers the reckoning up of Modou's personal attributes a religious duty, one which, because she has devoted all the adult years of her life to Modou, she undertakes with considerable trepidation:

> The *mirasse* commanded by the Koran requires that a dead person be stripped of his most intimate secrets; thus is exposed to others what was carefully concealed. These exposures crudely explain a man's life. With consternation, I measure the extent of Modou's betrayal. (9)

In 'stripp[ing Modou] of his most intimate secrets', however, Ramatoulaye also unwittingly exposes her own secret fears and wishes and reveals the extent of her own betrayal of the principles she espouses.

As Ojo-Ade says, *So Long a Letter* 'smacks of Beauvoirism'. But it is not, as he claims, Bâ's portrayal of the radical Aissatou that is immediately evocative of Beauvoir's *The Second Sex* but rather her depiction of the conservative Ramatoulaye. Through her portrayal of Ramatoulaye, Bâ takes up the issue of women's education, a theme which, like polygyny, has been suppressed in the dominant tradition. Ramatoulaye believes that she has been lifted 'out of the bog of tradition, superstition and custom' by her colonial education (15). She is, in fact, genuinely opposed to any Islamic practice, including polygyny, that denies dignity to women. But in accepting the colonialists' derogatory estimation of her culture, she also accepts their view of women's role and status in society. The traditions, superstitions, and customs of one patriarchal culture, have, in other words, merely been replaced by those of another, and these have been so completely assimilated that living her life in terms of them has become Ramatoulaye's prerequisite for happiness. A victim of French colonial education, Ramatoulaye seems to spring full-blown from Beauvoir's analysis of the condition of middle-class French women.

The reason Ramatoulaye advances for not choosing 'the right' and 'dignified solution' of obtaining a divorce is 'the immense tenderness I felt towards Modou Fall' (45). The story she tells reveals otherwise – that she has, in Beauvoir's terms, interiorized her dependence. Considering herself 'one of those who can realize themselves fully and bloom only when they form part of a couple' (55–6), Ramatoulaye contemplates the fate of divorced women of her generation:

> I knew a few whose remaining beauty had been able to capture a worthy man, a man who added fine bearing to a good situation and who was considered 'better, a hundred times better than his predecessor'. . . . I knew others who had lost all hope of renewal and whom loneliness had very quickly laid underground. (40)

She then examines herself in the mirror and finds, like Beauvoir's 'ageing woman', that 'her flesh no longer has fresh bounties for men' (Beauvoir 590): 'I had lost my slim figure, as well as ease and quickness of movement. My stomach protruded from beneath the wrapper. . . . Suckling had robbed my breasts of their round firmness. I could not delude myself: youth was deserting my body'. (41)

Ramatoulaye is unable to face the consequence of divorcing Modou: the loss of marital security. When, by severing all ties with her and the children, Modou in effect thrusts this fate upon her, Ramatoulaye is plunged into emotional turmoil. Believing, on the one hand, that her heart remains 'faithful to the love of [her] youth' (56), she at the same time calls out 'eagerly to "another man" to replace Modou' (53). After Modou's death, a number of men answer this call, only one of whom, Daouda Dieng, a doctor and a deputy at the National Assembly, she considers at all suitable. But after playing the part of the coquette – 'rolling [her] eyes round' in order 'to arouse interest' (60) – she rejects his proposal just as she has all of the others. Taking refuge in what Beauvoir calls 'retrospective romances' (589),

Ramatoulaye does, in a fashion, remain 'faithful to the love of [her] youth'. Reliving that thrilling moment of thirty years past when she first saw the 'tall and athletically built' Modou, full of 'virility' and with fine features 'harmoniously blended', she bursts forth in ecstatic apostrophe: 'Modou Fall, the very moment you bowed before me, asking me to dance, I knew you were the one I was waiting for' (13). When her true-story romance deviates from its fictional origins, she is emotionally and sexually paralysed.

Although she is a professional woman, Ramatoulaye gives little attention to that aspect of her life, focusing instead on her status as wife and mother. In defining the role of the mother, she echoes Beauvoir's description of 'the sainted Mother', the mother as 'the mediatrix between the individual and the cosmos', as 'the very incarnation of the Good' (204–6):

> [O]ne is a mother in order to understand the inexplicable. One is a mother to lighten the darkness. One is a mother to shield when lightning streaks the night, when thunder shakes the earth, when mud bogs one down. One is a mother in order to love without beginning or end. (82–3)

Ramatoulaye resembles even more closely the French middle-class housewife as Beauvoir describes her. For this type of woman, according to Beauvoir, '[r]eality is concentrated inside the house':

> [The house] decorations . . . provide an expression of her personality; she is the one who has chosen, made, hunted out furnishings and knick-knacks, who has arranged them in accordance with an aesthetic principle in which regard for symmetry is usually an important element; they reflect her individuality while bearing public witness to her standard of living. . . .
>
> In domestic work . . . woman makes her home her own, finds social justification, and provides herself with an occupation, an activity, that deals usefully and satisfyingly with material objects – shining stoves, fresh clean clothes, bright copper, polished furniture. (469–70)

Ramatoulaye, too, treats her home as an expression of her personality, as a work of art that she has created. 'I loved my house', she writes in her letter. 'You can testify to the fact that I made it a haven of peace where everything had its place, that I created a harmonious symphony of colours' (56). She also endeavours to make housework seem essential, an end, and not merely a means, in itself, and to transform the repetitive, unremunerated drudgery of daily domestic tasks into rewarding work:

Those women we call 'house'-wives deserve praise. The domestic
work they carry out, and which is not paid in hard cash, is essential
to the home. Their compensation remains the pile of well ironed,
sweet-smelling washing, the shining tiled floor on which the foot
glides, the gay kitchen filled with the smell of stews. Their silent action
is felt in the least useful detail: over there, a flower in bloom placed
in a vase, elsewhere a painting with appropriate colours, hung up in
the right place. (63)

In her obsession with cleanliness and order, Ramatoulaye is the model
of Beauvoir's 'maniac housekeeper' (471), resenting the entry into her home
of other human beings as they bring dirt and disorder. Thus, when Modou
dies, she is, it would seem, even more disturbed by the state of the house
following the inundation of mourners than she is by his death: 'Cola nuts
spat out here and there have left red stains: my tiles, kept with such
painstaking care, are blackened. Oil stains on the walls, balls of crumpled
paper. What a balance sheet for a day!' she groans (7).

As she begins her period of confinement, Ramatoulaye makes the
following entry in her diary: 'The walls that limit my horizon for four
months and ten days do not bother me. I have enough memories in me to
ruminate upon. And these are what I am afraid of, for they smack of
bitterness' (8). The walls do not bother her because the immaculately kept
and tastefully decorated house is an expression or an extension of her
personality and essential to the image of female fulfilment that directs her
life. The house is also all that remains of her romantic dream. As wife,
abandoned wife, and widow, she dwells in that house, and unlike Modou
who comes and goes – 'He never came again', she says sadly after his second
marriage (46) – it is a permanent feature. But it is precisely those walls, and
not her bitter memories, that Ramatoulaye should fear. By obstructing her
view of life's other and larger possibilities, they in effect become her prison.
Unable to conceive of a life beyond those walls, Ramatoulaye remains
trapped in her dead-end romance and her domestic enclosure.

Aissatou is in a literal sense Ramatoulaye's *alter ego* – her other self or
double. For when her husband, Mawdo Bâ, takes a second wife, she does
precisely what Ramatoulaye knows she ought to have done. 'And you left',
Ramatoulaye writes. 'You had the surprising courage to take your life into
your own hands. You rented a house and set up home there' (32). Like Adaku
in Emecheta's *The Joys of Motherhood*, Aissatou both literally and figuratively
storms the walls that confine her. Having 'rented a house' and 'set up home
there' for herself and her children, in this case boys, she proceeds, again like
Adaku, to find a means of becoming economically independent and,

though warned that 'boys cannot succeed without their father' (31), to raise her sons successfully 'contrary to all predictions' (34). Returning to college, Aissatou upgrades her qualifications which eventually leads to her appointment at a Senegalese embassy. And from her salary, Aissatou is able to supply Ramatoulaye with precisely what Ramatoulaye knows she ought to be able to provide for herself: she replaces with a brand-new model the car Modou has deprived Ramatoulaye of by handing it over to his second wife.

Through the bond of friendship between Ramatoulaye and Aissatou, a bond that is expressed through the form as well as the content of the novel, Bâ celebrates female solidarity. At the same time, she portrays Ramatoulaye as being ambivalent in her feelings toward Aissatou, thus revealing her conservative heroine's internalization of her oppression. Ramatoulaye, herself, valorizes friendship over romantic love in her letter: 'Friendship has splendours that love knows not. It grows stronger when crossed, whereas obstacles kill love. Friendship resists time, which wearies and severs couples. It has heights unknown to love' (54). But her narrative also reveals that while she has remained faithful to Modou, she has repeatedly betrayed Aissatou's friendship. Most notably, although she knows of Mawdo's plan to take a second wife, she does not warn Aissatou. And while she praises Aissatou for breaking off relations with Mawdo, she herself retains him as a confidant and as the family doctor.

In narrating her own and Aissatou's stories, Ramatoulaye also relates the stories of other women, in the telling of which she unconsciously reveals more of her own fears and weaknesses. Through these stories, Bâ extends the convention of the paired women to encompass multiple pairings, employing the convention in its extended form to reaffirm the choice made by her radical heroine.

In the telling of her friend Jacqueline's story, Ramatoulaye comes as close as she will get to acquiring an understanding of her own. Having interjected this story into her own just prior to its climax, Ramatoulaye wonders why she has done so. While her narrative tactics indicate an embarrassed reluctance to admit her choice openly, the substance of Jacqueline's story is even more revealing. Jacqueline, herself a victim of marital neglect and deceit, has had a nervous breakdown. What the narrative sequence implies is that it is Ramatoulaye's fear of this that determines her choice – her fear of being afflicted by the same disorder if she leaves the security of wifehood in Modou's tidy and immaculate house. As a result of psychiatric treatment, Jacqueline finds for herself 'a reason for living' (45). If Ramatoulaye's story is also to have a happy ending, a breakdown, at least in the figurative sense, is precisely what she requires in order to break out of her confinement in her debilitating image of women. She, too, needs to find an independent 'reason for living'.

As well as providing *So Long a Letter* with its narrative framework, the convention of the paired women is also an integral part of the action of the novel. For Ramatoulaye is, in addition, paired with her co-wife Binetou. But the convention appears in a different mode in the juxtaposition of these two characters, taking the form in which, as we shall see, it occurs in *Scarlet Song*. Ramatoulaye and Binetou are what might be called 'twin doubles', for although Ramatoulaye doesn't recognize it, she and her co-wife closely resemble each other. Because of the disparity in age and class background, each is envious of the other, Binetou of the material well-being Ramatoulaye derives from being married to Modou, and Ramatoulaye of her rival's 'shapely contours' (35) which are what attract Modou to her. In their efforts to gain or to keep Modou, both compromise their integrity, Binetou succumbing to her mother's pressure to leave school and marry the affluent Modou, and Ramatoulaye abandoning her principles in choosing to remain within the marriage. Ramatoulaye recognizes that Binetou is 'a victim' (48), 'a lamb slaughtered on the alter of affluence' (39). What she fails to see in her co-wife is a mirror image of herself. For she, too, is a sacrificial victim, though of somewhat different social forces.

The story of Aissatou's mother-in-law, Aunty Nabou, is the most cautionary tale of all for a woman like Ramatoulaye. A widow, Aunty Nabou has come into power by virtue of having outlived all the males who could exercise it over her. And this she wields with a fury on her offspring, manipulating their lives with no view to their happiness, but with the utmost determination to have her own way. Schooled in the patriarchal dictums and the class distinctions of her society, Aunty Nabou becomes an aggressively assertive agent on their behalf. Having seen her daughters 'well married', she is enraged when Mawdo, 'her "one and only man"', marries Aissatou without her consent (26); Aissatou is a mere goldsmith's daughter who will 'tarnish her noble descent' (28). Scheming and wheedling, whining that 'shame kills faster than disease' she knows no rest until, it must be admitted, a not entirely reluctant Mawdo, has agreed to take a second wife, a young girl of his mother's class and choice (30).

A thoroughly obnoxious character, Aunty Nabou is, if not Ramatoulaye's actual twin double, her potential one, for Ramatoulaye, who has already joined Aunty Nabou in widowhood, displays some of her suspect traits. A telling sign is her shock and dismay when she, 'who wanted to control everything', catches her teenage daughters smoking (77). Another is her chiding of her son-in-law for spoiling his wife by sharing the housework with her. She also exposes the same class bias as Aunty Nabou in her remark about Aissatou, that 'Mawdo raised you up to his own level, he the son of a princess and you the child from the forges' (19). And her antipathy to Binetou's mother, whom she spitefully refers to as 'Lady Mother-in-Law', seems to arise more from outrage at the fact that this lower-class woman has acquired the very amenities that she so cherishes – 'delicious jets of hot water [to] massage her back', 'ice cubes [to] cool the water in her glass' – than at the means she has employed to do so (49). Aunty Nabou is a grim parody of Ramatoulaye and a grim reminder of what she is in danger of becoming if she does not seek the power to liberate herself. Ramatoulaye's final diary entry is filled with optimism:

> I have not given up wanting to refashion my life. Despite everything – disappointments and humiliations – hope still lives on within me. . . .
> The word 'happiness' does indeed have meaning, doesn't it? I shall go in search of it. (89)

But she also reveals that she has 'obtained an extension of [her] widow's leave' (88). Ramatoulaye has been on 'wife's leave' from full participation in human affairs throughout her adult life. As Daouda Dieng retorts when she complains that there are too few women in the National Assembly: '[Y]ou who are protesting; you preferred your husband, your class, your children to public life' (62). While her period of confinement figuratively represents her psychological condition, it is also literally little more than an extension of her prior mode of existence. This second 'extension' contains the unhappy suggestion that Ramatoulaye will never succeed in breaking out of conventional gender definitions. For by remaining secluded within her domestic enclosure, she avoids the challenge of self-definition.

The source of Ramatoulaye's disequilibrium is, as Bâ makes clear, the western model of womanhood she has assimilated in the course of her colonial education. Psychologically entrapped in this model's debilitating definitions of her gender, she becomes susceptible to victimization by indigenous patriarchal practices. Thus, despite the compromises she makes, the rewards of conformity elude her. By contrast, Aissatou refuses to be constrained by western gender definitions, even though, as Bâ emphasizes, she has been educated at the same schools as Ramatoulaye. At the same time, she is able to use the skills she acquired to further her own goals. Even though her actions result in social disapprobation, she has the courage to confront male domination without compromise. And she is rewarded by her author for her nonconformity with professional and parental success.

Like her female predecessors, then, Bâ portrays women realistically, grounding her female characters in society and making them subject to historical forces. Her portrayal of men, however, is also, like that of her predecessors in some of their novels, problematic. Ojo-Ade is particularly bitter in his complaint about her representation of his gender. 'Man, the

unfaithful husband', he writes; 'Man, the womanizer; Man, the victimizer
– Bâ's novel describes him in all his negative forms, without an exception
to console his pride' (73–4). But perhaps Ojo-Ade overstates the case. For
while Modou and Mawdo tend to be stereotypical male figures, philander-
ers, crass and indolent in their egotism, Ramatoulaye's suitor, Daouda
Dieng, and her son-in-law, Abou, conform less readily to the stereotype. As
we have already seen, Daouda confronts Ramatoulaye with the falseness of
her own position and he also reminds her of his own pro-feminist stance
on issues in the National Assembly:

> 'Whom are you addressing, Ramatoulaye? You are echoing my
> speeches at the National Assembly, where I have been called a
> "feminist". I am not, in fact, the only one to insist on changing the
> rules of the game and injecting new life into it. Women should no
> longer be decorative accessories, objects to be moved about, com-
> panions to be flattered or calmed with promises. . . . Women must
> be encouraged to take a keener interest in the destiny of the country.'
> (61–2)

Daouda's statement contains the only overt criticism of Ramatoulaye to
occur in the novel. And although Ramatoulaye does not take up Daouda's
challenge to participate in public life – it is Aissatou who, in her employment at a Senegalese embassy, takes part in shaping 'the destiny of the
country' – Bâ's attribution to a male character of such unorthodox views
on women's role in society is revisionary. Daouda, however, reverts to type
in the marriage proposal he makes to Ramatoulaye, for he is unapologetic
in his attempt to engage her in a polygynous union. In her portrayal of
Abou, Bâ breaks much more decisively with the stereotype, assigning to
him radical views on the role and status of women in marital relations.
Offering an alternative model of marriage, Abou sharply counters
Ramatoulaye's accusation that he is spoiling his wife. 'Daba,' he says, 'is my
wife. She is not my slave, nor my servant' (73). Abou is, however, a marginal
character in the novel.

So Long a Letter has two main ideological functions: to foreground
polygyny and women's education as issues in contemporary African society
and to refute the orthodoxies of male literary representation. The convention of the paired women is Bâ's main 'weapon' in this novel. Through it,
she presents contrasting models of female identity. Polygyny brings the lives
of both Ramatoulaye and Aissatou to a crisis and wrecks their happiness.
But whereas Aissatou is able to use her education to achieve independence,
Ramatoulaye retains the negative aspects of her colonial education. Having
internalized western gender norms, she is unable to find independence and

freedom. As the author of the letter which makes up the novel, Ramatoulaye conforms quite readily to a slightly modified version of Ojo-Ade's (perverse) characterization of women writers such as Ogot and Nwapa: she complains of her sufferings as subject of the male master, but seeks solace in a middle-class society that has proclaimed woman the mother and housewife. Ramatoulaye is unable to write her own story. By pairing her with Aissatou, Bâ rewrites the text of what is acceptable for women, providing a positive fiction of female identity, the story of a woman who does not compromise with the forces of patriarchy.

Scarlet Song takes the events of 1968 in France and Senegal as its primary historical reference point. The novel is set mainly in Dakar, and its leading protagonists, Mireille de La Vallée, a French national, and Ousmane Gueye, a Senegalese, both participate in the student-led uprisings in their respective countries. As she does in *So Long a Letter* with the nationalist and feminist movements of the 1950s, so in *Scarlet Song* Bâ considers the extent to which the ideals of 1968 were maintained by participants in the years that followed. What she reveals once again is the betrayal of those ideals: the French students' failure to maintain their resistance to bourgeois values and the Senegalese students' later lack of commitment to creating 'a just and fair society' (45).

The convention of the paired women features in this novel too, though rather less prominently, taking the same form as it does in the pairing of Ramatoulaye and Binetou. Ousmane marries Mireille, he the son of a poor but high-caste family, she the only child of a French diplomat with an aristocratic heritage. Later Ousmane takes as a second wife his childhood sweetheart, Ouleymatou, whose background is the same as his own. Although coming from different cultures and classes, the co-wives Mireille and Ouleymatou are in many respects mirror images of each other. Like Ramatoulaye and Binetou, each wants what the other possesses. Attracted by Ousmane's position and possessions, Ouleymatou is determined to wrest him away from Mireille so that she can satisfy her desire for 'fine furniture, cars, tiled bathrooms, rustling gowns' (105). Employing all of the feminine wiles at her disposal, she also attempts to play the role of the western middle-class housewife. 'The *Toubabs* are so clean', she says to herself as she rubs, scrubs, and polishes in anticipation of Ousmane's first visit (114). On her part, Mireille envies Ouleymatou her 'experience in the arts of love'. And she, too, attempts, though unsuccessfully, to compete with her rival:

> She went to endless lengths to refurbish her armoury of seduction and win back Ousmane. She brushed her hair till it shone, rouged her cheeks, outlined her eyebrows and eyelashes. She drowned herself

in costly perfumes: the little packets of incense which Ouleymatou bought at the market for the ridiculous price of twenty-five francs, cancelled out all her efforts. (159)

During her student days, Mireille takes on the role of rebel, demonstrating her opposition to the values of French middle-class society by taking part in the 1968 uprising in Paris. In one of the letters she writes to Ousmane during this period, she speaks of her 'hatred of convention' (43), and although she is prevented by her father from participating fully in events, she is wholeheartedly committed to the overthrow of bourgeois values and institutions:

[S]he felt as passionately involved as her student friends who were, for the most part, middle-class youngsters like herself, who belonged to the most militant wing of the demonstrators.

They abhorred the traditional nuclear family. They considered it an institution to be demolished, its contents revised, its power restricted, its limits redefined. (42)

In her relationship with Ousmane, Mireille also considers herself to be in revolt against her society. But as soon as she marries him the values she has repudiated reassert themselves and she emerges from her student days as the very model of the bourgeois housewife. Like Ramatoulaye, she brings 'a personal note' to her house and arranges the furnishings according to aesthetic principles: 'she tidied up and moved around the furniture and knick-knacks to find the best way of setting them off' (82). Like Ramatoulaye, too, she resents the dirt and disorder that outsiders inevitably bring into her well-kept house. Angry at the work they create for her, she attempts to ban visits from Ousmane's friends and family: 'Table napkins were grey after they used them. The basin in the bathroom was like a kitchen sink, stained with grease after they had washed their hands' (86). Inflexible in her adherence to western middle-class cultural practices, she also tries to impose them on Ousmane, condemning behaviour such as the use of a spoon or hand in preference to a knife and fork as 'lack of breeding' or 'vulgarity' (93).

Despite the revolutionary ideology she espoused as a student, she also demonstrates her allegiance to the nuclear family. Thus, although Ousmane tries to persuade her otherwise, she considers unannounced visits from his relatives and friends as an invasion of privacy. 'Mireille had her own concept of family life', we are told (87); and 'habit prevails' is the narrator's comment on her efforts to treat her in-laws in accordance with Senegalese conceptions of family relations (97). Feeling she is being exploited, she also resents the customary financial obligations she is reminded she owes to her in-laws.

Although Mireille is a victim of Ousmane's duplicity and of his mother's scheming, her own intransigence, her refusal to adapt to Senegalese customs, also contributes to the breakdown of the marriage. She takes no interest in her husband's culture, decorating the flat with paintings she has brought with her from France and preferring to see a film than to attend the performance of religious songs that Ousmane's father is presiding over. And although she is aware that Ousmane has acquired considerable knowledge of French culture through his western education, when he attempts to explain to her the significance of Senegalese music and the contribution Africans have made to civilization, she does not listen: 'Mireille had long ago disappeared into the kitchen', not 'deign[ing] to abandon her domestic activities' (92–3).

On learning that Ousmane has married Ouleymatou, Mireille provides an astute analysis of the motives, as well as the fate, of women who decide to remain with their husbands in such circumstances:

> [T]he reason they do not leave is cowardice, fear of assuming responsibility for themselves. They are kept prisoner by the habit of not thinking for themselves, not taking any decisions, not seeing with their own eyes, of letting others take over. It's not long before they crumble. They are eaten up with suffering. They don't know the meaning of liberty. (161)

But like Ramatoulaye, she decides against her reason: 'Pathetically Mireille chose to stay [within the marriage]' (162). Rationalizing her choice on the grounds that she has no other options – to go back home would be a humiliating experience and in any case her parents would not accept the child that has resulted from the union – she never considers that she might easily strike out on her own, that she could, on the basis of her educational qualifications, support herself and the child and live independently. What prevents her from coming to this realization is her emotional dependence on Ousmane whom she still loves despite his double-dealing: 'bewitched and ungrateful as Ousmane was, she would be living, feeling beside him' (161). Thus, although at the outset she had claimed equality of status in marital relations, in the end she conspires in bringing about her own oppression, her situation being not unlike that of her mother: 'In [Mathilde de La Vallée's] life, only her husband counted. She pampered him, obeyed him and anticipated his slightest whim' (78). Like her mother, too, her dependence gives rise to a feeling of 'total isolation' (78) and '[s]uffering [becomes] an integral part of the rhythm of her existence' (163). Verifying, through her own behaviour, the statement she made about women who remain faithful to philandering husbands, she is eventually 'eaten up with suffering' and she crumbles, killing the baby and stabbing Ousmane.

Mireille's breakdown also brings to the fore her latent racism. When defending her love for Ousmane against her father's racist attacks, she had before her marriage been 'upheld by a sincere belief in the equality of all men' (28). But with the failure of her marriage, she reverts to more conventional western views of Africans, referring to Ouleymatou as a 'painted Negress' (159) and to Ousmane, in precisely the terms her father had used, as 'that object' (158). And although she reminds herself that 'black men are not the only ones who are unfaithful to their wives' (162), the terms of racial abuse with which she assaults Ousmane indicate that she identifies his behaviour with his race.

Thus despite her apparent commitment to social change and hatred of convention, Mireille remains a product of her culture. Like her mother, she chooses to conform to western middle-class definitions of her gender and to accept her subordination in marriage; like her father, she lapses into racist epithets when put to the test. And through her adherence to the values of her culture, she alienates Ousmane who resents her criticism and her attempt to make him adopt French social practices.

Ouleymatou, too, conforms to the categories of her culture, the main difference between the two women being that whereas Mireille considers herself a rebel, Ouleymatou has no illusions about her own values in relation to those of her society. Like her own and Ousmane's mother, she views marriage as a means of social and material enhancement. Determined to share in Ousmane's success, she uses 'all the artful dodges' she has learned through 'contact with experienced women' in order to seduce the man she had earlier rejected (105). Like other women in her community, too, she takes polygyny for granted: 'She was not averse to sharing. Sharing a man was the common lot of women in her circle and the idea of finding a man for herself alone had never crossed her mind' (106). And in her attitude to Mireille, '[t]he *Toubab* wife' (105), she reflects the prejudices of her society.

Scarlet Song offers no positive fictions of female identity, but the negative function of the models provided is emphasized in the narrative. As punishment for her conservatism, Mireille loses her reason. Ouleymatou, on the other hand, is portrayed as an unpleasant character, grasping and selfish. Furthermore, the end of the novel suggests that she, too, will lose a highly valued asset: her new-found source of material well-being. For although Ousmane survives the wounds that Mireille inflicts, he repents of the deeds that have led to the stabbing: 'A feeling of nausea and self-disgust flooded over him. It was he who had been mad and had contaminated Mireille. Only madness could explain his blindness and his actions' (165).

Ousmane is the main character of the novel, as its title with its reference to his bleeding wounds suggests: 'A scarlet song welled up from Ousmane's wounds, the scarlet song of lost hopes' (166). While Ousmane is partly to blame for his own tragedy, as well as for the degradation of Mireille and Ouleymatou, his actions are determined by the socio-historical conditions he meets as a youth growing up in Dakar in the 1950s. By the end of the novel he acquires heroic stature through his recognition of the inadequacy of his response to those conditions.

Like Emecheta's *Double Yoke*, *Scarlet Song* is a novel of male development. The male-authored text to which it seems to be most directly addressed is *The African Child*, Camara Laye's classic narrative of boyhood in Guinea. Like so many of the male-authored texts we have examined, *The African Child* is a 'national allegory'. It can also be classified, though the categories are far from being mutually exclusive, as a novel of (male) self-affirmation[3] written in the Negritude mode, a testimony to the African boy-child's success in meeting the requirements of the French colonial education system and its policy of cultural assimilation. The narrative closes with Laye on a plane bound for Paris, the winner of the ultimate prize: a scholarship to study at a French university. While his achievement costs him the knowledge of indigenous traditions, it has almost no effect on his character as it manifests itself in social interaction. With the exception of his mother who resents her son's moving away from her, his relationships with others – father, grandmother, uncles, playmates, girlfriends – are without tension. And in the end even his mother is reconciled to his leaving her for the world his academic success has opened up to him.

Scarlet Song responds with resistance to such self-affirming fictions of male development, to their idealization of the African past as well as of the male character. For much of their stories, Laye and Ousmane share a similar personal and family history. Like Laye, Ousmane is the favourite child of his mother. Although both come from Muslim homes, each is sent by his father to a French school where he excels in his studies. They also both experience adolescent love, undergo the rites of circumcision in order to prove their manhood, and travel to Paris as part of a programme of self-validation. And from the perspective of adulthood, both look back on childhood with nostalgia. But Ousmane's personal or sexual life, unlike Laye's, is in a state of almost perpetual tension or crisis.

Bâ's response to the idealization of the male character in works such as Laye's is to represent a less romanticized image. She also addresses the romantic depiction of traditions and of the past in the novel of self-affirmation. The primary concern of her novel is with the negative influence of the colonial situation on the male personality, particularly as this effects men's attitudes to and relationships with women. But *Scarlet Song* is also concerned with the influence of patriarchy, in its indigenous form, on the male personality. As a result of the pressures created by his social circumstances, Ousmane is both racially and sexually insecure, and the idyllic romances he dreams of (and Laye writes of) become in his experience exploitative and violent relationships.

In the attitudes he adopts in response to his social conditions, Ousmane generally conforms to the characteristics of the colonized black man as described by Fanon in *Black Skin White Masks*. In Fanon's terms, Ousmane suffers from both inferiority and dependency complexes, the outcome of his contact with western civilization in a colonial context. One of the manifestations of Ousmane's feelings of racial inferiority is his reluctance to tell Mireille about his background. Even though he comes from noble stock and his parents are highly respected in the Senegalese community, he holds back because of the relative poverty of his family: 'He erected a mental barrier between the aristocratic Mireille and the red earth walls of his parents' hut' (20). At the same time, his relationship with Mireille is his way of dealing with the problem of racial insecurity. The relationship also helps him overcome his sexual insecurity, the result of Ouleymatou's rejection of him on the grounds that she is not interested in a boy who spends all his time helping his mother: 'Mireille easily wiped out any lingering memory of Ouleymatou. She was the antidote to the poison in Ousmane's heart; she restored his confidence; she overcame his defences' (22).

Ousmane's trip to Paris is, like Laye's, a validation of his success in meeting the challenges of western education. But for him the ultimate prize is not a scholarship but a white wife. 'If Mireille chose him', he thinks earlier on in the relationship, 'the prophecies of his mother's friends would be fulfilled. They had predicted, "When a son is devoted to his parents, there will always be room for him at the top"' (35). In Fanon's account of colonial education, the black (male) child 'subjectively adopts a white man's attitude', identifying with the white heroes in the books he reads and against his own people (104). Out of this identification arises the need to be acknowledged as white. '[W]ho', Fanon asks, 'but a white woman can do this for me?': 'By loving me she proves that I am worthy of white love. I am loved like a white man. . . . I marry white culture, white beauty, white whiteness' (46). In making his decision to marry Mireille, Ousmane compares himself to 'the hero of a Corneille drama' who is forced to choose between the woman he loves and his own people (36).4 But in his own later analysis, he sees himself as having been 'led astray' when he was a student, 'stuffed with reading and slogans, bewitched by the novelty of the siren song' (150). He also admits that he had been drawn to Mireille 'by the need to assert himself, to rise intellectually and socially' (123). And certainly what attracts him to Mireille is her whiteness, 'her silky golden hair', 'her grey-blue eyes' (16), her 'milk-white neck' (17), 'her milky skin' (63) – every time Ousmane meets Mireille, he is dazzled by her whiteness.

Ousmane also conforms to Fanon's description in becoming a proponent of Negritude in an effort to free himself from white standards:

> He must immerse himself in the heart of his own race, to live according to black values and the rhythmic beat of the tomtom. He was drawn by his past, by his nature, to assume with fervour his own cultural heritage. (92)

In Fanon's view, the assertion of the primacy of black values is an inadequate response to the black man's dilemma. Like Soyinka, he sees it as a defensive reaction which merely reverses the conventional manichean allegory of race. Bâ attacks Negritude on the same grounds through her portrayal of Ousmane in whose conception Mireille and Ouleymatou are antithetical in character because of their different racial heritage. But Bâ reserves her harshest criticism for the sexual allegory that informs Negritude ideology. *Scarlet Song* thus functions intertextually as a critique of critiques which, like Fanon's and Soyinka's, do not take gender into account in their analysis.

Bâ makes explicit the gender codes of Negritude discourse. By exposing some of the internal contradictions of Negritude ideology, she also makes evident the ideological function of those codes: to maintain the status quo of male domination. Seeing his relationship with Ouleymatou as an affirmation of his identity as an African, Ousmane not only, in typical Negritude fashion, apostrophizes the black woman and 'confuses' her (in Bâ's terminology) with Mother Africa, but also casts himself as her liberator:

> 'Ouleymatou, the symbol of my double life!' Symbol of the black woman, whom he had to emancipate; symbol of Africa, one of whose 'enlightened sons' he was.
>
> In his mind he confused Ouleymatou with Africa, 'an Africa which has to be restored to its prerogatives, to be helped to evolve!' When he was with the African woman, he was the prophet of the 'word made truth', the messiah with the unstinting hands, providing nourishment for body and soul. And these roles suited his deep involvement. (149–50)

But as one of Africa's 'enlightened sons', Ousmane is more concerned with maintaining his own male prerogatives than he is with emancipating the black woman whose oppression is sanctioned by the very traditions with which he identifies her. Ouleymatou accepts her oppression because it means an improvement in her material conditions. Her 'liberator', Ousmane defines the limits of her freedom: 'At Ouleymatou's he was lord and master' (148).

Ouleymatou's stature as 'symbol of Africa' contrasts sharply with her lowly status in her relationship with Ousmane and, more generally, in Senegalese society. By pointing up the contrast, Bâ uncovers one of the strategic operations of Negritude literature: to mask the fact of women's oppression by the patriarchal structures of African societies. As Bâ says in the interview quoted earlier: 'There is still so much injustice. . . . In the family, in the institutions, in society, in the street, in political organizations, discrimination reigns supreme' (Schipper 46). In the fictional world of Bâ's novel, Ousmane, contrary to his stated intentions, contributes to the perpetuation of sexual discrimination. In the view of her neighbours, Ouleymatou is 'merchandise that [has] gone to the highest bidder' (135), and they congratulate her on her success in escaping from poverty. A victim of what Cham calls 'distorted cultural nostalgia' (39), Ousmane does not see the extent to which the traditions he celebrates have been deformed by crass materialism. Nor does he have any concept of Ouleymatou's true character, any notion of what living on the margins of society – of being 'badly nourished, badly housed, having to be satisfied when she needed clothes with her mother's rare hand-outs' (105) – has done to her. And in any case, her economic dependence suits his purposes. Transformed in her presence into 'the prophet of "the word made truth", the messiah with the unstinting hands', he finds in her the ideal Other.

At the same time, Ousmane's cultural nostalgia destroys his relationship with Mireille. For her racial otherness, her 'blond beauty' (105), takes on negative value. In his view, he 'would have done better to marry an illiterate black woman' (149). He has no affection for the 'mixed-race' child he has fathered, and he sees any compromise with Mireille as 'the abdication of his own personality' (99). In Fanon's terms, rather than seeking 'to create the ideal conditions of existence for a human world', Ousmane has 'lock[ed him]self into a world of retroactive reparations' (165). And although one of his friends points out to him that he has become as racist in his views as Mireille's father, it is not until he is confronted by Mireille in her madness that he recognizes her humanity and begins to see the limitations of the perspective he has adopted: 'Of what uncompromising dogma had he set himself up as the apostle. . .?' he asks himself (165).

The main ideological function of *Scarlet Song* is to refute Negritude ideology. Bâ responds to Negritude's idealization of the male character by portraying men realistically. Her portrayal of Ousmane can also be seen as a response to the tendency toward male stereotypes in women's fiction. In Cham's view, Bâ's novels are exceptions to the general rule of 'crude, uninformed and sweeping generalizations and stereotypes about male oppression of women in Africa' (35). This assertion is certainly valid in the case of *Scarlet Song*. Ousmane's character is marked, his views are shaped, by the racial and sexual manicheism of his society.

Ousmane's western education has taken him through the process of acculturation. His values have also been shaped in the context of indigenous patriarchy. One of the consequences is that he can see women only in terms of racialized sexual stereotypes. Through her portrayal of Mireille and Ouleymatou, Bâ undercuts these stereotypes by grounding the characters in the societies which have produced them. The two women resemble one another because they both have internalized the norms of their patriarchal societies. Like all good authors of the Negritude school (including Laye), Ousmane objectifies the African woman as 'symbol of Africa', as the embodiment of the cultural values to which he yearns to return. Bâ renders the gender codes underlying the Mother Africa trope explicit through her portrayal of Ousmane's relationship with Ouleymatou. Through her treatment of Ouleymatou, Bâ also counters the idealized image of the African woman engendered by the trope, replacing it with a realistic image.

In *Scarlet Song*, realism is the main weapon that Bâ uses in the struggle against male domination. Realism also plays a role in *So Long a Letter* in that the earlier novel, too, portrays women realistically. The strategic value of these portrayals is twofold. They allow Bâ to raise issues that are of crucial importance to debates on the status and role of women in society. The themes she emphasizes are polygyny, the socialization of women, and women's education. Through these portrayals Bâ also revises conventional male representations of women.

However, in *So Long a Letter*, as we have seen, her portrayal of men is problematic in that her male characters tend toward stereotypes or else they are backgrounded in the narrative. As we have also seen, stereotypical male characters are a trend in women's fiction, one which does not solve the problems of gender, although it does involve a reversal of the manichean allegory of gender and hence is subversive. In *Scarlet Song*, however, a male *bildungsroman*, Bâ seeks to transcend the allegory, just as Emecheta does in *Double Yoke*. Both authors help to resolve the problems of gender by 'making room' within their novels for men.

Part III

MEN WRITE BACK

7

GENDER ON THE AGENDA
Novels of the 1980s by Ngũgĩ and Achebe

Some men writers, 'men of good will' as Mariama Bâ would call them,[1] have also attempted to transcend the sexual allegory and hence to resolve the problems of gender in ways that run counter to the biases embedded in the contemporary African male literary tradition. In my first two chapters, I sought to uncover some of those biases, to probe from the perspective of gender the 'unconscious' of the male tradition in order to reveal what that tradition, as it is embodied in both literature and criticism, has tried to conceal: its social determination in patriarchy. The literary texts that were examined in those chapters were published over a thirty-year period, beginning in 1945 with the appearance of Senghor's 'Femme noire' and ending in 1977 with the publication of Ngũgĩ's *Petals of Blood*. In this, my last chapter, I will examine two male-authored novels that were published in the 1980s, Ngũgĩ's *Devil on the Cross* (1982)[2] and Achebe's *Anthills of the Savannah* (1987). These novels signal an important new departure in contemporary African literature: men writers' engagement with women writers in a dialogue on gender. They also mark a new departure in Ngũgĩ's and Achebe's work, for in each an attempt is made to transform the status of women from that of object to that of subject.

Both Ngũgĩ and Achebe have made statements of authorial intention with regard to the role of their central female characters, statements which indicate a commitment to gender reform. Ngũgĩ opens *Detained*, his prison diary, by hailing Waríínga as his inspiration: 'Waríínga heroine of toil . . . there she walks haughtily carrying her freedom in her hands' (3). Later, he tells of the decision he made regarding her characterization: 'Because the women are the most exploited and oppressed section of the entire working class, I would create a picture of a strong determined woman with a will to resist and to struggle against the conditions of her present being' (10). In an interview he gave shortly after the publication of *Anthills*, Achebe also takes up the theme of women's oppression. His heroine, Beatrice, he suggests, provides a model of womanhood in the role she performs as the harbinger of a new social order:

> We have created all kinds of myths to support the suppression of the woman, and what the group around Beatrice is saying is that the time has now come to put an end to that. . . . The position of Beatrice as sensitive leader of that group is indicative of what I see as necessary in the transition to the kind of society which I think we should be aiming to create.
>
> (Rutherford 4)

Devil on the Cross and *Anthills of the Savannah* both look back to earlier novels by their respective authors, the intertextual relation in each case indicating a desire to correct or to revise earlier images of women. Wariinga's life runs parallel to Wanja's – up to a point. Both women hail from Ilmorog. Both go to Nairobi when a schoolgirl pregnancy blasts their dreams of academic success. Like Wanja, Wariinga has been seduced by a wealthy businessman, a friend of the family, who denies responsibility for the pregnancy. Both have difficulty finding work and both are tempted to resort to prostitution. The similarities end there, for while Wanja succumbs to the temptation, Wariinga does not.[3] Eventually she takes on the role the earlier novel assigns to Karega, that of revolutionary leader. *Anthills* finds in *Things Fall Apart* one of its main intertextual sources. Beatrice alludes to the earlier work in attempting to explain her mysterious influxes of power: 'I do sometimes feel like Chielo in the novel, the priestess and prophetess of the Hills and Caves' (114). Beatrice is, in fact, a priestess of the goddess Idemili, and whereas the novel opens with the machinations of a male elite obsessed with power, it closes with a naming ceremony presided over by women. But *Devil on the Cross* and *Anthills of the Savannah* offer less of a change in sexual coding than might at first glance be evident. Patriarchal thought patterns, it seems, are deeply entrenched. For closer scrutiny shows that, from the perspective of gender, there is considerable continuity between these more recent novels and Ngũgĩ's and Achebe's earlier work, and, more generally, within the male tradition.

Devil on the Cross is a female *bildungsroman*, in this case one written by a male author. It tells the story of Wariinga's development as she passes from girlhood into adulthood and recognizes her identity and role in the world. At the Devil's Feast, a competition among modern thieves and robbers to choose the best means of exploiting the masses, Wariinga faces a spiritual crisis. Challenged by the devil in a dream to account for her passivity in the face of her former lover, the Rich Old Man's treatment of her, she defends her reaction by appealing to conventional notions of her gender: 'I'm a woman. I'm weak. There was nothing I could do' (191). As a result of her enlightenment at the Feast, she undergoes a transformation:

> Today's Wariinga has decided that she'll never again allow herself to be a mere flower, whose purpose is to decorate the doors and windows and tables of other people's lives, waiting to be thrown on to a rubbish heap the moment the splendour of her body withers. The Wariinga of today has decided to be self-reliant all the time, to plunge into the middle of the arena of life's struggles in order to discover her real strength and to realize her true humanity. (216)

But despite his evident concern with gender reform, Ngũgĩ's portrayal of Wariinga, in both her original and her transformed character, can be seen to operate in the interest of preserving patriarchal relations, the very relations that confirm Wariinga's status as sexual object, 'a mere flower' in the lives of men.

This paradox emerges from Ngũgĩ's commitment to a class analysis of history and theory of revolution, a commitment that leads him to conflate patriarchy and neo-colonialism and to impose a single narrative on his heroine's struggle against her oppression: that of class conflict. Robert Young's critique of orthodox Marxism applies equally well to Ngũgĩ's analysis:

> The straightforward oppositional structure of capital and class does not necessarily work any more: if we think in terms of Hegel's master/slave dialectic, then rather than the working class being the obvious universal subject-victim, many others are also oppressed: particularly women, black people, and all other so-called ethnic and minority groups. Any single individual may belong to several of these, but the forms of oppression, as of resistance or change, may not only overlap but may also differ or even conflict. (5)

Ignoring the heterogeneity of subject constitution, Ngũgĩ subordinates gender (as well as all other social distinctions) to class. For him, 'post-colonial' Kenyan history operates according to a single dialectic. The content of *Devil on the Cross*, he asserts in *Detained*, will be '[t]he Kenyan people's struggles against the neo-colonial form and stage of imperialism' (8). A marginalized category in his novel, gender is reconstituted to meet the requirements of the master narrative.

Gender functions as a metaphor for class in the first section of *Devil on the Cross*. Sexually abused and exploited by the men of the new ruling class, Wariinga provides a useful symbol for the degraded state of neo-colonial

Kenya. In order to secure employment, she must first satisfy the demands of the boss whose 'target is [always her] thighs' (19). The conclusion she comes to on the basis of her experience of looking for secretarial work is identical to the one Wanja reaches about women: 'the day on which they are born is the very day on which every part of their body is buried except one – they are left with a single organ' (26). Social values, too, have been reduced and debased, as the leader of the radical students' movement explains to Wariinga:

> [Neo-colonial countries] have been taught the principle and system of self-interest and have been told to forget the ancient songs that glorify the notion of collective good. They have been taught new songs, new hymns that celebrate the acquisition of money. (15).

The analogy becomes explicit when one of the contestants at the Devil's Feast, a man with nationalist loyalties, exhorts foreign investors 'to go back home and rape your own mothers, and leave me to toy with my mother's thighs' (168).

While women serve as an index of the state of the nation, men make up the nation's citizenry. Not only the ruling elite but also 'the people', the workers whose plight Wariinga represents, are defined as male. This identification is implied by the inflections for gender in the oration on the struggle to dominate nature delivered by Mūturi, the one male character in the novel to acquire heroic stature – by the generic pronouns and nouns he uses, as well as by the conventionally male-defined types of 'human' accomplishment he celebrates, and it betrays the patriarchal basis of Ngũgĩ's class perspective:

> Look at the fruits of the combined labour of many hands: roads, and rails, and cars, and trains, and many other types of wheel that permit man to run faster than the hare or the swiftest animal in the forest; aeroplanes that give man wings more powerful and faster than those of any bird in the sky; missiles faster than sound and lightning; . . . telephones, radios, televisions, devices that are able to capture the voice and substance of a human being, so that his face and his voice remain alive even after his body is dead and buried and has decayed. (52)

It is therefore not surprising that when, in the latter part of the novel, Wariinga 'discover[s] her real strength' and 'realize[s] her true humanity', she almost literally develops male characteristics.

Wariinga, 'heroine of toil', 'has said *goodbye* to being a secretary' (218) and has qualified as an engineer and motor mechanic. Not even contemplating the organization of a stenographers' trade union, she enthusiastically takes up a male-defined profession and becomes active in promoting the cause of its (male) workers. In Ngũgĩ's conception, secretaries are not 'workers', a concept which he defines from an exclusively male perspective, hence excluding what are traditionally considered to be women's occupations (clerical work, as well as mothering and prostitution) from his definition. His heroine is also required to undergo a transformation in character – to convert stereotypical feminine qualities into equally stereotypical masculine ones. Whereas the younger Wariinga is passive in her response to her oppressors, the mature Wariinga is aggressive – even violent. A master of the martial arts, she assaults her opponents 'with so many judo kicks and karate chops' (221). An expert marksman, too, she sometimes shoots to kill and sometimes merely shatters kneecaps.

Ngũgĩ leaves the reader in no doubt as to the significance of the weapon with which he equips his heroine. For the conventional symbolic association of the gun with phallic power is made explicit. As Wariinga reminds the Rich Old Man just before she shoots him, she has taken over the role he used to perform when they played the game of 'the hunter and the hunted' (253). In the version they played when they were lovers, the game reached its climax when the Rich Old Man fired his pistol into the sky to announce his sexual conquest. According to the dictates of Ngũgĩ's narrative, Wariinga must become an honourary male before she can acquire heroic stature. With a gun in her possession, she is suitably equipped to participate in the struggle for a more equitable social system for men.

Gender is also a function of class in Ngũgĩ's representation of the opposing sides in the conflict. One of the defining characteristics of the ruling elite is its objectification, as well as commodification, of women. Peasants and workers, on the other hand, are portrayed as being sexually egalitarian. Thus, whereas the boss of the company where Wariinga seeks employment as a secretary first 'eyes [her] from top to toe' and then suggests that they retire to 'the Modern Love *Bar and Lodging*' to sign the contract (19), the mechanics at the garage where she eventually finds work respect her for her ability: 'a deep friendship developed between Wariinga and the other workers' (221). Ngũgĩ's image of gender equality in peasant and working class society bears no relation to reality as he himself seems to admit when, in another context, he urges workers and peasants to unite 'without sexist prejudices' (*Barrel* 41).

Even more problematic is Ngũgĩ's own tendency to objectify women. As Elleke Boehmer observes, Wariinga does not sacrifice her sexual attractiveness to the struggle for a more equitable society ('"Master's Dance"' 16–17). Nor, we might add, does she lose her fashion consciousness. In fact, the manner in which she expresses her new-found revolutionary consciousness tends to be reduced to an improvement in her fashion awareness: 'These days all her clothes fit her perfectly. . . . [T]hey always suit the shape, colour and movement of her beautiful body' (217-18). But even in her ill-chosen secretarial garb, Wariinga is so beautiful that she 'stop[s] men in their tracks' (11). Dressed as a 'worker', she is even more striking, for now '*people* stop to watch her' (217, emphasis added). She is also, as is already evident, frequently caught in the authorial male gaze: 'Her body was a feast for the eyes. [W]hen she walked along the road . . . her breasts sway[ed] jauntily like two ripe fruits in the breeze' (11).

How, then, do we situate Ngũgĩ in his text? How do we explain the contradiction, not only between his stated desire to privilege women and his tendency toward male titillation, but also between his positioning of himself on the side of the peasants and the workers in the struggle and his manifestation of what he himself has designated a bourgeois characteristic? Such contradictions point to the androcentrism of Ngũgĩ's master narrative. He deviates into sexism because his class dialectic leaves no room for the female other. The only way in which he is able to challenge the manichean allegory of gender is to make the other the same as men – equal but with no difference from them. This is what he attempts in his portrayal of Wariinga as a gun-toting revolutionary. From his class perspective, 'a strong determined woman' is to all intents and purposes a man.

The identification of his heroine with masculine values is Ngũgĩ's response to the question of how to create a female national subject, a resolution which is quite different from that of Ogot and Emecheta. For rather than rewriting nationalism, he rewrites woman. As we have seen, the heroine of *Destination Biafra* also, at least briefly, adopts masculine values. But although, like Wariinga, Debbie relishes the power that the possession of a gun gives her – 'I did enjoy making those men obey me', she admits (93) – she comes to adopt a different attitude as a result of her experience, one which marks Emecheta's attempt to incorporate feminine values into the definition of nationalism. By contrast, in Ngũgĩ's representation, such values remain excluded and nationalism is reinscribed as a patriarchal ideology.

The identification of the heroine in masculine terms is, nonetheless, a subversive manoeuvre, albeit a problematic one, for it does at least initiate a reversal of the sexual allegory. But from the perspective Ngũgĩ adopts, woman also remains available for recruitment into the service of the class struggle as the female Other. For his master narrative requires that the demands of all other oppressed groups be sacrificed to those of the workers' struggle. From Ngũgĩ's point of view, there are no contradictions. But as

Young observes, 'forms of oppression, as of resistance' often 'differ or even conflict'. Thus although Wariĩnga determines that 'she'll never again allow herself to be a mere flower', she remains the object of the male gaze. She is the 'flower' of Ngũgĩ's text.

While Ngũgĩ's concern in *Devil on the Cross* is with neo-colonialism and class, in *Anthills of the Savannah* Achebe takes up the issue of state power, exploring in fictional form many of the ideas he deals with more directly in his pamphlet *The Trouble with Nigeria*. As C. L. Innes indicates in her discussion of *Anthills*, Ngũgĩ is one of the implied literary antagonists in Achebe's novel, which, through the character of Ikem, a newspaper editor as well as a creative writer, provides a critique of Marxist readings of recent African history (160). In their place Ikem, who had himself once been a proponent of Marxism, offers what he calls a 'new radicalism', from the perspective of which he views the practice of 'heap[ing] all our problems on the doorstep of capitalism and imperialism' as absurd and irresponsible (158). He also ridicules '[t]hose who would see no blot of villainy in the beloved oppressed nor grant the faintest glimmer of humanity to the hated oppressor' (100), and condemns Marxist revolutionary theory as presumptuous and narrowly dogmatic in its self-assured prescriptions. 'I cannot', he tells the students he is addressing, 'decree your pet, text-book revolution. I want instead to excite general enlightenment by forcing all the people to examine the condition of their lives. . . . As a writer I aspire only to widen the scope of that self-examination. I don't want to foreclose it with a catchy, half-baked orthodoxy' (158). In Ikem's reformed view of social transformation, analyses based on a single oppositional structure are reductive and simplistic. 'There is no universal conglomerate of the oppressed', he asserts. 'The most obvious practical difficulty is the magnitude and heterogeneity of the problem' (98–9).

As Innes likewise observes, Achebe's 'own early works and pronouncements also come under scrutiny' (151). For Achebe himself, in an endorsement of Ikem's views, seeks 'to widen the scope of [his] self-examination'. Of his earlier works, the one which Achebe most obviously interrogates is *Things Fall Apart*. While acknowledging the canonical status of his own first novel through intertextual citation,[4] he nonetheless goes on to revise it through his critique of patriarchal ideology and practices.

Anthills both repeats and negates *Things Fall Apart*. Though they are set in different periods and were written almost thirty years apart, the same kind of historical perspective shapes both narratives. If the main issue to be dealt with in *Things Fall Apart* is the reason for the rapid capitulation of Igbo society to the invading colonial forces, in *Anthills* it is the reason for the equally rapid slide into a corrupt and brutally authoritarian form of government shortly after independence. Beatrice's question near the end of *Anthills* applies to the circumstances in both novels: 'What must a people do to appease an embittered history?' (220). For blame is also similarly attributed, in both cases explicitly not to the potency of external forces, but to an internal weakness: to an imbalance in the local governing ethos between masculine and feminine values. In *Anthills*, this theme is most fully elaborated in symbolic terms, through the juxtaposition of Ikem's prose poem, 'Hymn to the Sun' (30–3), and the myth of Idemili (102–5), in the telling of which Achebe corrects his earlier error in gender ascription. Masculine images of violence and arrogance are set against feminine ones of 'peace and modesty':

> In the beginning Power rampaged through the world, naked. So the Almighty, looking at his creation through the round undying eye of the Sun, saw and pondered and finally decided to send his daughter, Idemili, to bear witness to the moral nature of authority by wrapping around Power's rude waist a loincloth of peace and modesty. (102)

But there is a major difference between the way in which gender is represented in the two novels. For in *Anthills*, agency is granted to women.

While *Anthills* challenges the authority of its author's own earlier and Ngũgĩ's later writing, Achebe seeks rapprochement with the female literary tradition. Beatrice, too, is a writer and the narrator of part of the story, taking on the task of 'bringing together as many broken pieces of this tragic history' as she can (82). Of even greater significance, however, is the fact that she initiates a dialogue on gender with Ikem who is Kangan's most renowned writer and, we are told, 'one of the finest [poets] in the entire English language' (62). In its self-reflexivity, *Anthills* is reminiscent of Emecheta's *Double Yoke* in which, as we have seen, another woman writer, Miss Bulewao, engages in this case a would-be male author, Ete Kamba, in a dialogue on gender. Achebe thus acknowledges the existence of a female literary tradition. He also acknowledges gender as an issue in the African literary tradition, as the site of conflict between men and women writers.

Beatrice is also a feminist, and one whose views have been shaped, not by the western women's movement, even though she has spent many years abroad as a student, but by her experience while she was growing up. 'There was', she says, 'enough male chauvinism in my father's house to last me seven reincarnations' (88). Furthermore, she is transformed in the course of events into a priestess of Idemili, thus undergoing, in her incarnation as a water deity, the same kind of metamorphosis as Nwapa's Efuru does.

It is Beatrice who, through her criticism of his political thinking, leads Ikem to extend the terms and range of his analysis of Kangan political structures and to reconsider the position he has taken up in his writing:

'giving women today the same role which traditional society gave them of intervening only when everything else has failed' (91). Acknowledging his indebtedness to Beatrice for the insight, Ikem goes beyond the distinction Uchendu makes in *Things Fall Apart* between the idealization of motherhood and the subordinate role of women in society and exposes the hypocrisy of his forebears' gender ideology:

> '*Nneka*, they said. Mother is supreme. Let us keep her in reserve until the ultimate crisis arrives and the waist is broken and hung over the fire. . . . Then, as the world crashes around Man's ears, Woman in her supremacy will descend and sweep the shards together.' (98)

As Ikem explains, making it evident that it is his female characters he is reviewing, he has only just realized 'that a novelist must listen to his characters who after all are created to wear the shoe and point the writer where it pinches' (97).

Beatrice is also instrumental in the process whereby her boyfriend, Chris, broadens his conception of state leadership and power. The Commissioner for Information in the cabinet of his and Ikem's former classmate, Sam, Chris is even slower than Ikem to realize the importance of establishing 'vital inner links with the poor and dispossessed' (141). His dying words are 'a coded message' to Beatrice acknowledging the justness of her accusation of conceit on the part of the old school friends in their attitude to rulership, as well as the accuracy of her prediction that their obsession with power would destroy all three of them. 'The last green bottle' (231), the last member of '[t]he trinity who thought they owned Kangan' (191), has fallen.

After the death of Ikem, Chris, and Sam, power continues to rampage through the Kangan world of public affairs as another male elite seizes control of the state. But in the novel's final chapter, Achebe changes the focus of his narrative from the domain of power politics to the social sphere where Beatrice, in her new role as the priestess of Idemili, assumes power. The group that gathers in Beatrice's flat for a naming ceremony is carefully constituted, a reminder of Ikem's observations on the multi-faceted nature of oppression. Signalling, in Achebe's words, 'the possibility of a new beginning' (Rutherford 3), the assembly embraces class, religious, ethnic, and sexual difference. But gender is the category Achebe most favours in his representation of an alternative politics. Three female figures move into the narrative space formerly occupied by the male trinity: Beatrice, Ikem's lover, Elewa, and Elewa's baby. Seizing the traditional male role of naming the child, Beatrice gives the baby girl a boy's name, Amaechina, 'May-the-path-never-close' (222). It is to women, then, that Achebe assigns the task of '[appeasing] an embittered history'.

At the same time, Achebe's representational strategies manifest striking contradictions and ambivalences – tensions which reveal the novel's social determination in patriarchy. For while gender is his privileged (though not exclusive) category, and feminine values are valorized over masculine ones, women are repeatedly subordinated to men in the narrative. As a consequence, Achebe avoids addressing the question which is posed in such novels as *The Graduate*, *Destination Biafra* and *Devil on the Cross* of how to create a female national subject. He is, it would seem, prepared to answer this charge by claiming, as Ikem does, that it is up to women to define for themselves the new role they will perform in the nation. 'I should never have presumed to know [what that role will be]', Ikem tells Beatrice. '*You* have to tell us. We never asked you before' (98). As Boehmer states in her discussion of *Anthills*, 'Achebe's refusal to dictate' to women the roles they are to assume in public affairs 'represents a significant advance in the African novel' ('Of Goddesses' 108). However, he leaves very little space in his narrative for female subjectivity.

This is, perhaps, nowhere so clearly evident than in Achebe's continuing refusal to generalize gender reference to include women as significant humans. Particularly telling is the passage in which the importance of metaphor or art as a basis for understanding is stressed. For while it refers to the cultural encoding of the goddess Idemili, it implicitly excludes women from the creative process:

> Man's best artifice to snare and hold the grandeur of divinity always crumbles in his hands, and the more ardently he strives the more paltry and incongruous the result. So it were better he did not try at all; far better to ritualize that incongruity and by invoking the mystery of metaphor to hint at the most unattainable glory by its very opposite, the most mundane starkness. (103)

In the main narrative, too, women operate on the periphery of the creative process, lacking, it would seem, the imaginative faculty and intellectual force necessary to create such things as poetry or political visions themselves. Even though Beatrice is a writer, her primary function in the novel is to inspire, support, and celebrate great men. Ikem quite explicitly casts her in the role of muse to his creative powers when, on his last visit to her flat, he pays tribute to Christopher Okigbo by describing the artist's path to immortality as leading him through 'the complex and paradoxical cavern of Mother Idoto' (101). And it is Ikem who formulates an alternative politics and Chris who first translates Ikem's ideas into action. Furthermore, the biblical allusions that pervade the novel confirm men's exalted status in that Ikem, who is killed when he makes his views public, is defined as John the Baptist, 'the precursor' who '[makes] straight the way' (114), while Chris, who dies attempting to save a young woman from rape, takes on the role of redeemer, as his name suggests.

In Achebe's estimation, women's true creativity would seem to be confined to child-bearing. At least this appears to be the case with Elewa, a shop-assistant whose sole significance in the first instance is that she is 'Ikem's girl'. For when it emerges, after the violent and tragic events, that she is 'carrying . . . a living speck of [Ikem] within her', she is transformed 'into an object of veneration' (184). But while 'Mother' remains 'Supreme', women are marginalized even in the reproductive process. For, as Boehmer observes, 'the implicit idea . . . of masculine influence as life-giving' runs through the novel ('Of Goddesses' 108). Thus not only is it 'a living speck' of Ikem that Elewa carries, but the name Amaechina is translated as 'The Shining Path of Ikem' (222).

Beatrice's significance, too, is determined primarily by her sex. Her relationship not only with Chris but also with Ikem and Sam is essentially sexual. Ikem responds to his muse's excitation with passionate kisses which leave Beatrice 'trembling violently' (101), while Sam responds to her more overtly sexual gestures with 'a gigantic erection' (81). Moreover, in contrast to the men, she has no same-sex relationships until she is, under the influence of Ikem's thinking, prompted to cross class boundaries and befriend Elewa. Nor is her character defined by her work, as the men's are, even though she, too, occupies a high-level government position. We never see Beatrice on the job and none of the scenes is set in her office. In fact, the only space she occupies is that which is conventionally considered domestic, social, and/or sexual. The sex scenes in the novel, of which there are several, are in themselves revealing of Achebe's ambivalence about gender equality. Although Beatrice is said to be in control during sex – 'this was her grove and these her own peculiar rites over which she held absolute power' (114) – her own experience is left out of the narrative, while Chris's is described in considerable detail. Elewa's and Ikem's sexual encounters are narrated from the same perspective. While she commands the action, it is he who has sex.

In the novel's final scene a woman acquires full subject status. But even then she is, in contrast, say, to Juanina in Ogot's *The Graduate*, allowed to exercise power only within certain limited boundaries which confirm the separate spheres of the sexes. Moreover, it is not until after the demise of the trinity that Beatrice assumes power. Thus while, on the one hand, Achebe challenges traditional gender relationships by calling into question the role in public affairs that is customarily assigned to women, on the other, he sanctions conventional arrangements by imposing the same old pattern on his narrative: 'as the world crashes around Man's ears, Woman in her supremacy . . . descend[s] and sweep[s] the shards together'.

The version of the myth of Idemili that is told in *Anthills* conforms to the same model, as well as to strict notions of what are masculine and feminine in politics.[5] As part of the same logic, this version of the myth assigns to Idemili the stereotypical female role of civilizing men. For Idemili's function, as Achebe defines it, is not to empower women but to moderate male power: 'to bear witness to the moral nature of authority by wrapping around Power's rude waist a loincloth of peace and modesty'. Thus, although Beatrice is, like Efuru, defined by a water deity myth, the myth, in this case, attests less to the legitimacy of even a limited form of female power than it does to the need for men to revise their ideas of leadership and power.[6] By the same token, one might ask whether Beatrice's apotheosis at the end of the novel is not mainly a vehicle for Achebe's resolution to the problems of male power.[7]

At the same time, in her role as Idemili's priestess, Beatrice seems to embody her author's continuing ambivalence toward female power. For she bears some of the familiar markings of the femme fatale and hence resembles Chielo and Idoto in ways other than those that are overtly expressed in the narrative. Once again female sexuality is associated with destruction and death. Encountering 'that other [goddessy] Beatrice' (199) during their love-making, Chris finds himself, rather as Egbo does in his encounters with Simi, 'always almost sucked . . . into fatal depths' by the 'deep over-powering eddies of [her] passion' (105). Threatened by her sexuality, Chris fears that he will be deprived of his power. '[W]ould he be found worthy? Would he survive?', he anxiously wonders (114). Both questions are answered in the negative, for Beatrice's prophecy of the demise of the trinity, a prophecy which is not only divinely inspired but is also the main means by which the narrative is structured, is a death warrant. Like Idemili whom she serves, Beatrice 'sends death to smite him' who, in her eyes, is 'unworthy' (104).[8]

In possessing vatic, as well as sexual, power, Beatrice also resembles a number of her literary predecessors, including Chielo. Considering that she is a writer, she seems to incarnate (male) authorial anxieties about female literary power. For through the destructive power of her words, she kills off the men who have power over the production and distribution of the word in Kangan, including Ikem, the nation's foremost man of letters. But in what can be seen as a compensatory gesture, Achebe minimizes the danger posed by literary women by identifying Beatrice with Idemili and hence with oral culture. Elewa, the only other female character of any significance, is barely literate.

169

From the point of view of the female characters, then, 'the shoe' still 'pinches'. There is not much room for women in *Anthills of the Savannah*. They are mainly vehicles for the resolution to issues in male ideology. In time-honoured fashion, Elewa bears a baby, symbol of a better future and witness to the potency of the authorial vision as it is conveyed in Ikem's 'new radicalism'. In similar fashion, Beatrice embodies cultural values which, in her author's view, will generate renewal. *Devil on the Cross* makes more space for woman herself to be the subject of transformation, but the transformation requires what amounts to a sex-change on the part of the heroine.

Both *Devil on the Cross* and *Anthills of the Savannah* bear the marks of the pressure that has been brought to bear on male authors by women's writing and feminist criticism. The nature of the influence of the female literary tradition on these texts is in the main positive. While Ngũgĩ creates a heroine who is more courageous, resourceful, and intelligent than any of the men in his novel, Achebe takes on gender as a category of socio-political analysis and privileges feminine values. Moreover, both authors represent women as being in the forefront of history. While Wariinga takes the lead in engaging in class warfare, Beatrice presides over an assembly which signals the possibility of a new social order coming into being.

There is, however, continuity as well as discontinuity between these novels and their male predecessors. For both authors fall back into familiar patterns and hence on to the manichean allegory of gender. Nonetheless, the range of representations of women in the male literary tradition is considerably broadened with the advent of Wariinga and Beatrice. Mechanical engineer, revolutionary leader, top civil servant, writer, and feminist are added to what is a paltry list – daughter, wife, mother, prostitute. . . .

It is, however, by engaging with women writers in a dialogue on gender that Ngũgĩ in *Devil on the Cross* and Achebe in *Anthills of the Savannah* make their most significant contribution to the development of African literature. For by writing back to women writers from their position as canonical authors, they transform the status of gender from that of a covert category to that of an officially recognized and important item on the agenda of African men's literature.

CONCLUSION
Redefining the African literary tradition

As JanMohamed claims, a dialogue on race with colonial discourse is 'a fundamental component of contemporary African literature'. Colonialism is, in other words, as he and other critics have demonstrated, a factor which has influenced the development of African literature. What I have tried to show is that a dialogue on gender is also a definitive feature of the African literary tradition, that patriarchy, too, is an important factor in the development of African literature. It is a factor that has been ignored by critics who, like JanMohamed, theorize African literature as having been shaped by the socio-political conditions of its production. For them, colonialism or, as with Ngũgĩ, neo-colonialism – and these only in their racial or class aspects – constitute the sole political context of African culture and history. The exclusion of patriarchy as a determinate historical, social, and political condition has a number of interrelated consequences for current theories of African literature. These include an obscuring of the complexity of the interaction between colonial and African (male) literature; and the construction of a literary tradition from which women's writing is excluded.

Gender is a submerged category in colonial discourse, a status that it has maintained until recently in African men's literature. While African men writers challenge the racial codes of colonial discourse and attempt to subvert them, they adopt certain aspects of the gender coding of their supposed adversaries in their representation of African women. Thus what Busia calls 'the voicelessness of the black woman' is a trope with a very long history, one which can be traced from Shakespeare's *The Tempest* through colonial texts like Conrad's *Heart of Darkness* to African representations of the colonial encounter such as Achebe's *Things Fall Apart*. The genesis of the Mother Africa trope, a trope that pervades the African male literary tradition from Senghor to Soyinka, can also be seen as colonial literature.

Such figures illustrate the way in which colonial and African (male) literary discourse sometimes interlink. The relationship between them is not, as JanMohamed, following Jameson's characterization of the dialogical, claims, solely an antagonistic one. For even though the figures fulfil a different ideological function in African than they do in colonial writing (serving as a means in the latter for legitimating colonialism and in the former for legitimating 'post-colonial' male domination), the form of the dialogical is essentially affirmative. What is revealed by such instances of what is basically non-parodic reiteration is the patriarchal nature of both European imperialism and African nationalism, a coincidence of interests and complicity between two groups of men who share a will to power.

Following Fanon, JanMohamed posits the trope of the racial allegory as a field of interchangeable oppositions between white and black, good and evil, superiority and inferiority, subject and object, self and other. I posit a somewhat different figure, that of the sexual allegory, as another field of oppositions, in this case between male and female, good and evil, superiority and inferiority, subject and object, self and other. What I have tried to show is the difference between the ways in which African men and women writers have negotiated this field: while men writers tend to valorize the sexual allegory, women writers attempt to subvert it.

For Jameson, ideology consists of '*strategies of containment*, whether intellectual or (in the case of narratives) formal' (*Political Unconscious* 52–3). The function of such strategies is to legitimate the power position of one's self and group. The burden of my reading of the African male literary tradition has been to reveal the strategies of containment to which men writers have resorted in their attempt to legitimate patriarchal ideology. These include the embodiment of Africa in the figure of a woman, one of the most enabling tropes of 'post-colonial' male domination as well as of colonialism; the portrayal of women as passive and voiceless, images that serve to rationalize and therefore to perpetuate inequality between the sexes; and the romanticization and idealization of motherhood, a means of masking women's subordination in society. They also encompass the assignment of different roles in the anti-colonial struggle to men and women – the allocation to the former of the task of mending the breach in the historical continuum and to the latter of embodying African cultural values; the assumption of the primacy of the male subject; the objectification of women; their identification with tradition and with biological roles; the representation of female sexuality as dangerous and destructive; and the resolution of narrative tension with the theme of redemption through repatriation to the village. These strategies of containment, the 'unconscious' from the perspective of gender of the male literary tradition, are as characteristic a feature of that tradition as are the strategies of intervention or subversive manoeuvres that (mainly) define its relation to colonial discourse.

The common struggle against racism unites men and women writers. Thus writers of both sexes attempt to transcend the racial allegory. But even here there are differences in representational strategies. For the colonized woman is doubly oppressed, enmeshed in the structures of an indigenous patriarchy and of a foreign masculinist-colonialism. Thus, women writers interrogate the sexual as well as the racial codes of colonial discourse. Thus, too, whereas the tendency in male literature is to counter colonial misrepresentations with valorizations of indigenous traditions, women writers are as critical of those traditions as they are of colonialism. And while the historical fact of women's resistance both to colonial and indigenous male domination is suppressed in the male literary tradition, it is highlighted in women's writing.

African women's writing is a multi-voiced discourse. As McLuskie and Innes observe: 'When women began publishing their work in the mid-sixties in Africa, they faced the problem not only of speaking for the experience of women in their own right . . . but also of combatting the orthodoxies of colonial and anti-colonial writing' (4). In fact, by merely writing when they did, Ogot and Nwapa challenged a number of orthodoxies: 'the voicelessness of the black woman', for instance, and her lack of subjectivity and historical reference, as well as the definition of female creativity as residing solely in the womb and its corollary: the notion of writing as an exclusively male activity. As we have seen, the response of the critical establishment was to read their texts according to its ingrained sexual prejudices.

While the interrogation of colonial texts is one of the undertakings of African women's literature, its primary engagement is with the African male literary tradition. In this system of exchange, the form of the dialogical is mainly, but not entirely, antagonistic. Adversarial interaction takes a number of different forms, including straightforward denunciation. Such confrontational tactics are, however, much less prevalent than are strategies of negotiation or intervention. Of these, the one which women writers most frequently employ in their attempt to subvert patriarchal ideology is inversion. Negotiation occurs at more than one level, as both thematic and formal categories are placed under revision.

Inversion often operates in conjunction with appropriation. Thus the process of discrediting the Okonkwo-type hero in *The Promised Land* and *Efuru* works by merging or replacing positive images, appropriated from the dominant discourse, with negative ones; and that of legitimating female power in several of Nwapa's novels involves the replacement of negative representations with positive ones, taken from the established literary order. Thus, too, the convention of the paired women depends on the appropriation for what is conventionally represented as deviant behaviour of positive identifications: freedom, fulfilment, integrity. The refiguration of the topos of the mother and that of the prostitute works in a similar manner, as does the re/de-construction of heroic values in *Destination Biafra*, of Negritude ideology in *Scarlet Song*, and of the male novel of development, the creation of a female form of the genre.

Inversion is also, as we have seen, the basis of male/female character portrayal in a number of novels. Its operation is, perhaps, most clearly seen in Ogot's debasement of the male and elevation of the female subject, but it is also evident in such works as *Efuru*, *The Joys of Motherhood*, and *So Long a Letter* in the juxtaposition of male stereotypes and female protagonists who are complex characters. As we have also seen, male critics have objected to women writers' derogatory portrayals of their gender. They have not, however, it should be noted, raised the issue of men writers' portrayal of women.

As has been indicated in earlier chapters, both Fanon and Soyinka regard inversion, as it is practised in Negritude discourse, as an inadequate strategy. For, they argue, it replicates and hence reinstates the oppressive structure of white/black binary opposition that characterizes colonial discourse. The inversion of patriarchal manicheism in African women's literary discourse does not resolve the problems of gender, but it does at least unmask the strategies of containment in which men writers engage, thus exposing the strategic operations of the discursive field produced by the sexual allegory. The same kind of argument can, of course, be made with regard to the inversion of colonial manicheism. It can also be argued that inversion is a necessary stage in the process of resistance, a view that has been advanced by Jonathan Dollimore:

> Jacques Derrida reminds us that binary oppositions are 'a violent hierarchy' where one of the two terms forcefully governs the other. A crucial stage in their deconstruction involves an overturning, an inversion 'which brings low what was high'. The political effect of ignoring this stage, of trying to move beyond the hierarchy into a world quite free of it, is simply to leave it intact in the only world we have. (190)

Inversion is the basis of male/female character portrayal throughout Ogot's and Nwapa's fiction. Emecheta and Bâ have, however, in at least one novel each, moved beyond this stage in the process of deconstructing the gender hierarchy. It is, perhaps, not insignificant that it is the more recent

174

arrivals on the literary scene, rather than 'the old guard', who have undertaken this project. The male protagonists of Emecheta's *Double Yoke* and Bâ's *Scarlet Song* are both complex characters. Neither is reduced to a stereotype and each is portrayed as having been shaped by particular social, political, and historical conditions. In addition, *Double Yoke* and *Scarlet Song* are male *bildungsromane*, that is novels that put male subjectivity in process. The portrayals in these novels can thus be seen as an attempt on the part of Emecheta and Bâ to reduce the level of antagonism in the literary dialogue on gender. In representing the male other as a subject, Emecheta and Bâ also attempt to transcend the manichean allegory of gender.

The female tradition in African fiction that emerges through the writing of Ogot, Nwapa, Emecheta, and Bâ is in part defined by its antagonistic relationship with colonial and African men's literature. As these authors belong to different generations and come from two different regions and three different countries in Africa, their works can be taken as paradigmatic. The interrogation of the racial and sexual codes of colonial discourse and the subversion of African male literary discourse are characteristic features of African women's fiction.

But as McLuskie and Innes indicate, African women also write out of their own needs and not only out of a concern with the colonial or African male other. Their literature is in a dialogic relation with other discourses that circulate in their societies. Nwapa, for instance, draws on the Igbo tradition of female power in *Efuru*, and Bâ on Islamic discourse in *So Long a Letter*. They also engage with each other's texts, the manifest intertextuality between several of Nwapa's and Emecheta's works being one of the clearest indications of the emergence of a female literary tradition. Their literature also displays a certain thematic and formal coherence. Marriage, motherhood, emotional and economic independence, women's education, their political and economic marginalization, their resistance to oppression and role in the nation-state are among the recurring motifs of African women's fiction. And while the convention of the paired women operates as a strategy of resistance, it also has a history within women's literature, as does the female novel of development.

By actively participating in the dialogue on gender, Ngũgĩ and Achebe acknowledge women's literary expression not only as an existing, parallel tradition, but also as part of African literature. They are, however, only partly successful in the attempt they make in *Devil on the Cross* and *Anthills of the Savannah* to dismantle the gender codes of African male literary discourse. The main strategy of intervention that we see in operation in these works is, as in women's writing, inversion. But in each case the inversion is reversed in the narrative. In Ngũgĩ's text, sexual objectification is combined with

CONCLUSION

the subversive, though problematic, manoeuvre of identifying the heroine in masculine terms. Achebe's treatment of gender is full of contradictions. Women are portrayed as being in the forefront of history and feminine values are privileged over masculine ones. At the same time, women are repeatedly subordinated to men in the narrative and female sexuality is identified in negative terms. Despite their reinscription of conventional gender codes, or possibly even because of it, their texts are particularly graphic in their exposure of the operations of the manichean allegory of gender.

Women writers have earned a place in African literary history. Writing in the main against the canon, they have redefined the African literary tradition. Uncovering gaps and silences, exposing biases and prejudices, they have renamed it a male tradition and declared the canon an artificial construct. They have also altered the conditions of reading African literature. Furthermore, by initiating a dialogue on gender, women writers have occasioned a change in the orientation of African literature. Gender and gender relations have been an issue in contemporary African literature from the beginning. As I have tried to show, one of the 'necessities' out of which it evolved was that of rationalizing male domination. The difference now is that gender is ceasing to be a submerged category in men's writing and is becoming more and more an issue that must be dealt with explicitly by both writers and critics.

The critical practice of excluding women's literary expression from African literature is in Jameson's terms 'a socially symbolic act'. It reproduces in symbolic form, and therefore reinforces, institutional forms of exclusion that operate to marginalize women in society. What I have tried to do is to write women's writing back into the African literary tradition, a task that has also been undertaken by a number of the authors, men as well as women, whose works I have examined. Its antagonistic relationship with colonial literature is a characteristic feature of this tradition. For whatever differences there may be in representational strategies, the struggle against racism is one which engages both men and women writers. The affirmative aspects of the African literary dialogue on gender is also a defining feature of the contemporary African literary tradition. As we have seen, writers of both sexes have made moves to reduce the level of antagonism in the dialogue on gender. In so doing, they produce fiction that belongs primarily neither to a male nor to a female literary tradition, but rather to an African one. The joint effort to transcend the manichean allegory of gender marks a new moment in African literature, one that looks forward to the (re)emergence of more sexually egalitarian societies.

NOTES

INTRODUCTION
Exclusionary practices

1   For a critique of Taiwo's book, see Ama Ata Aidoo, 'To be an African woman writer—an overview and a detail', in Kirsten Holst Petersen (ed.) *Criticism and Ideology: Second African Writers' Conference, Stockholm 1986*, Uppsala, Scandinavian Institute of African Studies, 1988: 155–72. Aidoo aptly characterizes Taiwo's book as 'patronizing', 'self-righteous', and 'insensitive'. She also exposes his androcentrism and his careless reading of women's novels.

2   In their concern with (white) western women writers' exclusion from the canon, Nina Bahm, 'Melodramas of beset manhood: how theories of American fiction exclude women authors', in Elaine Showalter (ed.) *The New Feminist Criticism: Essays on Women, Literature, and Theory*, London, Virago, 1986, 63–80; and Lillian S. Robinson, 'Treason our text: feminist challenges to the literary canon', in Showalter, op. cit.: 105–21, make the same point as Krupat.

3   Ashcroft and his colleagues subsume both race and gender into coloniality in their attempt to make their theory applicable to 'all post-colonial literatures' (2). For a critique of their model in terms of its conflation of 'first-' and 'third-world' colonialist experience, see Arun P. Mukherjee, 'Whose post-colonialism and whose postmodernism?', *World Literature Written in English*, 1990, 30.2: 1–9.

4   See Ifi Amadiume, *Male Daughters, Female Husbands: Gender and Sex in an African Society*, London, Zed, 1987; Kwame Arhin, 'The political and military roles of Akan women', in Christine Oppong (ed.) *Female and Male in West Africa*, London, George Allen & Unwin, 1983: 91–8; Kamene Okonjo, 'Sex roles in Nigerian politics', in Oppong, op. cit.: 211–22; Kamene Okonjo, 'Women's political participation in Nigeria', in Filomena Chioma Steady (ed.) *The Black Woman Cross-Culturally*, Cambridge, Mass., Schenkman, 1981: 79–106; Mona Etienne, 'Gender relations and conjugality among the Baule', in Oppong, op. cit.: 303–19; Jeanne K. Henn, 'Women in the rural economy: past, present, and future', in Margaret Jean Hay and Sharon Stichter (eds) *African Women South of the Sahara*, London, Longman, 1984: 1–18; Jean O'Barr, 'African women in politics', in Hay and Stichter, op. cit.: 140–55; and Omolara Ogundipe-Leslie, 'African women, culture and another development', *Présence Africaine*, 1987, 141.1: 129–32.

5   For evidence of the under-representation of girls and women in African educational systems in the period 1960–75, see Helen Ware, 'Female and male life-cycles', in Oppong, op. cit.: 10–15. See also Ayesha Imam, 'The myth of equal opportunity in Nigeria', in Miranda Davies (ed.) *Third World – Second Sex*, vol. 2, London, Zed, 1987: 99–103; and Carolyne Dennis, 'Women and the state in Nigeria', in Haleh Afshar (ed.) *Women, State, and Ideology*, Albany, State University of New York Press, 1987: 17–18.

6   Kamene Okonjo, 'Sex roles in Nigerian politics', in Oppong, op. cit.: 211–22; Amadiume, op. cit.: 147–72.

7   Of course, 'first-world' states are also defined by their experience, in this case as agents, of imperialism; and their literature is replete with ideological valorizations of this experience. Jameson also classifies 'all third-world texts' as 'non-canonical' (65), a classification that operates on the assumption that other cultures do not have literary traditions.

8   For Achebe, see *Morning Yet on Creation Day*, London, Heinemann, 1975: 55–62; and *Hopes and Impediments: Selected Essays 1965–1987*, Oxford, Heinemann, 1988: 40–1. For Ngũgĩ, see *Decolonizing the Mind: The Politics of Language in African Literature*, London, James Currey, 1986.

9   For a brief discussion of Achebe's engagement of African Marxists in *Anthills of the Savannah*, see C. L. Innes, *Chinua Achebe*, Cambridge, Cambridge University Press, 1990: 159–60. In Chapter 7, I also consider Achebe's critique of Marxism in *Anthills*. For Soyinka, see *Kongi's Harvest*, Oxford, Oxford University Press, 1967; and *Opera Wonyosi*, London, Rex Collings, 1981, especially the foreword. For Ngũgĩ, see *Writers in Politics*, London, Heinemann, 1981: 71–81; and *Petals of Blood*, London, Heinemann, 1987, especially 199–200.

10   See, for example, Barbara Smith, 'Toward a Black feminist criticism', in Showalter, op. cit.: 168–74; Deborah E. McDowell, 'New directions for Black feminist criticism', in Showalter, op. cit.: 186–8; Alice Walker, *In Search of Our Mothers' Gardens: Womanist Prose*, London, Women's Press, 1984: 371–6; Gayatri Chakravorty Spivak, 'Three women's texts and a critique of imperialism', in Henry Louis Gates Jr (ed.) *'Race', Writing, and Difference*, Chicago, University of Chicago Press, 1986: 262–80; Hazel V. Carby, ' "On the threshold of woman's era": lynching, empire, and sexuality in Black feminist theory', in Gates, op. cit.: 301–16; Amadiume, op. cit.: 3–10; and Kamene Okonjo, 'The dual-sex political system in operation: Igbo women and community politics in Midwestern Nigeria', in Nancy J. Hafkin and Edna G. Bay, (eds) *Women in Africa: Studies in Social and Economic Change*, Stanford, Stanford University Press, 1976: 45.

11   See Alison Perry, 'Meeting Flora Nwapa', *West Africa*, 18 June 1984: 1262; and Buchi Emecheta, 'Feminism with a small "f"!', in Petersen, op. cit.: 173–81.

12   Recently several studies have appeared which examine the gender codes of colonial literature. See, for example, David Bunn, 'Embodying Africa: women and romance in colonial fiction', *English in Africa*, 1988: 15.1: 1–28; Abena P. A. Busia, 'Silencing Sycorax: on African colonial discourse and the unvoiced female', *Cultural Critique*, 1989–90: 14: 81–103; and Sandra M. Gilbert and Susan Gubar, *Sexchanges*, vol. 2 of *No Man's Land: The Place of the Woman Writer in the Twentieth Century*, New Haven, Yale University Press, 1989: 3–46.

13   This trope clearly participates in several systems. In her discussion of representations of African women, Kathleen M. McCaffrey observes that 'the image

of the mother, as fertile and bountiful as the African earth itself, is found everywhere' in African sculpture and orature. From this perspective, it is an oral form that contemporary men writers engage and transform. See Kathleen M. McCaffrey, 'Images of women in West African literature and film: a struggle against dual colonization', *International Journal of Women's Studies*, 1980, 3.1: 76. More recently, Manthia Diawara has argued that the trope, as it occurs in such contemporary Mande texts as Camara Laye's *The African Child*, is a redeployment of the metaphor of woman as mother Mande which is found in classical Mande narratives such as *The Epic of Soundiata*. See Manthia Diawara, 'Canonizing Soundiata in Mande literature: toward a sociology of narrative elements', *Social Text*, 1992, 31/2: 154–68.

1 HOW COULD THINGS FALL APART FOR WHOM THEY WERE NOT TOGETHER?

1   These figures were provided by the moderator for the Annual South Bank Show Lecture for 1990, delivered by Achebe on 18 January 1990.

2   For Achebe's view of Cary, see Dennis Duerden and Cosmo Pieterse (eds) *African Writers Talking*, London, Heinemann, 1975: 4; and Chinua Achebe, *Morning Yet on Creation Day*, London, Heinemann, 1975: 70.

3   A considerable amount of useful biographical information on Achebe is provided by C. L. Innes, *Chinua Achebe*, Cambridge, Cambridge University Press, 1990: 4–12.

4   Flora Nwapa's *Idu* (1970) interrogates *Things Fall Apart* on this matter by expanding the Ndulue–Ozoemena story into a novel in which women are represented as having substantial social and economic power. '[Idu and Adiewere] understand each other so well', the townspeople say, 'that nobody ever hears their quarrel' (2). When Adiewere dies suddenly, Idu wills herself to die, too.

5   See also Eustace Palmer, *An Introduction to the African Novel*, London, Heinemann, 1972: 52–3; Gerald Moore, *Twelve African Writers*, London, Hutchinson, 1980: 125; and Lewis Nkosi, *Tasks and Masks: Themes and Styles of African Literature*, Harlow, Longman, 1981: 36.

6   See, for example, Abdul R. JanMohamed, *Manichean Aesthetics: The Politics of Literature in Colonial Africa*, Amherst, University of Massachusetts Press, 1983: 162–5; Carole Boyce Davies, 'Motherhood in the works of male and female Igbo writers: Achebe, Emecheta, Nwapa and Nzekwu', in Carole Boyce Davies and Anne Adams Graves (eds) *Ngambika: Studies of Women in African Literature*, Trenton, New Jersey, Africa World Press, 1986: 245–6; and Innes, op. cit.: 25–9.

7   See, for example, Palmer, op. cit.: 53; Nkosi, op. cit.: 35; Kofi Awoonor, *The Breast of the Earth: A Survey of the History, Culture, and Literature of Africa South of the Sahara*, Garden City, New York, Anchor/Doubleday, 1975: 253; and JanMohamed, op. cit.: 183.

8   Loesch's definition of these terms is cited in Casey Miller and Kate Swift, *Words and Women*, New York, Anchor, 1977: 44.

9   For a brief account of women's engagement in the anti-colonial struggle in Ghana, Kenya, Nigeria, and Zambia, see Robin Morgan (ed.) *Sisterhood is Global: The International Women's Movement Anthology*, Garden City, New York, Anchor/Doubleday, 1984: 257, 393, 497–8, and 741. See also Maria Rosa Cutrufelli, *Women of Africa: Roots of Oppression*, trans. Nicolas Romano, London,

Zed, 1983: 170–5; Agnes Akosua Aidoo, 'Asante Queen Mothers in government and politics in the nineteenth century', in Filomena Chioma Steady (ed.) *The Black Woman Cross-Culturally*, Cambridge, Mass., Schenkman, 1985; 74–5; Judith Van Allen, '"Aba Riots" or "Women's War"? ideology, stratification, and the invisibility of women', in Nancy J. Hafkin and Edna G. Bay (eds) Women in Africa: Studies in Social and Economic Change, Stanford, Stanford University Press, 1976: 59–85; and Ifi Amadiume, Male Daughters, Female Husbands: Gender and Sex in an African Society, London, Zed, 1987: 120–2 and 138–40.

10   For a summary of this argument, see JanMohamed, op. cit.: 42. I draw on this summary in the discussion that follows.

11   Nuruddin Farah identifies *Things Fall Apart* as one of the pre-texts for his fourth novel, *Sardines* (1981), by making reference to this folktale in the opening pages. The novel's main protagonist Medina, we are told, has 'given the interpretive title "He" 'to a folktale she has 'adapted from Chinua Achebe's Things Fall Apart' (3). What we learn about Medina's adaptation of the tale suggests that Farah has subverted its conventional meaning by transforming the story into a satire on male egoism. What we have here, then, is an instance of intertextuality between men writers' texts. Furthermore, Farah's treatment of the tale suggests that men writers have also engaged each other in a dialogue on gender.

2   THE MOTHER AFRICA TROPE

1   I have borrowed this image from Omolara Ogundipe-Leslie, 'The female writer and her commitment', *African Literature Today*, 1987, 15: 7. Ogundipe-Leslie uses it to characterize Lawino in Okot's *Song of Lawino*.

2   I have used Len Orzen's English translation of Sembène's 'La noire de . . .', though not the misleading title he gives the story: 'The promised land'.

3   Denunciations of Senghor and Okot can be found in Ogundipe-Leslie, op. cit.: 6–7; and Mineke Schipper, 'Mother Africa on a pedestal: the male heritage in African literature and criticism', *African Literature Today*, 1987, 15: 43–4. Sembène, Farah, Beti, and Ngũgĩ have been praised for their portrayals of women in Abioseh M. Porter, 'Ideology and the image of women: Kenyan women in Njau and Ngũgĩ', *Ariel*, 1981, 12.3: 69–72; Jennifer Evans, 'Mother Africa and the heroic whore: female images in *Petals of Blood*', in Hal Wylie, Eileen Julien, and Russell J. Linnemann (eds) *Contemporary African Literature*, Washington, Three Continents Press, 1983: 57–65; Karen Smyley-Wallace, 'Women and alienation: analysis of the works of two francophone African novelists', in Carole Boyce Davies and Anne Adams Graves (eds) *Ngambika: Studies of Women in African Literature*, Trenton, New Jersey, Africa World Press, 1986: 64–5 and 70–1; Katherine Frank, 'Women without men: the feminist novel in Africa', *African Literature Today*, 1987, 15: 15; and Arlette Chemain-Degrange, *Emancipation féminine et roman africain*, Dakar, Nouvelles Editions Africaines, 1980: 352. Soyinka is commended in Sylvia Bryan, 'Images of women in Wole Soyinka's work', *African Literature Today*, 1987, 15: 122. He is condemned in Carole Boyce Davies, 'Maidens, mistresses and matrons: feminine images in selected Soyinka works', in Davies and Graves, op. cit.: 81–4; and Florence Stratton, 'Wole Soyinka: a writer's social vision', *Black American Literature Forum*, 1988, 22.3: 544–5 and 551–2.

3 MEN FALL APART
Grace Ogot's novels and short stories

1   Also see Jane Bryce, 'Inventing autobiography: some examples from fiction and journalism by Nigerian women writers', *Seminar on Aspects of Commonwealth Literature: 1989–1990*, London, Institute of Commonwealth Studies, 1990: 5–6; and Adeola James (ed.) *In Their Own Voices: African Women Writers Talk*, London, James Currey, 1990: 10.

2   'The year of sacrifice', *Black Orpheus*, 1962, 11: 41–50; 'Ward nine', *Transition*, 1964, 3.13: 41–5.

3   'The old white witch', as well as 'Elizabeth', 'The green leaves', 'Tekayo', and 'The hero', stories which are also discussed in this chapter, are found in Grace Ogot, *Land Without Thunder*, Nairobi, East African Publishing House, 1968.

4   'The wayward father', as well as 'Allan Mjomba', 'Island of tears', and 'Love immortalised', are found in Grace Ogot, *The Island of Tears*, Nairobi, Uzima Press, 1980.

5   'The other woman', as well as 'Pay day', 'The ivory trinket', and 'Fishing village', are found in Grace Ogot, *The Other Woman*, Nairobi, Transafrica Publishers, 1976.

6   The strategy of discrediting the male subject is also central to 'Pay day', 'The ivory trinket', and 'Fishing village'.

7   My sources for information on the constitution of the Kenyan Parliament are *Keesings Contemporary Archives*, vols 14–26, Bristol, Keesings Publications; and *Uhuru: Kenya Year Book*, vols 14–16, Nairobi, Newspread International.

4 FLORA NWAPA AND THE FEMALE NOVEL OF DEVELOPMENT

1   It should be noted that Achebe is, at the same time, critical of Jones for upholding 'the dogma of universalism'. See Chinua Achebe, *Morning Yet on Creation Day*, London, Heinemann, 1975: 52.

2   See Ernest N. Emenyonu, Review of *Efuru* by Flora Nwapa, *Ba Shiru*, 1970, 1.1: 58–61; and 'Who does Flora Nwapa write for?', *African Literature Today*, 1975, 7: 28–33.

3   Such passages occur on the following pages of *The Concubine*: 16, 26, 51–2, 61–2, and 64.

4   Alastair Niven's more recent study of *The Concubine* suggests the extent to which critical attitudes and practices are entrenched. His reading of the novel is almost identical to Jones's and Palmer's. See Alastair Niven, *Elechi Amadi's The Concubine: A Critical View*, London, Collins/British Council, 1981.

5   For Bryce, see 'Inventing autobiography: some examples from fiction and journalism by Nigerian women writers', *Seminar on Aspects of Commonwealth Literature: 1989–1990*, London, Institute of Commonwealth Studies, 1990: 1–9; and 'Conflict and contradiction in women's writing on the Nigerian Civil War', *African Languages and Cultures*, 1991, 4.1: 29–42.

6   In an interview Nwapa stated that both *Efuru* and *Idu* are set in her home town, Oguta. See Adeola James (ed.) *In Their Own Voices: African Women Writers Talk*, London, James Currey, 1990: 115.

7   Andrade sets *Efuru* 'at the turn of the century' (98). Textual allusions, such as the one to the conscription of Nigerians into the British Army (186) and to motor boats on the lake (202), indicate a much later setting. Nwapa has also stated that *Efuru* and *Idu* are set in the late 1940s and early 1950s. See James, op. cit.: 115.

8   According to Joyce Cary, the colonial government in Southern Nigeria was financed by taxes on imported gin. See Malcolm Foster, *Joyce Cary: A Biography*, London, Michael Joseph, 1969: 152.

9   In a discussion following a seminar she gave at SOAS in 1989, Amadiume said that she thought it likely that Uhamiri was related to, or another name for, Idemili.

10   Andrade's reading of this tale seems to be the product of wishful thinking on the part of a critic. For she claims that the girl (who remains nameless in Nwapa's version of the story but whom Andrade names Nkwo) *is saved by her sister Orie*. Because, as Andrade observes, 'Orie day is Uhamiri's day', she is then able to link the story to Efuru's relationship with Uhamiri: 'Through Orie, the tale points to the rescuing function that the deity, Uhamiri, will have in Efuru's life' (99). In Nwapa's version of the story, it is Nkwo who rescues her sister from the evil spirit after the other sisters, Eke, Orie, and Afo, have refused to help: '[Orie] banged the door in her face' just as Eke had done before her (109).

11   See Tsitsi Dangarembga's *Nervous Conditions*, London, Women's Press, 1988. Dangarembga's portrayal of the two sisters, Tambudzai's mother and her Aunt Lucia, is based on the same formula as Nwapa's portrayal of Ossai and Ajanupu. Tambudzai and her cousin Nyasha represent a changed form of the convention.

12   Archdeacon Crowther Memorial Girls' School. See Flora Nwapa, *Women Are Different*, Enugu, Tana Press, 1986: 3. For biographical information on Nwapa, see Hans M. Zell, Carol Bundy, and Virginia Coulon (eds) *A New Reader's Guide to African Literature*, London, Heinemann, 1983: 439–40.

13   As reported in Jane Bryce, 'Nigerian popular fiction, popular writing by women in Nigeria: the Pacesetter Series', unpublished paper, 1990: 2.

5 'THEIR NEW SISTER'
Buchi Emecheta and the contemporary African literary tradition

1   Only two of these novels do not have an explicitly Nigerian setting: *The Rape of Shavi* which is set in an imaginary African kingdom, and *Gwendolen* which is set in Jamaica and London.

2   These awards include the Daughter of Mark Twain Award in 1975, the Jock Campbell–*New Statesmen* Award in 1977, the Best Third World Writer for 1976–1979 Award, the *Afro-Caribbean Post*'s Golden Sunrise Award in 1977, and the Best Black Writer in Britain Award in 1980. See Davidson Umeh and Marie Umeh, 'An interview with Buchi Emecheta', *Ba Shiru*, 1985, 12.2: 19.

3   According to Donatus Nwoga, Emecheta uses '*chi*' in this novel as it is conceptualized among Western Igbo: to refer not only to an individual's 'personal god' but also to 'the person who has reincarnated the individual'. The individual is then assumed to be 'supervised, ruled and guided' in life by 'the circumstances of the . . . *chi*'s life in his or her previous world existence' (64–5).

4   See also Marie Umeh, 'African women in transition in the novels of Buchi Emecheta', *Présence Africaine*, 1980, 116.4: 190–201; Katherine Frank, 'The death

of the slave girl: African womanhood in the novels of Buchi Emecheta', *World Literature Written in English*, 1982, 21.3: 476–97; Ernest N. Emenyonu, 'Technique and language in Buchi Emecheta's *The Bride Price*, *The Slave Girl*, and *The Joys of Motherhood*', *Journal of Commonwealth Literature*, 1988, 23.1: 130–41; Catherine Obianuju Acholonu, 'Buchi Emecheta', in Yemi Ogunbiyi (ed.) *Perspectives on Nigerian Literature: 1700 to the Present*, Lagos, Guardian Books, 1988: 216–22; and Rolf Solberg, 'The woman of Black Africa, Buchi Emecheta: the woman's voice in the new Nigerian novel', *English Studies*, 1983, 64: 247–62.

5   See also Emenyonu, op. cit., 131.
6   Emecheta was the first writer Nwapa named when she was asked in an interview about the authors she reads. See Adeola James (ed.) *In Their Own Voices: African Women Writers Talk*, London, James Currey, 1990, 116.
7   See also Cyprian Ekwensi, *Survive the Peace*, London, Heinemann, 1976.
8   Of the historians I consulted, only O. B. C. Nwolise broaches the subject of rape in the Nigerian Civil War and he does so only in passing. See O. B. C. Nwolise, 'The social consequences of the Civil War in Biafra', *Proceedings of the National Conference on Nigeria Since Independence, Zaria, March 1983*, 3, Zaria, Panel on Nigeria Since Independence History Project, 1984: 37–8.

6 'LITERATURE AS A . . . WEAPON'
The novels of Mariama Bâ

1   See also Ojo-Ade's 'Female writers, male critics', *African Literature Today*, 1983, 13: 158–79.
2   A more detailed analysis of Sembène's 'allegory' is provided by Fírinne Ní Chréacháin-Adelugba in her 'Self and Other in Sembène Ousmane's *Xala*', in Kolawole Ogungbesan (ed.) *New West African Literature*, London, Heinemann, 1979: 91–103.
3   Kenneth W. Harrow classifies it as such, though he neglects to mark the genre for gender. In my discussion of *The African Child*, I draw on his analysis. See Kenneth W. Harrow, 'A formal approach to African literature', *Research in African Literatures*, 1990, 21.1: 86–8.
4   If the Corneille tragedy Bâ has in mind is *The Cid*, then Ousmane quite clearly identifies against himself. For 'the Cid' makes himself worthy of the woman he loves by becoming 'the scourge of the Moors'. See Pierre Corneille, 'The Cid', in *Pierre Corneille: Seven Plays*, trans. Samuel Solomon, New York, Random House, 1969: 75.

7 GENDER ON THE AGENDA
Novels of the 1980s by Ngũgĩ and Achebe

1   'Men of good will' is part of Bâ's dedicatory inscription to *So Long a Letter*.
2   *Devil on the Cross* was published originally in Gĩkũyũ under the title *Caitaani Mũtharaba-inĩ* (1980) which was written during Ngũgĩ's one year detention in prison in Kenya.
3   However, in Ngũgĩ's most recent novel, *Matigari* (1987), the old pattern reemerges: the main female character, Gũthera, is a prostitute.

4 Beatrice's comparison of herself to 'Chielo in the novel' (114) provides the most obvious example. Her father is also cast in the same mould as Okonkwo (85–7); and Ikem, as we shall see shortly, takes up the issue introduced by Uchendu in the earlier novel of the supremacy of motherhood.

5 Ifi Amadiume raises questions about the gender markings in this version of the myth too. Once again her observations suggest that Achebe's requirements necessitated accommodation to the demands of patriarchy. She does not know, she says, 'any direct translation from Igbo which would render God a "he,"' or any version of the myth in which Idemili is given a father. See Ife Amadiume, 'Class and gender in Anthills of the Savannah', *P A L Platform*, 1989, 1.1: 9.

6 In claiming that Achebe 'draws on the same redemptive Igbo tradition of female devotion and worship as did Nwapa in *Efuru*', Boehmer overlooks the difference between the functions that have been assigned to Idemili and Uhamiri by their respective authors. There is no suggestion in *Efuru* that worshipping Uhamiri 'demands retreat from everyday life' as Boehmer claims. In fact, considering that Uhamiri symbolizes women's economic independence, it would seem to require the very opposite. See Elleke Boehmer, 'Of Goddesses and stories: gender and a new politics in Achebe's *Anthills of the Savannah*', *Kunapipi*, 1990, 12.2: 107 and 110.

7 Boehmer raises the same issue when she suggests that 'gender in Achebe remains a vehicle: woman is the ground of change or discursive displacement but not the subject of transformation'. See Boehmer, op. cit.: 103. David Maughan-Brown goes one step further. In his view, Beatrice's role as priestess makes little or no 'contribution to the novel's examination of political leadership'. See David Maughan-Brown, '*Anthills of the Savannah* and the ideology of leadership', *Kunapipi*, 1990, 12.2: 141.

8 On this same point, it is not incidental that Chris dies attempting to save 'a most attractive girl whose striking features had earlier . . . made not a fleeting impression' on him (202). Of course, the 'girl's' appearance raises another set of issues, such as the question as to whether Chris would have intervened if she had not been attractive.

BIBLIOGRAPHY

Achebe, Chinua, 'African literature as restoration of celebration', *Kunapipi*, 1990, 12.2: 1–10.

——*Anthills of the Savannah* (1987) Oxford, Heinemann, 1988.

——Arrow of God, London, Heinemann, 1964.

——'Girls at war', *Girls at War and Other Stories*, London, Heinemann, 1972.

——*Hopes and Impediments: Selected Essays 1965–1987*, Oxford, Heinemann, 1988.

——'An image of Africa', *The Massachusetts Review*, 1977, 18.4: 782–94.

——*Morning Yet on Creation Day*, London, Heinemann, 1975.

——'The role of the writer in a new nation', in G. D. Killam (ed.) *African Writers on African Writing*, London, Heinemann, 1973, 7–13.

——*Things Fall Apart* (1958) London, Heinemann, 1968.

——*The Trouble with Nigeria*, London, Heinemann, 1984.

Acholonu, Catherine Obianuju, 'Buchi Emecheta', in Yemi Ogunbiyi (ed.) *Perspectives on Nigerian Literature: 1700 to the Present*, vol. 2, Lagos, Guardian Books, 1988: 216–22.

Ahmad, Aijaz, 'Jameson's rhetoric of otherness and the "National Allegory" ', *Social Text*, 1987, 17: 3–25.

Aidoo, Agnes Akosua, 'Asante Queen Mothers in government and politics in the nineteenth century', in Filomena Chioma Steady (ed.) *The Black Woman Cross-Culturally*, Cambridge, Mass., Schenkman, 1985: 65–77.

Aidoo, Ama Ata, 'To be an African woman writer – an overview and a detail', in Kirsten Holst Petersen (ed.) *Criticism and Ideology: Second African Writers' Conference, Stockholm 1986*, Uppsala, Scandinavian Institute of African Studies: 1988, 155–72.

Akare, Thomas. *The Slums*, London, Heinemann, 1981.

Amadi, Elechi, *The Concubine* (1966) London, Heinemann, 1982.

——*Ethics in Nigerian Culture*, Ibadan, Heinemann, 1982.

Amadiume, Ifi, 'Class and gender in *Anthills of the Savannah*', *P A L Platform*, 1989, 1.1: 8–9.

——*Male Daughters, Female Husbands: Gender and Sex in an African Society*, London, Zed, 1987.

Amuta, Chidi, 'History, society and heroism in the Nigerian War novel', *Kunapipi*, 1984, 6.3: 57–70.

——'Literature of the Nigerian Civil War', in Yemi Ogunbiyi (ed.) *Perspectives on Nigerian Literature: 1700 to the Present*, vol. 1, Lagos, Guardian Books, 1988: 85–92.

——'The Nigerian Civil War and the evolution of Nigerian literature', in Hal Wylie,

Eileen Julien, and Russell J. Linnemann (eds) *Contemporary African Literature*, Washington, Three Continents Press, 1983: 83–93.

Andrade, Susan Z., 'Rewriting history, motherhood, and rebellion: naming an African women's literary tradition', *Research in African Literatures*, 1990, 21.1: 91–110.

Arhin, Kwame, 'The political and military roles of Akan women', in Christine Oppong (ed.) *Female and Male in West Africa*, London, George Allen & Unwin, 1983:91–8.

Armah, Ayi Kwei, 'An African fable', *Présence Africaine*, 1968, 68.4: 192–6.

——Two Thousand Seasons, Nairobi, East African Publishing House, 1983.

Ashcroft, Bill, Gareth Griffiths, and Helen Tiffin, *The Empire Writes Back: Theory and Practice in Post-Colonial Literatures*, London, Routledge, 1989.

Ashcroft, W. D., 'Intersecting marginalities: post-colonialism and feminism', *Kunapipi*, 1989, 11.2: 23–35.

Awoonor, Kofi, *The Breast of the Earth: A Survey of the History, Culture, and Literature of Africa South of the Sahara*, Garden City, New York, Anchor/Doubleday, 1975.

Bâ, Mariama, *Scarlet Song*, trans. Dorothy S. Blair, Harlow, Longman, 1985, trans. of *Un chant écarlate*, Dakar, Nouvelles Editions Africaines, 1981.

——So Long a Letter, trans. Modupé Bodé-Thomas, London, Virago, 1982, trans. of *Une si longue lettre*, Dakar, Nouvelles Editions Africaines, 1980.

Bahm, Nina, 'Melodramas of beset manhood: how theories of American fiction exclude women authors', in Elaine Showalter (ed.) *The New Feminist Criticism: Essays on Women, Literature, and Theory*, London, Virago, 1986: 63–80.

Bakhtin, Mikhail, *The Dialogic Imagination*, ed. Michael Holquist, trans. Caryl Emerson and Michael Holquist, Austin, University of Texas Press, 1981.

——Problems of Dostoevsky's Poetics, ed. and trans. Caryl Emerson, Manchester, Manchester University Press, 1984.

Beauvoir, Simone de, *The Second Sex*, ed. and trans. H. M. Parshley, Harmondsworth, Penguin, 1972.

Beti, Mongo, *Perpetua and the Habit of Unhappiness*, trans. John Reed and Clive Wake, London, Heinemann, 1978, trans. of *Perpétue et l'habitude du maleur*, Paris, Buchet/Chastel, 1974.

Boehmer, Elleke, 'Of Goddesses and stories: gender and a new politics in Achebe's *Anthills of the Savannah*', *Kunapipi*, 1990, 12.2: 102–12.

——' "The master's dance to the master's voice": revolutionary nationalism and the representation of women in the writing of Ngũgĩ wa Thiong'o', *Seminar on Aspects of Commonwealth Literature: 1988-1989*, London, Institute of Commonwealth Studies, 1989: 1–19.

Brown, Lloyd W., *Women Writers in Black Africa*, Westport, Connecticut, Greenwood Press, 1981.

Bryan, Sylvia, 'Images of women in Wole Soyinka's work', *African Literature Today*, 1987, 15: 119–30.

Bryce, Jane, 'Conflict and contradiction in women's writing on the Nigerian Civil War', *African Languages and Cultures*, 1991, 4.1: 29–42.

——'Inventing autobiography: some examples from fiction and journalism by Nigerian women writers', *Seminar on Aspects of Commonwealth Literature: 1989–1990*, London, Institute of Commonwealth Studies, 1990: 1–9.

——'Nigerian popular fiction, popular writing by women in Nigeria: the Pacesetter Series', unpublished paper, 1990.

Bunn, David, 'Embodying Africa: woman and romance in colonial fiction', *English in Africa*, 1988, 15.1: 1–28.

Burness, Don (interviewer and ed.) *Wanasema: Conversations with African Writers*, Athens, Ohio, Centre for International Studies, Ohio University, 1985.

Busia, Abena P. A., 'Silencing Sycorax: on African colonial discourse and the unvoiced female', *Cultural Critique*, 1989–90, 14: 81–103.

'The Cabinet: second woman', *The Weekly Review*, 3 January 1986: 8.

Carby, Hazel V., ' "On the threshold of woman's era": lynching, empire, and sexuality in Black feminist theory', in Henry Louis Gates, Jr.(ed.) *'Race', Writing, and Difference*, Chicago, University of Chicago Press, 1986: 301–16.

Case, Frederick Ivor, Review of *So Long a Letter* by Mariama Bâ, *World Literature Written in English*, 1982, 21.3: 538–40.

Cham, Mbye Baboucar, 'The female condition in Africa: a literary exploration by Mariama Bâ', *A Current Bibliography on African Affairs*, 1984-1985, 17.1: 29–51.

Chemain-Degrange, Arlette, *Emancipation féminine et roman africain*, Dakar, Nouvelles Editions Africaines, 1980.

Chinweizu, Onwuchekwa Jemie, and Ihechuwu Madubuike, *Toward the Decolonization of African Literature*, vol. 1, Enugu, Fourth Dimension, 1980.

Chréacháin-Adelugba, Fírinne Ní, 'Self and Other in Sembène Ousmane's *Xala*', in Kolawole Ogungbesan (ed.) *New West African Literature*, London, Heinemann, 1979: 91–103.

Conde, Maryse, 'Three female writers in modern Africa: Flora Nwapa, Ama Ata Aidoo and Grace Ogot', *Présence Africaine*, 1972, 82.2: 132–43.

Conrad, Joseph, *Heart of Darkness* (1902) London, Penguin, 1989.

Cook, David, *African Literature: A Critical View*, London, Longman, 1977.

Corneille, Pierre, 'The Cid', in *Pierre Corneille: Seven Plays*, trans. Samuel Solomon, New York, Random House, 1969.

Cutrufelli, Maria Rosa, *Women of Africa: Roots of Oppression*, trans. Nicolas Romano, London, Zed, 1983.

Dangarembga, Tsitsi, *Nervous Conditions*, London, Women's Press, 1988.

Davies, Carole Boyce, 'Feminist consciousness and African literary criticism', in Carole Boyce Davies and Anne Adams Graves (eds) *Ngambika: Studies of Women in African Literature*, Trenton, New Jersey, Africa World Press, 1986: 1–23.

——'Maidens, mistresses and matrons: feminine images in selected Soyinka works', in Carole Boyce Davies and Anne Adams Graves (eds) *Ngambika: Studies of Women in African Literature*, Trenton, New Jersey, Africa World Press, 1986, 75–88.

——'Motherhood in the works of male and female Igbo writers: Achebe, Emecheta, Nwapa and Nzekwu', in Carole Boyce Davies and Anne Adams Graves (eds) *Ngambika: Studies of Women in African Literature*, Trenton, New Jersey, Africa World Press, 1986, 241–56.

Dennis, Carolyne, 'Women and the state in Nigeria: the case of the Federal Military Government, 1984-1985', in Haleh Afshar (ed.) *Women, State, and Ideology*, Albany, State University of New York Press, 1987, 13–27.

Diallo, Nafissatou, *A Dakar Childhood*, trans. Dorothy S. Blair, London, Longman, 1982, trans of *De Tilène au Plateau: une enfance Dakaroise*, Dakar, Nouvelles Editions Africaines, 1975.

Diawara, Manthia, 'Canonizing Soundiata in Mande literature: toward a sociology of narrative elements', *Social Text*, 1992, 31/2: 154–68.

Diop, David Mandessi, *Hammer Blows and Other Writings*, ed. and trans. Simon Mpondo and Frank Jones, Bloomington, Indiana University Press, 1973.

Dollimore, Jonathan, 'The dominant and the deviant: a violent dialectic', *Critical Quarterly*, 1986, 28.1–2: 179–92.

Duerden, Dennis and Cosmo Pieterse (ed.) *African Writers Talking*, London, Heinemann, 1975.

Ekwensi, Cyprian, *Jagua Nana* (1961) Oxford, Heinemann, 1987.

——*Survive the Peace*, London, Heinemann, 1976.

Ellmann, Mary, *Thinking About Women*, New York, Harcourt Brace & World, 1968.

Emecheta, Buchi, *The Bride Price*, New York, George Braziller, 1976.

——*Destination Biafra* (1982) Glasgow, Fontana/Collins, 1983.

——*Double Yoke*, London, Ogwugwu Afor, 1982.

——'Feminism with a small "f"!', in Kirsten Holst Petersen (ed.) *Criticism and Ideology: Second African Writers' Conference, Stockholm 1986*, Uppsala, Scandinavian Institute of African Studies, 1988: 173–81.

——*Gwendolen*, London, William Collins Sons, 1989.

——*Head Above Water*, London, Fontana, 1986.

——*The Joys of Motherhood* (1979) London, Heinemann, 1980.

——*Rape of Shavi*, London, Ogwugwu Afor, 1983.

——*Second-Class Citizen* (1974) Glasgow, Fontana/Collins, 1980.

——*The Slave Girl*, New York, George Braziller, 1977.

Emenyonu, Ernest N., *Cyprian Ekwensi*, London, Evans, 1974.

——Review of *Efuru* by Flora Nwapa, *Ba Shiru*, 1970, 1.1: 58–61.

——'Technique and language in Buchi Emecheta's *The Bride Price*, *The Slave Girl*, and *The Joys of Motherhood*', *Journal of Commonwealth Literature*, 1988, 23.1: 130–41.

——'Who does Flora Nwapa write for?', *African Literature Today*, 1975, 7: 28–33.

Etienne, Mona, 'Gender relations and conjugality among the Baule', in Christine Oppong (ed.) *Female and Male in West Africa*, London, George Allen & Unwin, 1983: 303–19.

Evans, Jennifer, 'Mother Africa and the heroic whore: female images in *Petals of Blood*', in Hal Wylie, Eileen Julien, and Russell J. Linnemann (eds) *Contemporary African Literature*, Washington, Three Continents Press, 1983, 57–65.

Fanon, Frantz, *Black Skin White Masks*, trans. Charles Lam Markmann, London, Paladin, 1970.

Fapohunda, Eleanor R., 'Female and male work profiles', in Christine Oppong (ed.) *Female and Male in West Africa*, London, George Allen & Unwin, 1983: 32–53.

Farah, Nuruddin, *From a Crooked Rib* (1970) London, Heinemann, 1977.

——*Sardines*, London, Allison & Busby, 1981.

Felski, Rita, *Beyond Feminist Aesthetics: Feminist Literature and Social Change*, London, Hutchinson Radius, 1989.

Fido, Elaine Savory, 'Okigbo's *Labyrinths* and the context of Igbo attitudes to the female principle', in Carole Boyce Davies and Anne Adams Graves, *Ngambika: Studies of Women in African Literature*, Trenton, New Jersey, Africa World Press, 1986: 223–39.

Foster, Malcolm, *Joyce Cary: A Biography*, London, Michael Joseph, 1969.

Frank, Katherine, 'The death of the slave girl: African womanhood in the novels of Buchi Emecheta', *World Literature Written in English*, 1982, 21.3: 476–97.

——'Women without men: the feminist novel in Africa', *African Literature Today*, 1987, 15: 14–34.

Gilbert, Sandra M. and Susan Gubar, *Sexchanges*, vol. 2 of *No Man's Land: The*

Place of the Woman Writer in the Twentieth Century, New Haven, Yale University Press, 1989.

Haggard, H. Rider, *King Solomon's Mines* (1885) ed. Dennis Butts, Oxford, Oxford University Press, 1989.

——*She* (1887) ed. Daniel Karlin, Oxford, Oxford University Press, 1991.

Harrow, Kenneth W., 'A formal approach to African literature', *Research in African Literatures*, 1990, 21.1: 79–89.

Henn, Jeanne K., 'Women in the rural economy: past, present, and future', in Margaret Jean Hay and Sharon Stichter (eds) *African Women South of the Sahara*, London, Longman, 1984: 1–18.

Ike, Chukwuemeka, *Sunset at Dawn*, London, Collins, 1976.

Imam, Ayesha, 'The myth of equal opportunity in Nigeria', in Miranda Davies (ed.) *Third World – Second Sex*, vol. 2, London, Zed, 1987: 99–103.

Innes, C. L., *Chinua Achebe*, Cambridge, Cambridge University Press, 1990.

Innes, C. L. and Bernth Lindfors, Introduction, in C. L. Innes and Bernth Lindfors (eds) *Critical Perspectives on Chinua Achebe*, Washington, Three Continents Press, 1978:1–8.

Irele, Abiola, 'Literary Lyricism', Review of *Une si longue lettre* by Mariama Bâ, *West Africa*, 14 April 1980: 661–2.

Iroh, Eddie, *Forty-Eight Guns for the General*, London, Heinemann, 1976.

Jabbi, Bu-Buakei, 'Fire and transition in *Things Fall Apart*', in C. L. Innes and Bernth Lindfors (eds) *Critical Perspectives on Chinua Achebe*, Washington, Three Continents Press, 1978: 135–47.

James, Adeola, Review of *An Introduction to the African Novel* by Eustace Palmer, *African Literature Today*, 1975, 7: 147–52.

——(ed.) *In Their Own Voices: African Women Writers Talk*, London, James Currey, 1990.

Jameson, Fredric, *The Political Unconscious: Narrative as a Socially Symbolic Act*, Ithaca, Cornell University Press, 1981.

——'Third-world literature in the era of multinational capitalism', *Social Text*, 1986, 15: 65–88.

JanMohamed, Abdul R., *Manichean Aesthetics: The Politics of Literature in Colonial Africa*, Amherst, University of Massachusetts Press, 1983.

Jeyifo, Biodun, 'The nature of things: arrested decolonization and critical theory', *Research in African Literatures*, 1990, 21.1: 33–48.

Jones, Eldred, 'Locale and universe', Review of *The Concubine* by Elechi Amadi, *Efuru* by Flora Nwapa, and *A Man of the People* by Chinua Achebe, *Journal of Commonwealth Literature*, 1967, 3: 127–31.

Keesings Contemporary Archives, vols 14-26, Bristol, Keesings Publications.

Killam, Douglas, 'Kenya', in Bruce King (ed.) *Literatures of the World in English*, London, Routledge & Kegan Paul, 1974: 116–35.

Kitchener, Julie, 'Author in search of an identity', *New African*, December 1981: 61.

Kolodny, Annette, 'A map for rereading: gender and the interpretation of literary texts', in Elaine Showalter (ed.) *The New Feminist Criticism: Essays on Women, Literature, and Theory*, London, Virago, 1986: 46–62.

Krupat, Arnold, *The Voice in the Margin: Native American Literature and the Canon*, Berkeley, University of California Press, 1989.

Larson, Charles R., Review of *The Promised Land* by Grace Ogot, *Africa Report*, 1967, 12.9: 44–5.

——'Things fall further apart – new African novels', *College Language Association Journal*, 1966, 10: 64–67.

Laye, Camara, *The African Child*, trans. James Kirkup, London, Collins, 1959, trans. of *L'enfant noir*, Paris, Plon, 1953.

Lindfors, Bernth, 'The famous authors' reputation test: an update to 1986', in János Riesz and Alain Ricard(eds), *Semper Aliquid Novi: Litérature comparée et littératures d'Afrique: Mélanges Albert Gérard*, Tübingen, Gunter Narr Verlag, 1990: 131–43.

——'Interview with Grace Ogot', *World Literature Written in English*, 1979, 18.1: 56–68.

——'The teaching of African literatures in anglophone African universities: an instructive canon', *Matatu*, 1990, 7: 41–55.

Little, Kenneth, *African Women in Towns: An Aspect of Africa's Social Revolution*, London, Cambridge University Press, 1973.

Liyong, Taban lo, Review of *Weep Not, Child* by James Ngũgĩ, *Africa Report*, 1965, 10.11: 42–4.

McCaffrey, Kathleen M., 'Images of women in West African literature and film: a struggle against dual colonization', *International Journal of Women's Studies*, 1980, 3.1: 76–88.

McDowell, Deborah E., 'New directions for Black feminist criticism', in Elaine Showalter (ed.) *The New Feminist Criticism: Essays on Women, Literature, and Theory*, London, Virago, 1986: 186–99.

McLuskie, Kathleen and Lyn Innes, 'Women and African literature', *Wasafiri*, 1988, 8: 3–7.

Maughan-Brown, David, '*Anthills of the Savannah* and the ideology of leadership', *Kunapipi*, 1990, 12.2: 139–48.

Miller, Casey and Kate Swift, *Words and Women*, New York, Anchor, 1977.

Miller, Nancy K., 'Emphasis added: plots and plausibilities in women's fiction', in Elaine Showalter, *The New Feminist Criticism: Essays on Women, Literature, and Theory*, London, Virago, 1986: 339–60.

Mohanty, Chandra, 'Under western eyes: feminist scholarship and colonial discourses', *Feminist Review*, 1988, 30: 61–88.

Moody, H. L. B., Elizabeth Gunner, and Edward Finnegan, *A Teacher's Guide to African Literature*, London, Macmillan, 1984.

Moore, Gerald, Review of *The Promised Land* by Grace Ogot, *Mawazo*, 1967, 1.2: 94–5.

——*Twelve African Writers*, London, Hutchinson, 1980.

Morgan, Robin (ed.) *Sisterhood is Global: The International Women's Movement Anthology*, Garden City, New York, Anchor/Doubleday, 1984.

Mukherjee, Arun P., 'Whose post-colonialism and whose postmodernism?', *World Literature Written in English*, 1990, 30.2: 1–9.

Munonye, John, *The Only Son*, London, Heinemann, 1966.

——*A Wreath for the Maidens*, London, Heinemann, 1973.

Mwangi, Meja, *Going Down River Road*, London, Heinemann, 1976.

Nasta, Susheila, Introduction, in Susheila Nasta (ed.) *Motherlands: Black Women's Writing from Africa, the Caribbean and South Asia*, London, Women's Press, 1991: xiii–xxx.

Ngũgĩ wa Thiong'o, *Barrel of a Pen: Resistance to Repression in Neo-Colonial Kenya*, London, New Beacon, 1983.

——*Decolonizing the Mind: The Politics of Language in African Literature*, London, James Currey, 1986.

——*Detained: A Writer's Prison Diary*, London, Heinemann, 1981.

——*Devil on the Cross*, London, Heinemann, 1982, author's trans. of *Caitaani Mũtharaba-inĩ*, Nairobi, Heinemann, 1980.

——*Matigari*, trans. Wangũi wa Goro, Oxford, Heinemann, 1989, trans. of *Matigari*, Nairobi, Heinemann, 1987.

——*Petals of Blood*, London, Heinemann, 1977.

——*Weep Not, Child*, London, Heinemann, 1964.

——*Writers in Politics*, London, Heinemann, 1981.

——'Writing against neo-colonialism', in Kirsten Holst Petersen (ed.) *Criticism and Ideology: Second African Writers' Conference, Stockholm 1986*, Uppsala, Scandinavian Institute of African Studies, 1988: 92–103.

Niven, Alastair, *Elechi Amadi's* The Concubine: *A Critical View*, London, Collins/British Council, 1981.

Nkosi, Lewis, *Tasks and Masks: Themes and Styles of African Literature*, Harlow, Longman, 1981.

Nwapa, Flora, *Efuru* (1966) London, Heinemann, 1978.

——*Idu*, London, Heinemann, 1970.

——*Never Again* (1975) Enugu, Tana Press, 1986.

——*One is Enough*, Enugu, Tana Press, 1981.

——*This is Lagos and Other Stories* (1971) Enugu, Nwankwo-Ifejika, 1979.

——*Wives at War and Other Stories* (1980) Enugu, Nwamife, 1984.

——*Women are Different*, Enugu, Tana Press, 1986.

Nwoga, Donatus Ibe, *The Supreme God as Stranger in Igbo Religious Thought*, Abiazu Mbaise, Imo State, Hawk Press, 1984.

Nwolise, O. B. C., 'The social consequences of the Civil War in Biafra', *Proceedings of the National Conference on Nigeria Since Independence, Zaria, March 1983*, vol. 3, Zaria, Panel on Nigeria Since Independence History Project, 1984.

O'Barr, Jean, 'African women in politics', in Margaret Jean Hay and Sharon Stichter (eds) *African Women South of the Sahara*, London, Longman, 1984: 140–55.

Obbo, Christine, *African Women: Their Struggle for Economic Independence*, London, Zed, 1980.

Obiechina, Emmanuel, *An African Popular Literature: A Study of Onitsha Market Pamphlets*, Cambridge, Cambridge University Press, 1973.

Ogot, Grace, 'The African writer', *East Africa*, 1968, 5.11: 35–7.

——The Graduate, Nairobi, Uzima Press, 1980.

——*Land Without Thunder*, Nairobi, East African Publishing House, 1968.

——*The Other Woman*, Nairobi, Transafrica Publishers, 1976.

——*The Promised Land* (1966) Nairobi, East African Publishing House, 1974.

——*The Strange Bride*, trans. Okoth Okombo, Nairobi, Heinemann, 1989, trans. of *Miaha*, Nairobi, Heinemann, 1983.

——'Ward nine', *Transition*, 1964, 3.13: 41–5.

——*The Island of Tears*, Nairobi, Uzima Press, 1980.

——'Women's world', Review of *Efuru* by Flora Nwapa, *East Africa Journal*, 1966, 3.7: 38–9.

——'The year of sacrifice', *Black Orpheus*, 1962, 11: 41–50.

Ogundipe-Leslie, Omolara, 'African women, culture and another development', *Présence Africaine*, 1987, 141.1: 123–39.

——'The female writer and her commitment', *African Literature Today*, 1987, 15: 5–13.

Ogunyemi, Chikwenye Okonjo, 'Womanism: the dynamics of the contemporary Black female novel in English', *Signs: Journal of Women in Culture and Society*, 1985, 11.1: 63–80.

Ojo-Ade, Femi, 'Female writers, male critics', *African Literature Today*, 1983, 13: 158–79.

——'Still a victim? Mariama Bâ's *Une si longue lettre*', *African Literature Today*, 1982, 12: 71–87.

Okigbo, Christopher, *Labyrinths*, London, Heinemann, 1971.

Okonjo, Kamene, 'The dual-sex political system in operation: Igbo women and community politics in Midwestern Nigeria', in Nancy J. Hafkin and Edna G. Bay (eds) *Women in Africa: Studies in Social and Economic Change*, Stanford, Stanford University Press, 1976, 45–58.

——'Sex roles in Nigerian politics', in Christine Oppong (ed.) *Female and Male in West Africa*, London, George Allen & Unwin, 1983: 211–22.

——'Women's political participation in Nigeria', in Filomena Chioma Steady (ed.) *The Black Woman Cross-Culturally*, Cambridge, Mass., Schenkman, 1981: 79–106.

Okot p'Bitek, *Africa's Cultural Revolution*, Nairobi, Macmillan, 1973.

——*Song of Lawino* (1966) Nairobi, East African Publishing House, 1968.

Okpewho, Isidore, *The Last Duty*, London, Longman, 1976.

Palmer, Eustace, 'The feminine point of view: Buchi Emecheta's *The Joys of Motherhood*', *African Literature Today*, 1983, 13: 38–55.

——*The Growth of the African Novel*, London, Heinemann, 1979.

——*An Introduction to the African Novel*, London, Heinemann, 1972.

——'A plea for objectivity: a reply to Adeola James', *African Literature Today*, 1975, 7: 123–7.

——Review of *The Concubine* by Elechi Amadi and *Efuru* by Flora Nwapa, *African Literature Today*, 1968, 1: 56–8, reprinted in *Journal of Commonwealth Literature*, 1968, 3: 127–31.

Parry, Benita, 'Problems in current theories of colonial discourse', *Oxford Literary Review*, 1987, 9.1–2: 27–58.

Perry, Alison, 'Meeting Flora Nwapa', *West Africa*, 18 June 1984: 1262.

Petersen, Kirsten Holst, Introduction, in Kirsten Holst Petersen (ed.) *Criticism and Ideology: Second African Writers' Conference, Stockholm 1986*, Uppsala, Scandinavian Institute of African Studies, 1988: 7–16.

Porter, Abioseh M., 'Ideology and the image of women: Kenyan women in Njau and Ngũgĩ', *Ariel*, 1981, 12.3: 61–74.

Robinson, Lillian S., 'Treason our text: feminist challenges to the literary canon', in Elaine Showalter (ed.) *The New Feminist Criticism: Essays on Women, Literature, and Theory*, London, Virago, 1986, 105–21.

Ruddy, Patricia, 'Prostitution', unpublished essay, 1989.

Rutherford, Anna, 'Interview with Chinua Achebe', *Kunapipi*, 1987, 9.2: 1–7.

Schipper, Mineke, 'Mother Africa on a pedestal: the male heritage in African literature and criticism', *African Literature Today*, 1987, 15: 35–54.

Sembène, Ousmane, *God's Bits of Wood*, trans. Francis Price, London, Heinemann, 1970, trans. of *Les bouts de bois de Dieu: Banty Mam Yall*, Paris, Livre Contemporain, 1960.

——'La noire de. . .', in Ousmane Sembène, *Voltaique*, Paris, Présence Africaine, 1962, trans. as 'The promised land', in Ousmane Sembène, *Tribal Scars and Other Stories*, trans. Len Ortzen, London, Heinemann, 1974.

——*Xala*, trans. Clive Wake, London, Heinemann, 1976, trans. of *Xala: roman*, Paris, Présence Africaine, 1973.

Senghor, Léopold Sédar, *Léopold Sédar Senghor: Prose and Poetry*, ed. and tran. John Reed and Clive Wake, London, Oxford University Press, 1965.

Shelton, Austin J., 'The articulation of traditional and modern in Igbo literature', *The Conch*, 1969, 1.1: 30–49.

Smith, Barbara, 'Toward a Black feminist criticism', in Elaine Showalter (ed.) *The New Feminist Criticism: Essays on Women, Literature, and Theory*, London, Virago, 1986: 168–85.

Smyley-Wallace, Karen, 'Women and alienation: analysis of the works of two Francophone African novelists', in Carole Boyce Davies and Anne Adams Graves (eds) *Ngambika: Studies of Women in African Literature*, Trenton, New Jersey, African World Press, 1986: 63–73.

Solberg, Rolf, 'The woman of Black Africa, Buchi Emecheta: the woman's voice in the new Nigerian novel', *English Studies*, 1983, 64: 247–62.

Soyinka, Wole, 'Ethics, ideology and the critic', in Kirsten Holst Petersen (ed.) *Criticism and Ideology: Second African Writers' Conference, Stockholm 1986*, Uppsala, Scandinavian Institute of African Studies, 1988: 26–51.

——*The Interpreters*, Glasgow, Fontana/Collins, 1972.

——*Kongi's Harvest*, Oxford, Oxford University Press, 1967.

——*Madmen and Specialists*, London, Methuen, 1971.

——*The Man Died: Prison Notes of Wole Soyinka*, London, Rex Collings, 1972.

——*Myth, Literature and the African World*, Cambridge, Cambridge University Press, 1978.

——*Opera Wonyosi*, London, Rex Collings, 1981.

——*Season of Anomy*, London, Rex Collings, 1980.

Spacks, Patricia Meyer, *Gossip*, New York, Alfred Knopf, 1985.

Spender, Dale, *Man Made Language*, London, Routledge & Kegan Paul, 1980.

Spivak, Gayatri Chakravorty, *In Other Worlds: Essays in Cultural Politics*, New York, Methuen, 1987.

——'Three women's texts and a critique of imperialism', in Henry Louis Gates, Jr (ed.) *'Race', Writing, and Difference*, Chicago, University of Chicago Press, 1986: 262–80.

Steady, Filomena Chioma, Introduction, in Filomena Chioma Steady (ed.) *The Black Woman Cross-Culturally*, Cambridge, Mass., Schenkman, 1981: 1–41.

Stratton, Florence, ' "Periodic embodiments": a ubiquitous trope in African men's writing', *Research in African Literatures*, 1990, 21.1: 111–26.

——'The shallow grave: archetypes of female experience in African fiction', *Research in African Literatures*, 1988, 19.2: 143–69.

——'Wole Soyinka: a writer's social vision', *Black American Literature Forum*, 1988, 22.3: 531–53.

Taiwo, Oladele, *Female Novelists of Modern Africa*, London, Macmillan, 1984.

Udechukwu, Obiora, 'Aesthetics and the mythic imagination: notes on Christopher Okigbo's *Heavensgate* and Uche Okeke's *Drawings*', in Donatus Ibe Nwoga (comp. and ed.) *Critical Perspectives on Christopher Okigbo*, Washington, Three Continents Press, 1984: 78–85.

Uhuru: Kenya Year Book, vols 14–16, Nairobi, Newspread International.

Umeh, Davidson and Marie Umeh, 'An interview with Buchi Emecheta', *Ba Shiru*, 1985, 12.2: 19–25.

Umeh, Marie, 'African women in transition in the novels of Buchi Emecheta', *Présence Africaine*, 1980, 116.4: 190–201.

——'The Joys of Motherhood: myth or reality?', Colby Library Quarterly, 1982, 18: 39–46.

——'Reintegration with the lost self: a study of Buchi Emecheta's Double Yoke', in Carole Boyce Davies and Anne Adams Graves (eds) Ngambika: Studies of Women in African Literature, Trenton, New Jersey, Africa World Press, 1986: 173–80.

Van Allen, Judith, ' "Aba Riots" or "Women's War"? ideology, stratification, and the invisibility of women', in Nancy J. Hafkin and Edna G. Bay (eds) Women in Africa: Studies in Social and Economic Change, Stanford, Stanford University Press, 1976: 59–85.

Walker, Alice, In Search of Our Mothers' Gardens: Womanist Prose, London, Women's Press, 1984.

Ware, Helen, 'Female and male life-cycles', in Christine Oppong (ed.) Female and Male in West Africa, London, George Allen & Unwin, 1983: 6–31.

Were, Miriam K., Your Heart is My Altar, Nairobi, East African Publishing House, 1980.

'Women in Parliament: no further ahead', The Weekly Review, 21 October 1983: 17.

Young, Robert, White Mythologies: Writing History and the West, London, Routledge, 1990.

Zell, Hans M., 'The first Noma Award for Publishing in Africa', Africa Book Publishing Record, 1980, 6.3–4: 199–201.

Zell, Hans M., Carol Bundy, and Virginia Coulon (eds) A New Reader's Guide to African Literature, London, Heinemann, 1983.

INDEX

Abrahams, Peter 3
Achebe, Chinua 2, 11, 19, 22–38, 90, 112, 113, 158–9, 164–70; *Anthills of the Savannah* 19, 27, 158–9, 164–70, 175–6; *Arrow of God* 89–90; canonical status 3, 6, 22–3; critical reception of 19, 22–3; 'Girls at war' 122–3; negative relations with colonial writers 23–4, 31, 37; positive relations with African women writers 158, 165, 170, 175; positive relations with colonial writers 30–2, 35; on the role of African writers 23–4; sexual politics of 24–38, 167–70; subversion of patriarchal ideology in 164–6, 170; *Things Fall Apart* 19, 22–8, 51, 61, 63, 67, 70–1, 80, 83, 84, 85, 87–90, 97, 99, 113, 116, 159, 164–6, 169, 171
Africa: feminization of 18, 19, 30–1, 37, 39–55, 60, 91, 153, 172, 178–9
African female literary tradition 58, 108, 111, 119, 132, 165; characteristics of 10, 11, 97, 128, 131, 173–5; intertextual relations within 18, 19, 111–12, 118–19, 125, 175; representation of men in 65–7, 70–2, 77–8, 79, 84, 87–8, 99, 117, 131, 145–6, 154, 174–5
African literary canon 3–6, 13, 176; all-male 3, 5
African literary tradition: characteristics of 1, 11–12, 127, 171, 176; development of 11–12, 132, 155, 170, 171, 176; place of women's writing in 1, 5, 9, 12, 13, 19, 55, 171, 176

African male literary tradition 158, 170; characteristics of 10–11, 39–40, 47, 50, 97, 107, 129, 136, 172–3; intertextual relations within 11, 40, 42–50, 159, 164–5 167, 169; representation of women in 29–32, 35–6, 41, 51–4, 60, 85–6, 91, 134, 162–4, 167–70, 171, 172, 175–6
African men: under colonialism 7–8, 151–3
African men writers: negative influence of colonial literature on 10–11, 24, 31, 37, 40, 171, 172–3; positive influence of African women's writing on 19, 158, 165, 170, 175, 176; positive influence of colonial literature on 18, 30–2, 35, 39–41, 171–2; on the status of women 51, 54, 158–9
African/national subject 158, 165–6, 167–70; constructed as male 7–10, 36, 41, 51–4, 60, 79, 160–2, 172; in women's writing 62–5, 70, 77–9, 99, 107; *see also* female national subject, writing subject
African societies and male domination 7–8, 14–17, 54–5, 154
African women: and the anti-colonial struggle 17, 35–6, 75; under colonialism 7–8, 14–16, 76–7, 87–8, 101, 104–6, 172–3; designated agents of moral corruption 15–17, 53; identified with tradition 8, 17, 36, 41, 52–3, 91, 97, 118, 134, 136, 153, 172; and national politics 10, 15, 17, 27, 72–3, 76; in 'post-colonial' societies 16–17, 54–5, 154; pre-colonial 7, 15; and

urban space 15–17, 76–7; and
western education 7–8, 76, 80,
88–9, 101, 104–6; *see also* Igbo
women
African women writers: and the
canon 3–4, 6, 12, 13, 58, 108–9,
133, 176; negative influence of
African men's writing on 10, 11,
19, 38, 50, 54, 61–7, 70–2, 79, 83,
87–8, 89–92, 97, 99, 100, 103–4,
107, 113, 116, 117–18, 119–20,
121–4, 126–7, 132, 137–8, 146,
151–2, 153–5, 173, 175; negative
influence of colonial literature on
11, 62–3, 83, 173, 175; positive
influence of African men's writing
on 120–2, 123–4, 126, 127, 131–2,
137, 154–5, 172, 175, 176; and
western feminism 13, 111
Ahmad, Aijaz 10
Aidoo, Ama Ata 2, 3, 4, 108, 134, 135
Akara, Thomas 53
Amadi, Elechi: *The Concubine* 81–6,
89, 91; sexual politics of 85–6, 91
Amadiume, Ifi: *Male Daughters, Female
Husbands* 7–8, 10, 13, 14, 16, 26–8,
35–6, 76, 90
Amuta, Chidi 120, 121–7
Andrade, Susan Z. 6–7, 13, 18, 58, 87,
92, 98, 102, 111, 113, 116
Armah, Ayi Kwei 3, 19, 44; 'An
African fable' 41, 44, 46–7, 51
Ashcroft, Bill, Gareth Griffiths and
Helen Tiffin: *The Empire Writes
Back* 2, 5, 6–7, 9, 10–11
Ashcroft, W. D. 9
Awoonor, Kofi 22, 40

Bâ, Mariama 19, 97, 108, 129,
133–55, 158, 175; critical
reception of 133–6; negative
relations with African men
writers 54–5, 137–8, 146, 151–2,
153–5; positive relations with
African men writers 137, 154–5;
on the role of African women
writers 54–5; *Scarlet Song* 137,
144, 147–55, 175; *So Long a
Letter* 133–49, 155, 174–5;

subversion of patriarchal ideology
in 137–55
Bakhtin, Mikhail 17–18, 188
Beauvoir, Simone de 135, 139–42
Beti, Mongo 19, 50–1; *Perpetua and the
Habit of Unhappiness* 41, 47–9, 52–3
Boehmer, Elleke 60, 162, 167, 168
Brown, Lloyd W.: *Women Writers in
Black Africa* 2, 28–9, 61–2, 68–70,
86–7, 92, 94, 96
Brutus, Dennis 3
Bryce, Jane 87, 104, 125
Bunn, David 31
Busia, Abena P. A. 35, 171

Cary, Joyce 23, 24, 29, 30, 36–7
Case, Frederick Ivor 133–5
Cham, Mbye Baboucar 139, 154
Chinweizu, Onwuchekwa Jemie and
Ihechukwu Madubuike 5, 11
Clark, John Pepper 3
colonial policies: and African women
7–8, 15–16, 76–7, 87
colonialism: negative influence on
African literature 6–8, 23–4, 40,
62, 67, 87–9, 99, 101, 104–6, 107,
109, 113–15, 116, 119–20, 171,
172; patriarchal character of 7–8,
14–16, 18, 88–9, 101, 172–3
Conde, Maryse 61–2
Conrad, Joseph 24; *Heart of Darkness*
23, 30, 35, 37, 171
convention of the paired women 97,
117–18, 138–45, 146–50, 173, 175
Cook, David 1, 4, 22
criticism of African literature: and
African women writers 1–13, 55,
58–61, 80–6, 92, 101–3, 108–11,
127, 133–6, 176; sexual politics of
1–4, 25, 29, 32–3, 35, 37, 59–61,
127, 133–6, 176; *see also* feminist
criticism, historicist criticism, New
Criticism

Dangarembga, Tsitsi: *Nervous
Conditions* 97, 107
Davies, Carole Boyce 7–8, 30–1
decolonization: literary 10–12

Dennis, Carolyne 16–17
Diallo, Nafissatou 107, 135
dialogism 17–18, 39–40, 171–2, 178–9;
forms of the dialogical 18;
gender-based 1, 11–12, 17, 18, 19,
61, 62, 64–5, 67, 70–1, 79, 83, 87–8,
89–92, 97, 99, 104–6, 113, 116–18,
119–20, 121–7, 129–32, 137–8, 146,
151–2, 154–5, 158, 159–60, 164–6,
170, 171, 173–6, 180; race-based
10, 11–12, 24, 37, 40, 62–3, 67, 87,
99, 107, 171, 172–3, 176
Diop, David Mandessi 40
Dollimore, Jonathan 174

Ekwensi, Cyprian 19, 50, 121; *Jagua
Nana* 53, 87, 90, 102–4, 113, 118
Ellmann, Mary 82
Emecheta, Buchi 13, 19, 97, 103,
108–32, 134, 135–6, 175; *The Bride
Price* 107, 108, 110, 112; critical
reception of 108–9; *Destination
Biafra* 108, 109–10, 111, 120–7,
163, 167, 174; *Double Yoke* 108,
111, 117, 127–32, 151, 155, 165,
175; *The Joys of Motherhood* 9, 18,
107, 108, 111–20, 131, 138–9, 142,
174; negative relations with
African men writers 113, 116–18,
119–20, 121–7, 132; positive relations
with African men writers 120–2,
123–4, 126, 127, 131–2; *The Slave
Girl* 107, 108, 109, 112; subversion
of patriarchal ideology in 111–32

Fanon, Frantz 6, 15, 17, 172; *Black Skin
White Masks* 152–4, 174
Fapohunda, Eleanor R. 10
Farah, Nuruddin 2, 19, 50–1; *From a
Crooked Rib* 41, 44–5, 47, 52–3
Felski, Rita 62
female national subject 78–9, 124–5,
163, 167; problems in the
representation of 78, 124
female novel of development: by African
men writers 159–64; by African
women writers 86–7, 107, 175; *see
also* male novel of development

female sexuality: representations of
30–1, 85–6, 91, 169, 172
feminism: African 13, 90–3, 101, 104,
107, 110, 111, 119, 165; designated
a western phenomenon 9, 12, 92,
102, 110, 135–6; western 12–13,
61, 109–11
feminist criticism 58, 59, 170;
problems with images mode of
50–1, 61–2; racial politics of
12–13, 61, 92, 101–2, 109–11, 136
Fido, Elaine Savory 91
Frank, Katherine 101–3, 109–11, 136

gender romance 36–7, 116, 136;
characteristics of 36–7
Gilbert, Sandra M. and Susan Gubar
30–1
good woman/whore dichotomy: in
men's writing 51–2, 53, 118, 136;
in women's writing 103, 118; *see
also* motherhood, prostitution

Haggard, H. Rider 23, 30–1, 37
Head, Bessie 2, 3, 12, 108, 134
historicist criticism: sexual politics of
6–12, 13–14, 18, 32, 171

ideology: literature and 14, 17, 62, 172
Igbo women: and the anti-colonial
struggle 35–6, 87; under
colonialism 94; pre-colonial 26–8;
and the struggle against male
domination 35–6
Ike, Chukwuemeka 126
Imam, Ayesha 80
Innes, C. L. 22, 29, 30, 32, 164
Innes, C. L. and Bernth Lindfors 22
inversion: as a strategy of intervention
62, 65, 67, 72, 78, 79, 84, 99, 117,
145–6, 153, 155, 173–5
Irele, Abiola 133–4
Iroh, Eddie 122, 126
Islam 15, 137, 138–40, 151, 175
Izevbaye, Daniel 5

Jabbi, Bu-Buakei 34
James, Adeola 81

Spender, Dale 60
Spivak, Gayatri Chakravorty 12
Steady, Filomena Chioma 13
Sutherland, Efua 135

Taiwo, Oladele 2–3, 59

Udechukwu, Obiora 91
Umeh, Marie 109–11, 113

Ware, Helen 10
water deity myths: in men's writing

26–8, 35–6, 86, 89–92, 165, 167,
169; sexual politics of 86, 89–92,
167, 169; in women's writing
89–99, 111–12, 119
Were, Miriam K. 107
Writing subject: constructed as male
7–11, 41, 51–4, 60–1, 79, 82,
167–8; as female 38, 54–5, 173, (in
Achebe) 165, 167–70, (in
Emecheta) 120–1, 127–8, 131–2

Young, Robert 160, 163–4